The Higher Learning in America

The Higher Learning in America

A Memorandum on the Conduct of Universities
by Business Men

The Annotated Edition

Thorstein Veblen

Edited with an Introduction and Notes by
RICHARD F. TEICHGRAEBER III

Johns Hopkins University Press
Baltimore

© 2015 Johns Hopkins University Press
All rights reserved. Published 2015
Printed in the United States of America on acid-free paper

2 4 6 8 9 7 5 3 1

Johns Hopkins University Press
2715 North Charles Street
Baltimore, Maryland 21218-4363
www.press.jhu.edu

Library of Congress Cataloging-in-Publication Data

Veblen, Thorstein, 1857–1929.
The higher learning in America : a memorandum on the conduct of universities
by business men / Thorstein Veblen ; edited with an introduction and notes by
Richard F. Teichgraeber III. — Annotated edition.
pages cm
Includes index.
ISBN 978-1-4214-1677-9 (hardcover : alk. paper) — ISBN 978-1-4214-1678-6
(pbk. : alk. paper) — ISBN 978-1-4214-1679-3 (electronic) — ISBN
1-4214-1677-8 (hardcover : alk. paper) — ISBN 1-4214-1678-6 (pbk. : alk.
paper) — ISBN 1-4214-1679-4 (electronic) 1. Education, Higher. 2. Universities
and colleges—United States. I. Teichgraeber, Richard F. II. Title.
LA226.V3 2015
378—dc23   2014030727

A catalog record for this book is available from the British Library.

*Special discounts are available for bulk purchases of this book. For more information,
please contact Special Sales at 410-516-6936 or specialsales@press.jhu.edu.*

Johns Hopkins University Press uses environmentally friendly book materials,
including recycled text paper that is composed of at least 30 percent
post-consumer waste, whenever possible.

CONTENTS

The first edition of *The Higher Learning in America: A Memorandum on the Conduct of Universities by Business Men* was published by B. W. Huebsch in New York in late 1918. In preparing the text of this new edition for the printer, I used a digitally scanned copy of the first edition that was carefully compared to a copy of the final corrected typescript manuscript Veblen delivered to his publisher in late September 1918.[1] Differences between these earlier texts are minor: misspellings, misprints, or scanning errors, which have been easily corrected. Some small liberties have been taken with this new edition. Veblen's numbered footnotes have been alphabetized to facilitate annotation. For the readers' convenience, Veblen's footnotes also have been emended to bring them in line with standard scholarly practice. His spelling, word division, and punctuation have been regularized both in his text and in his footnotes wherever it was possible to do so without encroaching on his tone or meaning.

For all the notice it has received, *The Higher Learning in America* has never been annotated. Publication of this first annotated edition seems an appropriate way to mark the centennial of Veblen's great book. The annotation is divided into two parts. Numbered notes placed on the appropriate pages identify—when identification proved possible—events, institutions, persons, and publications alluded to or mentioned in the text of *The Higher Learning in America*. Bracketed notes follow Veblen's now alphabetized footnotes and identify events, institutions, persons, and publications he alludes to or mentions in his footnotes. I supply a broad range of contexts but pay particular attention to the history of American higher education during the course of Veblen's lifetime. From time to time, my notes take issue with what Veblen has to say. He was an extraordinarily provocative observer of the cultural and intellectual currents in which he swam but not always a completely reliable one. Readers also will find a comprehensive index that directs them to recurrent themes in *The Higher Learning in America* as well

1. The original manuscript is in the Thorstein B. Veblen Papers, Carleton College Archives.

as to more particular subject matter in the text and in the footnotes. The general aim of this new edition is to produce a book that will assist readers of varied interests and tastes.

In preparing the annotation, I have relied frequently on Frederick Rudolph, *The American College and University: A History* (New York: Vintage Books, 1962); Laurence R. Veysey, *The Emergence of the American University* (Chicago: University of Chicago Press, 1965); Roger L. Geiger, *To Advance Knowledge: The Growth of American Research Universities, 1900–1940* (New York: Oxford University Press, 1986); and Joseph F. Kett, *The Pursuit of Knowledge under Difficulties: From Self-Improvement to Adult Education in America, 1750–1990* (Stanford, CA: Stanford University Press, 1994), chaps. 5–9. For details relating to the history of the University of Chicago, I have drawn from Richard J. Storr, *Harper's University: The Beginnings* (Chicago: University of Chicago Press, 1966); John W. Boyer, *Building for the Long Future: The Role of Trustees in the Early University*, Occasional Papers on Higher Education VI (Chicago: College of the University of Chicago, 2000); and *"Broad and Christian in the Fullest Sense": William Rainey Harper and the University of Chicago*, Occasional Papers on Higher Education XV (Chicago: College of the University of Chicago, 2005). My introduction was read and improved by Thomas Bender, John W. Boyer, Geoffrey Harpham, and Thomas Volet. Gary Cox, Public Services Archivist, University of Missouri–Columbia; David Hartwig, University Archivist, Stanford University; and Eric Hillerman, College Archivist, Carleton College have given every possible assistance. At Johns Hopkins University Press, I wish to thank Greg Britton (who hatched the idea for this book), Sara J. Cleary, Catherine Goldstead, and (especially) the copy editor, Andre M. Barnett, for working with me during the production process to improve the manuscript. Finally, I also want to acknowledge the able work done by Bob Land in assembling the index and generous support for my research provided by the Sean M. Berkowitz Endowed Fund at Tulane University.

There is no authoritative modern biography of Thorstein Veblen. The most comprehensive remains Joseph Dorfman's *Thorstein Veblen and His America* (1934). It should be read along with the 1966 reprinted edition (New York: Augustus M. Kelley), which contains corrections and new appendices. Among the best recent studies of particular episodes in Veblen's life are Christopher Capozzola, "Thorstein Veblen and the Politics of War, 1914–20," *International Journal of Politics, Culture, and Society*, 13, no. 2 (Winter 1999), 255–71; Clare Eby, "Boundaries Lost: Thorstein Veblen, *The Higher Learning in America*, and the Conspicuous Spouse," *Prospects: An annual journal of American cultural studies*, ed. Jack Salzman, 26 (2001), 251–94; Roxanne Nilan and Karen Bartholomew, "No More 'The Naughty Professor': Thorstein Veblen at Stanford," *Sandstone & Tile* (Stanford Historical Society), 31, no. 2 (Spring–Summer, 2007), 13–33. On Veblen's years at the University of Chicago and Stanford University, see also William J. Barber, "Political Economy in an Atmosphere of Academic Entrepreneurship: The University of Chicago," and Mary E. Cookingham, "Political Economy in the Far West: The University of California and Stanford," in *Breaking the Academic Mould: Economists in Higher Learning in the Nineteenth Century*, ed. William J. Barber (Middletown, CT: Wesleyan University Press, 1988), 241–90. Veblen was among the five professors at the University of Chicago who most influenced the four women graduate students whose successful careers are studied in Ellen Fitzpatrick, *Endless Crusade: Women Social Scientists and Progressive Reform* (New York: Oxford University Press, 1990).

Veblen's many writings, including his letters, his journalism, and his reviews, cry out for collection in an authoritative critical edition. The remarkable breadth of his intellectual interests is displayed in the bibliography of Dorfman's *Thorstein Veblen and His America*, 519–24. For a helpful guide to the secondary literature on Veblen, see Jerry L. Simich and Rick Tilman, *Thorstein Veblen: A Reference Guide* (Boston: G. K. Hall & Co.,1985), which can be supplemented by the bibliography in Rick Tilman, *The Intellectual Legacy of Thorstein Veblen* (Westport, CT:

Greenwood Press), 1996, 233–52. On the historical reception of Veblen's writings, see Rick Tilman, *Thorstein Veblen and His Critics: Conservative, Liberal, and Radical Perspectives* (Princeton, NJ: Princeton University Press, 1992).

For the general intellectual background, see Idus L. Murphree, "The Evolutionary Anthropologists: The Progress of Mankind; The Concepts of Progress and Culture in the Thought of John Lubbock, Edward B. Tylor, and Lewis H. Morgan," *Proceedings of the American Philosophical Society*, 105, no. 3 (June 27, 1961), 265–300; John P. Diggins, *The Bard of Savagery: Thorstein Veblen and Modern Social Theory* (New York: Seabury Press, 1978); Thomas L. Haskell, "Veblen on Capitalism: Intellectual History in and out of Context," *Reviews in American History*, 7, no. 4 (Dec. 1979), 553–60; Dorothy Ross, *The Origins of American Social Science* (Cambridge: Cambridge University Press, 1991); Geoffrey Hodgson, "Thorstein Veblen and Post-Darwinian Economics," *Cambridge Journal of Economics*, 16, no. 3 (Dec. 1992), 285–301.

On the "professors' literature of protest," see Mark Beach, "Professional versus Professorial Control of Higher Education," *Educational Record*, 9, no. 3 (Summer 1968), 263–73; Laurence R. Veysey, *The Emergence of the American University* (Chicago: University of Chicago Press, 1965), 381–93; and Clyde W. Barrow, *Universities in a Capitalist State: Corporate Liberalism and the Reconstruction of American Higher Education* (Madison: University of Wisconsin Press, 1990), 166–77. For a particularly good discussion of the historical background of *The Higher Learning in America*, see Peter Dobkin Hall, "*Noah Porter Writ Large?* Reflections on the Modernization of American Education and Its Critics, 1866–1916," in *The American College in the Nineteenth Century*, ed. Roger Geiger (Nashville, TN: Vanderbilt University Press, 2000), 196–220. For three carefully argued discussions of how the American research university and American business developed in tandem over the course of the late twentieth century, see Derek Bok, *Universities and the Marketplace: The Commercialization of American Higher Education* (Princeton, NJ: Princeton University Press, 2003); Christopher Newfield, *Ivy and Industry: Business and the Making of the American University, 1880–1980* (Durham, NC: Duke University Press, 2003); and David Hollinger, "Money and Academic Freedom a Half-Century after McCarthyism: Universities amid the Force Fields of Capital," in *Cosmopolitanism and Solidarity: Studies in Ethnoracial, Religious, and Professional Affiliation in the United States* (Madison: University of Wisconsin Press, 2006), 77–105.

This chronology highlights events, individuals, and institutions that have some bearing on Thorstein Veblen's education and professional career and on the composition and subject matter of *The Higher Learning in America*. Articles and books listed in "Suggested Readings" discuss Veblen's career and book in more detail.

Childhood and Education, 1857–91

1857   Born on July 30 in Cato Township, Manitowoc County, Wisconsin, sixth of twelve children of Kari Thorsteindatter Bunde and Thomas Anderson Veblen.

1874   Enrolls at Carleton College Academy, Northfield, Minnesota, at age seventeen; finishes course requirements in three years.

1876   Johns Hopkins University opens.

1877–81   Enrolls at Carleton College; completes bachelor of arts course requirement in three years. After graduation, Veblen teaches for a year at Monona Academy in Madison, Wisconsin.

1881–4   Enrolls as graduate student at Johns Hopkins in fall 1881 and begins studies in philosophy and political economy. After failing to receive financial aid, Veblen withdraws before the end of the fall semester and transfers to Yale to study philosophy under president Noah Porter (1811–92), then also a well-known American metaphysician and moral philosopher. Awarded a PhD in spring 1884. Veblen returns to Minnesota seriously ill after contracting malaria. Publishes first paper in July, "Kant's Critique of Judgment," in the *Journal of Speculative Philosophy*.

1885–90   Slowly recovers health and develops new and abiding interest in Anglo-American anthropology during convalescence in Minnesota. In April 1888, marries Ellen May Rolfe (1858–1926), niece of the president of Carleton College. Begins to seek full-time academic appointments in 1889, applying for positions at Michigan College of Agriculture and Applied Science, University of Iowa, and St. Olaf's College. Starts work on English translation of the Icelandic epic *The Laxdaela Saga*. Despite excellent recommendations, Veblen fails to find an appointment and decides to return to graduate study.

1891   At the start of the winter semester, begins graduate study in political economy, at age thirty-four, under J. Laurence Laughlin (1850–1933) at Cornell University. William Rainey Harper (1856–1906) appointed first president of University of Chicago in July. Stanford University opens in October. Veblen publishes "Some Neglected Points in the Theory of Socialism," in *Annals of the American Academy of Political and Social Science*, in November. In winter of 1891–92, Laughlin accepts position as chair of the Political Economy Department at the University of Chicago.

University of Chicago, 1892–1906

The most enduring myth about Veblen is that he was alienated from the prevailing academic culture of his time and bounced from job to job. The truth is that his professional career had considerably more ups than downs. Despite sometimes strained relations with University of Chicago's president William Rainey Harper, Veblen was one of only three regular appointments in the Political Economy Department that Harper chose to keep on the payroll during his twelve years in office. Veblen also gained the admiration and respect of many of his faculty colleagues and graduate students and later benefited in various ways from their loyalty. Among his Chicago graduate students were the first four women trained as social scientists in the new American university system created in the late nineteenth century.

1892–94   University of Chicago opens in October 1892. On Laughlin's recommendation, Veblen is awarded a fellowship in the Political Economy Department. Teaches courses on socialism, history of political economy, economic factors in civilization, and economics of agriculture. Promoted to tutor in political economy in 1894.

1895–96   Appointed managing editor of the *Journal of Political Economy*. His language skills enable him to review and translate French, German, and Italian economic studies. Writes all book reviews on the subjects of Marxism and socialism. Veblen's translation of Gustav Cohn's *The Science of Finance* (1895) helps to launch the Economic Studies of the University of Chicago book publication series. Promoted to instruc-

Figure 1. Thorstein Veblen, 1901. Carleton College Archives

tor in political economy in 1896. Request for legal separation from
his wife is denied.

1898   College of Commerce and Administration begins operations at the
University of Chicago.

1899–90   Publishes *The Theory of the Leisure Class: An Economic Study in the
Evolution of Institutions* in February 1899. Book receives immediate
and widespread notice, giving Veblen national prominence. Promoted to assistant professor in political economy in 1900.

1904–6   Publishes *The Theory of Business Enterprise*. In summer 1904, begins
writing a paper that will lead to *The Higher Learning in America*.
Chicago president William Rainey Harper dies in January 1906. In
April 1906, Veblen delivers four lectures to the Harvard Economics
Department, which are later published in *Quarterly Journal of
Economics* under title "The Socialist Economics of Karl Marx and
His Followers." In early April, begins negotiations with Stanford
University President David Starr Jordan (1851–1931) about a new
faculty appointment in the Economics and Social Sciences Depart-
ment. Earthquake strikes the San Francisco Bay area on April 18,
damaging Stanford campus and closing it for the spring semester.

In May, interim University of Chicago president Harry Pratt Judson
(1849–1927) confronts Veblen with his wife's allegations of marital
infidelity and neglect. Veblen refuses to respond and resigns from
Chicago to take an appointment as associate professor in political
economy at Stanford. Stanford reopens in the fall.

Stanford University, 1907–10

Although Veblen's years at Stanford were relatively uneventful, his arrival in the
fall of 1906 capped President David Starr Jordan's efforts to revive the university's
flagging Department of Economics and Social Sciences. Aware of rumors sur-
rounding his personal affairs, Jordan recruited Veblen with a five-year appointment as associate professor that permitted him to teach as little as he wanted in
order to devote time to writing.

1907	Begins teaching at Stanford in January. Principal course offerings are Economic Factors in Civilization and History of Economic Principles.
1908	Harvard Business School opens as first independent American professional school with full-time faculty to offer master's degrees in business administration.
1909–10	In April 1909, begins correspondence with former Chicago graduate student and faculty colleague Herbert J. Davenport (1861–1931) about the possibility of an appointment in the Economics Department at the University of Missouri. In December, Stanford president David Starr Jordan confronts Veblen with his wife's allegations of marital infidelity and neglect. Veblen again refuses to reply and resigns. At Jordan's urging, Stanford trustees agree to pay the remainder of Veblen's salary through spring semester 1910. In December 1909, accepts appointment as lecturer in economics at the University of Missouri and moves to Columbia, Missouri.

University of Missouri, 1911–8

Veblen's appointment as lecturer in the Economics Department at the University
of Missouri marked the beginning of a brief golden age for the department. His
colleagues included Herbert J. Davenport, who moved to Cornell in 1916 and
later was elected president of the American Economic Association, and Walter W.
Stewart (1885–1958) who moved to Amherst College in 1916 and later served on
the Federal Reserve and headed the Rockefeller Foundation. With the publication

of *Imperial Germany and the Industrial Revolution* in 1915, Veblen's intellectual productivity and public visibility also began to reach their peak.

1911–12   Starts teaching economics at Missouri in February. Former Stanford graduate students William Camp and Leon Ardzrooni follow Veblen to Missouri. Divorced by Ellen Rolfe Veblen in January 1912.

1914   Publishes *Instinct of Workmanship: And the State of the Industrial Arts*. School of Commerce founded at the University of Missouri. Marries Ann Fessenden Bradley (1877–1920) in July.

1915   Publishes *Imperial Germany and the Industrial Revolution*. American Association of University Professors (AAUP) founded in New York.

1916   Book-length manuscript of *The Higher Learning in America: A Memorandum on the Conduct of Universities by Business Men* substantially completed by March. Veblen's first effort to publish it is blocked by University of Missouri president Albert Ross Hill (1868–1943).

1917   United States breaks diplomatic relations with German in February; enters World War I in April. Veblen publishes *An Inquiry into the Nature of Peace and the Terms of Its Preparation*.

1918   Veblen takes leave of absence from University of Missouri in February to work in Statistical Division of the United States Food Administration in Washington, DC. In May, gives series of lectures at Amherst College based on materials later published as *The Vested Interests and the State*. In July, severs ties with University of Missouri and resigns position in the United States Food Administration to accept appointment as contributing editor of the *Dial* magazine. Moves to New York in the fall and publishes *The Higher Learning in American*. Armistice ending World War I signed in November.

New School for Social Research, 1919–26

The opening of the New School in 1919 drew nationwide attention partly because of the distinguished faculty it assembled, which included Veblen, as well as Charles Beard, James Harvey Robinson, and Wesley C. Mitchell (Veblen's former graduate student), all of whom had recently resigned from Columbia. They were referred to as the New School's "big four." Others on the first faculty of the New School included Leon Ardzrooni (another of Veblen's former graduate students), Horace Kallen, Harold Laski, Harry Elmer Barnes, and Roscoe Pound. John Dewey retained his Columbia professorship but agreed to lecture at the New School.

1919–22   Publishes *The Vested Interests: And the State of the Industrial Arts* and *The Place of Science in Modern Civilization and Other Essays* in 1919. Joins faculty of New School for Social Research, which opens in fall 1919. Resigns as contributing editor of the *Dial* in November but continues to write on current political and economic affairs for the *Freeman* magazine. Veblen's second wife, Ann Bradley Veblen, dies in July 1920. Publishes *The Engineers and the Price System* in 1922.

1923   Publishes *Absentee Ownership and Business Enterprise in Recent Times; The Case of America.*

1925–26   The American Economic Association tenders Veblen the nomination of its presidency in 1925, on the condition he give an acceptance speech. Veblen declines, explaining "they did not offer it to me when I needed it." Publishes *The Laxdaela Saga* (*The Epic of the Salmon River Valley*) in English translation from Icelandic with introduction. Retires from New School in 1926.

The Final Years

1927–29   Returns to California in January 1927. Visits his brother Andrew in San Diego and then settles in Menlo Park. Dies of heart disease at home on August 3, 1929, at age 72, with stepdaughter and other family members besides him. Veblen is cremated and his ashes scattered over the Pacific Ocean.

The Higher Learning in America

Introduction

Veblen in Historical Context

Every serious student of the modern American university system should come to terms with Thorstein Veblen's *The Higher Learning in America* (1918). Much of the book reads like a scathing indictment. Institutions that should be dedicated solely to the disinterested pursuit of knowledge, Veblen charged, had allowed themselves to become all things to all people. They pursued extraneous ends such as adult education, community service, and social work. They provided undergraduates with various "ways and means of dissipation" that included intercollegiate sports, fraternities, clubs, and an extensive range of extracurricular programs known as "student activities."[1] Such involvement in the world came at a high price, Veblen continued, because it prompted America's new universities to emulate the practices of modern business corporations to accomplish their many unrelated ends. Universities were ruled by boards of trustees dominated by well-to-do businessmen and by presidents who were essentially businessmen in academic dress. University boards and presidents presided over faculty and staff in a hierarchical structuring common to large business corporations. They employed unsavory techniques of self-promotion and salesmanship that informed the daily operations of competitive business enterprises. They reduced university professors to the status of business hirelings. All these practices, Veblen insisted, served not only to hide the American university's lost sense of purpose but also to constrain substantially the faculty's disinterested pursuit of knowledge. The bureaucratization of university affairs controlled the faculty from above. The constant promotional activity of university presidents ("captains of erudition," Veblen called them) put a premium on the faculty's intellectual acquiescence, and the faculty's legal status as employees-at-will undermined whatever remained of professional self-respect.[2]

1. Thorstein Veblen, *The Higher Learning in America*, 105–6. All page references given in parenthesis are to this edition of Veblen's text. I invite the reader to check up on me.
2. In 1918, faculty of all ranks were considered a university's "employees-at-will," meaning all faculty were subject to dismissal for inadequate performance of academic duties or personal misconduct,

Quite an indictment, and one that captures historians' and critics' assessment of *The Higher Learning in America*. But it tells us little about what Veblen intended when, in the spring of 1918, he decided to publish a manuscript that had been sitting in his files for more than a dozen years. Some readers of *The Higher Learning in America*, impressed more by the wit than by the substance of Veblen's indictment, have said that the book's ultimate aim was to ridicule rather than to offer constructive criticism. If so, what moved Veblen, a decided supporter of the United States' entry into World War I, to publish a book mocking institutions that had closed ranks after President Woodrow Wilson's April 1917 war message to Congress, pledging to do anything to secure the nation's military commitment? Furthermore, what do we make of the fact that Veblen knew he was hardly alone in condemning the encroachment of corporate business practices and values into the operation of the American university and the work lives of professors? Behind *The Higher Learning in America* lay more than three decades of writings by dozens of other American university professors that had voiced essentially the same criticism and complaint. At the book's outset, Veblen acknowledged the existence of their writings—work that one of its many authors labeled the "professors' literature of protest"[3]—and conceded that they "had their share in shaping" his views. But he also said that careful reading of *The Higher Learning in America* "would doubtless make it appear that the unacknowledged indebtedness greatly exceeds what so is accredited and accounted for" (35). How deep was Veblen's indebtedness to earlier and generally like-minded critics of the American university?

The literature on *The Higher Learning in America* is not extensive and offers little help in answering this question. It makes two principal claims about Veblen's book. The first is that he was pursuing a personal agenda. The Veblen legend, based on facts but wrapped in layers of inference that recent biographical research has largely stripped away, pictures him as an academic maverick whose personal indiscretions forced his dismissal from the University of Chicago in 1906 and from Stanford University in 1909. Accepting this image of Veblen suggests that he somehow used the book to distill his anger about his mistreatment into a cogent analysis of the American university's betrayal of its highest ideals and of the public it is supposed to serve.

---

regardless of whether they were responsible for any legal wrong. Authority to appoint and dismiss faculty belonged to boards of trustees, but the actual exercise of authority was delegated to college and university presidents.

3. The phrase was Joseph Jastrow's in "Academic Aspects of Administration," *Popular Science Monthly*, 73 (Oct. 1908), 326.

The second claim is that the book is satirical, that its primary purpose is to mock and ridicule the incoherent ambitions of the new American university system. This interpretation dates back to the earliest reviews of *The Higher Learning in America* and has remained a familiar approach ever since. In March 1919, an anonymous critic for the *North America Review* found reading Veblen "far superior to the run of fictional satirists" of the American university. "Mr. Veblen approaches more nearly the manner of Jonathan Swift than does any contemporary writer."[4] Modern scholars have come to similar conclusions. While Veblen's book remains a useful guide to the infiltration of salesmanship and other business practices into American academic life, David Riesman observed, it also has to be read as a "wonderfully witty and sarcastic book."[5]

Let's set aside these familiar characterizations to help readers of this new edition of *The Higher Learning in America* see the book in a new and brighter light—or, more precisely, to see it as I believe Veblen saw it at the time of its publication. By examining his decision to publish *The Higher Learning in America* in wartime and by sorting out his debts to earlier critics of the American university, I will probe two of the book's most important and least investigated sources. Not much digging is needed to discover that Veblen's immediate purpose in publishing *The Higher Learning in America* in late 1918 was not to settle any personal scores. Like many other prowar intellectuals at the time, he believed World War I might prove to be seedtime for fundamental reform in America. He also believed that the war provided American universities an opportunity to regain their bearings, and in the final section of the book's opening chapter, he sketched a now forgotten plan for how to accomplish this. More significant for my purposes, careful study of Veblen's debts to earlier critics of the American university will also show that he expressed beliefs and ideas that grew out of and had great resonance in American academic culture during the period between the turn of the century and World War I. In approaching *The Higher Learning in America* along these lines, my aim is to place Veblen's book at the scene of its writing, as well as to locate it more clearly in the history of modern American academic culture. I also want to draw attention to some neglected aspects of the book that speak directly to our time.

---

4. Review of *The Higher Learning in America* in *North America Review* (Mar. 1919), 417–20. Jonathan Swift (1667–1745) was an Anglo-Irish author, clergyman, and satirist, best known for *Gulliver's Travels* (1726).

5. David Riesman, *Thorstein Veblen: A Critical Interpretation* (New York: Scribner, 1953), 110.

The Composition of *The Higher Learning in America*

Summer 1904 is generally considered the starting point for *The Higher Learning in America*. Veblen was a forty-eight-year-old assistant professor in the Political Economy Department at the University of Chicago, where his career had begun in 1892. His work as the first managing editor of the University of Chicago–based *Journal of Political Economy*, which included contributing numerous scholarly articles and book reviews, had made his name relatively well known in academic circles. He also had published two books. The first—*The Theory of the Leisure Class* (1899)—had attracted immediate and widespread notice. We do not know precisely what made Veblen begin a paper exploring how business practices and values had infiltrated the American university. But there was nothing especially arresting or original about his choice of subject. During the last decades of the nineteenth century, the American university's ties to business had become familiar fare in newspaper stories and editorials across the country, as well as in a steady stream of articles published in the nation's leading monthly magazines. It also seems likely Veblen knew something of the contents of University of Chicago president William Rainey Harper's 1905 article "The Business Side of a University," which was partly a defense of a practice Harper had used to build the faculty of the University of Chicago: raiding leading faculty from other institutions.[6]

Veblen left the University of Chicago for Stanford University in 1906. During the twelve years that followed, the now lost 1904 paper, which became the 1918 book manuscript of *The Higher Learning in America*, was expanded and revised on at least four separate occasions.[7] The first was at Stanford, where Veblen shared an expanded draft with President David Starr Jordan, with whom he maintained a collegial relationship even after he was forced to resign and moved to the University of Missouri in 1909. At the University of Missouri, Veblen expanded and revised the Chicago paper for a second time. In 1916, he intended to publish a book-length manuscript in Missouri's in-house University Studies series, but the university president Ross Hill intervened and blocked publication. Hill explained to Veblen that he had found "so many paragraphs that reflected on educational leaders of the universities that I considered it might seem discourteous for the University of Missouri to become officially responsible for its publication and

6. See William Rainey Harper, *The Trend in Higher Education* (Chicago: University of Chicago Press, 1905), 161–85.

7. Archival information about *The Higher Learning in America* in the making is remarkably scant, rendering it impossible to answer all of our questions. Detailed reconstruction of Veblen's additions and revisions is impossible since only the final manuscript version of the book survives.

distribution."[8] Veblen accepted Hill's judgment that the time was not ripe for *The Higher Learning in America* and told a colleague that the book should be published posthumously.

He did not stick to this position for three reasons. First, he decided to take on a new publisher. Dissatisfied with how longtime publisher Macmillan Company had handled his earlier books, sometime in early 1918, Veblen arranged a meeting with B. W. Huebsch (1876–1964), the proprietor of a well-respected Chicago publishing house that specialized in British and translated European works on psychoanalysis and socialism, as well plays and other works of literature fashioned by the kind of new American, British, and European writers who more established American publishers hesitated to publish. Veblen struck up an amicable business relationship with Huebsch, who quickly arranged to take over the plates of the books held by Macmillan. Their relationship lasted through the publication of four new titles (beginning with *The Higher Learning in America*), new editions of his earlier books, extending to the end of Veblen's publishing life in 1923, and beyond the grave: Veblen was among several distinguished authors Huebsch took with him when he joined Viking Press in 1925.[9]

Two other decisions, made around the same time he switched publishers, also influenced Veblen's decision to publish *The Higher Learning in America* before his death. In February 1918, he accepted an appointment as a special wartime investigator for the Statistical Division of the United States Food Administration in Washington, DC; then, four months later, as he lost interest in that appointment, Veblen joined John Dewey (1859–1952) and Helen Marot (1865–1940) as one of three new contributing editors of the *Dial* magazine.[10] Given a leave of absence from his position at the University of Missouri, Veblen spent four months working for the Food Administration, where he authored a series of memoranda on different aspects of wartime domestic economic policy. Before formally ending his services there and moving to New York in June, he also completed a memorandum titled "The War and Higher Learning" that he personally distributed to leading educators across the country and, in July 1918, published as his second

8. Hill, as quoted in Joseph Dorfman, *Thorstein Veblen and His America* (New York: Viking Press, 1943), 353.

9. Over time, B. W. Huebsch's list of authors included Sherwood Anderson, Van Wyck Brooks, Randolph Bourne, Harold Laski, D. H. Lawrence, James Joyce, August Strindberg, and Maxim Gorky. Huebsch's 1916 edition of Joyce's *Portrait of the Artist as a Young Man* was the first edition of the novel published anywhere.

10. First published in Chicago in 1880, the *Dial* was the American voice of literary modernism and progressivism. In the summer of 1918, Martyn Johnson (1883–1934), the magazine's wealthy new owner and editor, moved operations to New York. Thompson charged Dewey, Marot, and Veblen with special responsibility to address what many progressive American reformers then believed—mistakenly—was a looming reconstruction at home and abroad.

contribution to the *Dial*. The piece was a call to action. While Veblen saw World War I as a grave threat to higher learning in Europe and in the United States, he also believed it presented an extraordinary opportunity for American universities. Because the United States had been spared the destruction and disorganizing experience of the war, he argued, it had the material means to conserve and reconstruct the Western world's disrupted joint enterprise in science and scholarship. American universities, in particular, could provide a free sanctuary for displaced European students and teachers, regardless of nationality, as long as they gave evidence of academic fitness. They also could cooperate in establishing an "international clearing house" that Veblen envisioned as a "focus, exchange, and center of diffusion for scholarly pursuits and mutual understanding" (38). Perhaps best of all, Veblen declared, by placing their financial and administrative resources at service to the Western world, American universities could find a new way of serving their ostensible purpose—"higher learning"—which they had served in name only.[11]

In May or June 1918, Veblen retrieved the manuscript he had returned to his files at the University of Missouri in 1916 and added an expanded version of his forthcoming *Dial* article to the end of its introductory chapter.[12] He also added a brief paragraph, dated 1918, to the preface he had written in 1916, alerting readers to "a new situation" (35) that his final addition addressed and then dispatched fair copy of the revised manuscript to Huebsch. However, a final revision remained. Two months later, Huebsch returned Veblen's preface with a letter informing him that, while he had put the rest of the manuscript in the printer's hands and expected proofs soon, he was holding back the preface at the suggestion of two unnamed but "friendly and sympathetic" readers. "It is their opinion and I agree with it," Huebsch explained, "that you do not help the book by stressing the personal note in the preface. The book itself is free from the color that the preface possesses and its impersonal tone gives it an effectiveness which the preface weakens." Veblen usually rejected editorial advice out of hand. In this case, however, we know Veblen welcomed Huebsch's comments, told him he would tone down those parts of his 1916 preface that addressed "the question of

11. During the four months Veblen spent in Washington, DC, talk of fundamental social reform was ubiquitous in American progressive assessments of World War I. By the time *The Higher Learning in America* appeared in autumn 1918, the nation was awash with reconstruction plans of the sort Veblen had in mind when he proposed the creation of an international academic clearinghouse. See Daniel T. Rodgers, *Atlantic Crossings: Social Politics in a Progressive Age* (Cambridge, MA: Belknap Press of Harvard University Press, 1998), 298–99.

12. "The War and Higher Learning," *Dial* (July 18, 1918), 45–49.

personalities," and then returned a revised 1916 preface to him without changing its date.[13]

The Professors' Literature of Protest

Presented with the history of its protracted composition, one has to wonder how Veblen viewed *The Higher Learning in America* when B. W. Huebsch published the first edition in late 1918. Was he ever puzzled by the question of what kind of book he had created over the course of fourteen years? In the 1916 preface, Veblen acknowledged that protracted composition of *The Higher Learning in America* had made for a "fragmented presentation" and a "repetitious" (33) argument. He saw no need to give examples, but they are not hard to find. Veblen's long "Introductory" chapter does not introduce the book so much as yoke together preliminary discussions of several loosely related topics. He went on to explore most of them at greater length in subsequent chapters, but he did not return to his compressed opening discussion of how the rise of the American university represented a new chapter in the history of "modern civilization" (42). Nor did he even mention again in passing his proposal to create a postwar international academic clearinghouse. As for repetitiveness, the book's long concluding chapter launches a final attack on the office of the American university presidency that made for some of the book's most memorable passages, and one that Veblen perhaps obviously enjoyed writing. What he accomplished here, however, was essentially a derisive rehearsal of points he had already developed—somewhat more soberly—in his discussion of academic administration and policy in chapter 3.

Apart from his brief acknowledgment that *The Higher Learning in America* was fragmented and repetitious, there is no evidence Veblen seriously considered the kind of book he had written. I want to do some of that for him here, however, first by briefly recounting the story of the sweeping transformation of American

13. B. W. Huebsch to Thorstein Veblen, Aug. 16, 1918, B. W. Huebsch Papers, MS Division, Library of Congress; and Thorstein Veblen to B. W. Huebsch, Aug. 24, 1918. Although the manuscript version of the 1916 preface has not surfaced, Jacob Warshaw, one of Veblen's colleagues at the University of Missouri, recalled its angry tone: "In the midst of characteristic Veblenian language appeared a short sentence referring to the University of Chicago and containing something like these words: 'Where the present writer was assassinated.'" Warshaw, as quoted in Clare Eby, "Boundaries Lost: Thorstein Veblen, *The Higher Learning in America*, and the Conspicuous Spouse," *Prospects: An Annual of American cultural studies*, ed. Jack Salzman, 26 (2001), 291, n. 65. Huebsch's papers in the Library of Congress contain no information about the exact month of publication of the first edition of *The Higher Learning in America*, nor its price or the number of copies printed. The final corrected typescript of the manuscript Veblen returned to Huebsch bears a stamp showing it was received on Sept. 30, 1918. It would seem, then, that Huebsch brought out the first edition either in late October or, more probably, in November.

higher education during the last three decades of the nineteenth century and then by exploring how the "professors' literature of protest" found its way into Veblen's thinking while he was writing *The Higher Learning in America*.

The story of the still astonishingly rapid construction of the American university system after the end of the Civil War can be traced in two phases. The line of demarcation falls in the early 1890s, when a variety of developments—the most conspicuous of which was the opening in quick succession of Clark University, Stanford University, and University of Chicago between 1889 and 1892—signaled the onset of the nation's first great "academic boom." For roughly two decades after 1865, a small handful of new and reformed institutions—Cornell University, Johns Hopkins University, and Harvard University—had stood out as daring but isolated experiments. Then other private and public institutions across the country rapidly began to adopt their two most important innovations: the elective system and graduate schools. At the same time, American colleges and universities turned the corner regarding enrollment. At the beginning of this period, the number of undergraduates was small: a total of 52,000. By 1890, there were 157,000, and the figure rose to 230,000 in 1900. The number of college and university professors also grew dramatically—from 5,533 in 1870 to 23,868 in 1910—and in the process, professors gained new measures of status and influence in American culture at large. The popularity of new and reformed institutions also prompted a new and continuous flow of private gifts for their aid, as well as larger and more dependable legislative appropriations.[14]

Another fundamentally important development historians trace back to the "academic boom" of the early 1890s was that the internal administrative structure of a typical American university gained the steeply hierarchical shape, which, in most respects, it has maintained to this day. By the turn of the century, the American university hierarchy comprised the board of trustees or regents, the president, deans, department chairs, and faculty members of several different ranks. In addition, an administrative staff grew with its own various purposes, from athletics to public relations and fund-raising, and its own internal gradations. With this new hierarchal structure, the phrase *the administration* first gained widespread use to refer to presidents, deans, business staff, department chairs,

14. In the early 1890s, American higher education also was the site of activity usually associated with the country's then so-called captains of industry. In Chicago, for example, William Rainey Harper enlisted several local millionaires in a friendly rivalry with John D. Rockefeller, which by 1916 provided the University of Chicago $8 million worth of land and buildings and $39 million in endowment (see figure 2). Rockefeller's huge gifts to the General Education Board (GEB), incorporated in 1903, also left a deep mark on the entire system of American higher education. By 1921, he had personally donated $129 million (the equivalent of $1.6 billion today) to the GEB's endowment, whose income was used to bolster college and university endowments across the country.

Figure 2. William Rainey Harper (*right foreground*), John D. Rockefeller (*left foreground*), trustee Martin A. Ryerson (*second from left*), and philanthropist Julius Rosenwald (*left*), 1901. University of Chicago Archives

and other senior professors who actively supported the policies and decisions of the president. Power usually flowed downward throughout the university. American college and university presidents routinely exercised preeminent power. In almost all cases, they determined salaries and made faculty appointments and promotions free of any procedural constraints. Presidents also appointed deans, who in turn appointed department chairpersons. A formal subservience to "the administration" was expected of the faculty, as well as informal deference.[15] The concept of *tenure* as a continuous faculty appointment, though not entirely unknown in this period, was accepted by very few college and university presidents. Professors also were usually barred from becoming members of boards of trustees, either at their own or at other institutions.

All this is a schematic recounting of developments that allowed the American university system to secure a prominent and stable place in our national affairs. These same developments also gave rise to the "professors' literature of protest." This now largely forgotten literature, as we shall see, found its heyday during the years that Veblen was writing *The Higher Learning in America.* But its origins date

15. An anonymous contribution to *Scribner's Magazine* in 1907 provided an early eyewitness account of this development. See "The Point of View," *Scribner's Magazine,* 42 (1907), 123–24.

back to the first phase of the construction of the American university system when Franklin W. Clarke (1847–1931), professor of chemistry and physics at the University of Cincinnati, published two articles in *Popular Science Monthly*, arguing that faculty control was the only appropriate basis for university governance. Looking for an explanation of why the traditional classical curriculum continued to dominate American higher education at the time, Clarke found it in administrative procedures, which dictated that American colleges and universities employ professors solely on the basis of presidents' individual recommendations to boards of trustees. Clarke did not call for a full transfer of appointive power from trustees to faculty, but he did maintain that the faculty, rather than the president, was the proper source of recommendations for all faculty appointments and promotions.[16]

Popular Science Monthly (during the last decades of the nineteenth century, America's most important and widely read nonspecialist science journal) and *Science* (the official journal of the American Association of Science) served as the main forums for professors' literature of protest well into the twentieth century. They were by no means the only ones. Articles criticizing the American system of university governance also began to appear in the nation's leading monthly magazines in the early 1880s. An anonymous contribution to the *Century Magazine* in 1883, for example, helped to launch the question of proper procedures for faculty appointments into broader public discussion. The article echoed Clarke in arguing that university presidents and boards of trustees should give faculties more power and an official consulting role in making appointments.[17] During the late 1880s and 1890s, a steady stream of similar articles by professors across the country, supplemented by numerous like-minded magazine and newspaper editorials, augmented and expanded Clarke's argument to include giving faculty more direct power in choosing presidents and in determining university budgets and policies.

For the most part, examples of the professors' literature of protest that Thorstein Veblen knew dated from the opening decade and a half of the twentieth century, by the end of which time it had become a well-established genre. The most widely circulated examples from this era were John J. Stevenson, "The Status of the American College Professor" (1904); James P. Munroe, "Closer Relations between Trustees and Faculty"(1905); George M. Stratton, "Externalism in the

16. Franklin W. Clarke, "American Colleges v. American Science," *Popular Science Monthly* 9 (1876), 476, and "The Appointment of College Officers," *Popular Science Monthly* 21 (1882), 171–78. Clarke was one of the founders of the American Chemical Society and served as its president in 1901.

17. "College Presidents and the Power of Appointment," *Century Magazine*, 26 (July 1883), 467–69.

American University" (1907); Stewart Patton, "University Administration and University Ideals" (1911); John Jay Chapman, "Professorial Ethics" (1910); George T. Ladd, "The Need of Administrative Changes in the American University" (1912); Joseph Jastrow, "The Administrative Peril in Education" (1912); and, above all, James McKeen Cattell, "Concerning the American University" (1902) and "University Control" (1906).

Stratton's piece was published in the *Atlantic Monthly*; the rest first appeared either in *Popular Science Monthly* or in *Science*. In March 1913, it was James McKeen Cattell (1860–1940), then the owner and editor of both *Popular Science Monthly* and *Science*, who helped to ensure all these "protests" received additional public notice when he collected them in a 482-page volume titled *University Control*. Cattell also led off the book with an expanded version of his 1906 article that provided the title of the collection. His long piece included the outline of a plan for a sweeping and democratic reorganization of American university governance that he had first published in *Science* in March 1906. In 1911, Cattell also had circulated his plan among hundreds of university scientists across the country, asking for unsigned written responses to his suggestions. He received almost three hundred replies, most of which agreed with his proposal that the powers of university presidents and trustees should be curtailed and faculty power increased. Cattell reprinted the anonymous replies verbatim in the May 12 issue of *Science* and then again in the pages that followed his lead article in *University Control*. He further enlarged the book by reprinting Cornell University president Jacob Schurman's "Faculty Participation in University," a statement drawn from Schurman's 1912 annual report to the Cornell trustees in which he strongly advocated greater faculty participation in the management and control of the university.

University Control was the most elaborate and wide-ranging discussion of American university governance to appear before *The Higher Learning in America*. It also was the book Veblen identified by name as having "been in mind throughout" the writing of his book, as well as serving "as ground and material" for much of its argument (49, note f).[18] Today, *University Control* is best remembered as a

18. Of all the figures who contributed to the professors' literature of protest, James McKeen Cattell (1860–1944) undoubtedly was the one who cut the broadest swath, both intellectually and personally. Best remembered for his uncompromising opposition to American involvement in World War I, he was the acknowledged (and often irascible) leader of the early twentieth-century push for great faculty control of the American universities. Financially independent, Cattell in those years was not only owner-editor of both *Science* and *Popular Science Monthly* but also owner and founder of the Science Press, which published the two magazines and *University Control*. Cattell used his money and his position as editor to lend power and support to what he believed was a national movement to supplant the increasing power of presidents and trustees with greater faculty control.

book that also prompted action that helped to provide the longest-lasting domain of the genre of the professors' literature of protest as the catalyst for the founding of the American Association of University Professors in 1915. Not simply the first national association fully controlled by professors, the AAUP provided professors with a new platform for expressing their ideas and opinions, as well as a new theater in which their debates about university affairs would play out in front of the public for decades to come. For a *précis* of the recurrent concerns of the professors' literature of protest, one could scarcely do better than "Faculty Share of University Control" (1915), a paper that John Dewey (1859–1952) wrote during the year he served as the first president of the AAUP and presented at the annual meeting of the Association of American Universities.[19]

The professors' literature of protest was mostly the work of figures, such as Cattell and Dewey, who had received their PhDs in the 1880s or early 1890s. They had begun their careers believing they were a welcome part of the booming new American university system who would contribute to defining its purpose and guiding its development. But things did not play out quite as they had envisaged. It is true that the principal contributors to *University Control* included several individuals who had helped to professionalize the organization and study of academic disciplines in the United States.[20] In 1888, John Stevenson was among the founders of the Geological Society of America. In 1892, Cattell, Dewey, Jastrow, and George Stratton were among the founders of the American Psychological Association. Cattell was elected the association's president in 1895, Jastrow in 1900, and Stratton in 1908. In 1892, John Creighton was the founding editor of the *Philosophical Review*; in 1902, he was founding president of the American Philosophical Association. Later Cattell joined Dewey in representing Columbia University at the landmark conference of university faculty that led to the establishment of the AAUP.

Within the universities that employed them, however, where fundamental control rested in the hands of university presidents and boards of trustees or regents with no immediate connection to either scholarship or teaching, even these once prominent figures were in much the same position as their colleagues elsewhere. They had no particular authority for developing institutional plans they were expected to carry out and were formally excluded from the process of select-

19. John Dewey, "Faculty Share of University Control," first published in *Journal and Proceedings and Addresses of the Seventeenth Annual Conference* (1915), 27–32; reprinted in *John Dewey: The Middle Works, 1899–1924*, ed. Jo Ann Boydston (Carbondale: Southern Illinois University Press, 1979), 109–22.

20. Veblen also made an important contribution to this work. As managing editor of the *University of Chicago–based Journal of Political Economy* from 1895 to 1905, he helped to promote and enrich national and international discourse among professional economists.

ing those who had authority to fashion such plans. In 1908, Jastrow declared that America had "developed or accepted a type of university administration, to which there is no close, hardly a distant, parallel elsewhere." He also decried it as "government by imposition."[21]

Veblen and the Professors' Literature of Protest

The belief that faculty had no responsible share in American university governance, and that almost all important educational and administrative questions were routinely settled without their participation, was choroused again and again by the many figures who contributed to the professors' literature of protest during the late nineteenth and early twentieth century. By the time *University Control* appeared in 1913, this belief informed a widespread and embittered protest.[22] It also was embedded in a discussion that had three recurring themes: (1) how to define the highest goals of the American university; (2) how the establishment of a corporate business model of governance endangered the development of the American university; and (3) how to overcome a variety of dangers constituted by that same model of governance, especially the overbearing power it assigned to the office of the university president. My initial purpose in this section is to survey how these themes were addressed by the ten named contributors to *University Control* and then to show how the same themes also formed much of what Veblen called the "ground and material" of *The Higher Learning in America*. Veblen's account of the condition of the American university, as we shall see, was by no means a carbon copy of what he found in *University Control*. If it were, his use of the book would be less interesting and less memorable. Veblen was not wide of the mark, however, when he said that his indebtedness to the contributors to *University Control* exceeded what he managed to accredit or account for in writing the book.

The principal contributors to *University Control* were one in their conviction that, if the American university was to have any hope of achieving its highest purpose,

---

21. Joseph Jastrow, "Academic Aspects of Administration," *Popular Science Monthly* (Oct. 1908), 328. Although largely powerless within institutions that employed them, American college and university professors did have relatively easy access to editorial columns and reviews and hence were not without a certain cultural authority of their own. The professors' literature of protest did not go unanswered. Reponses from colleges and university presidents appeared in many of the same popular magazines and professional journals that published that literature. Most conceded that the American system of university governance was autocratic and hierarchical but stressed the advantages of the arrangement.

22. As Dewey explained things tersely to American university presidents in 1915, "grown men with a high degree of intellectual training and wide reputation do not enjoy being treated like children." Dewey, "Faculty Share in University Control," in *John Dewey: The Middle Works, 1899–1924*, 111.

faculty must have an active and responsible share in its governance. They held strongly to this belief because they also maintained that the American university was—like its more long-standing counterparts in Britain and Europe—essentially a cultural institution whose highest purpose was to serve the needs of the faculty and their students. "The university is those who teach and those who learn and the work they do," Cattell declared. The health of the university, in his view, was primarily a matter of recruiting gifted and well-trained men to the faculty and providing them with the resources and freedom to do their work.[23] Jastrow echoed these sentiments when he declared that the university existed to "provide the collective facilities, the communal stimulus, the larger environment, in which intellectual products flourish" (319). The university was "first and foremost an educational institution ministered to by a company of scholars," he wrote, "no other test of values is relevant than the educational one; no sacrifice in any measure of educational to other interests can be justified" (333). Stratton repeated this belief when he declared that the "first duty" of the university was to "offer knowledge and the power of judgment" (429).

The same general belief that the university was a distinct institution, a domain of cultural authority whose practices and values should be insulated from external pressures, suffused *The Higher Learning in America*. Veblen declared that the university "is, and . . . has always been, a corporation for the cultivation and care of the community's highest aspirations and ideals" (59). "In the current common-sense apprehension of what is right and good, as it works out in the long run" he wrote, "the university is a corporation of learning, disinterested and dispassionate." It is "the one great institution of modern times that works to no ulterior end and is controlled by no consideration of expediency beyond its own work" (75). Later Veblen echoed Cattell and Jastrow in defining the university as "a body of scholars and scientists, each and several of whom necessarily goes to his work on his own initiative and pursues it in his own way" (94).

A second prominent element of continuity between the contributors to *University Control* and Veblen lay in their analysis of developments they believed were obstructing the American university in realizing its highest purpose. Here, too, they chorused the belief that the chief obstacles facing the American university were constituted by its distinctive system of governance. The "comprehensive and woeful wrong," as Jastrow put it, was that the forces directing American academic life did not express its "real intentions, demands and ideals . . . The rest is but a bill of particulars" (333). All the contributors to *University Control* recog-

23. J. McKeen Cattell, ed., *University Control* (New York: Science Press, 1913), 414. Subsequent page references are given in parenthesis in the text.

nized that American universities were organized as institutions in which ultimate authority rested in the hands of a small body of trustees or regents composed largely of businessmen who were not members of the university community. The board's chief point of contact with the university, that is, with its faculty and students, was through the university president to whom the board delegated not just *de jure* but also *de facto* authority in all personnel decisions. Some contributors acknowledged there were differences in how strictly the new American system of "university control" was applied. All agreed, however, that the typical American university operated, as Jastrow described in an earlier version of his *University Control* piece, as "little more than a corporation of an industrial type, in which groups of men have been employed to perform tasks."[24] They agreed too that the ascendancy of the corporate model of "university control" thus represented a complete repudiation of the long-standing British and European understanding of the university as a free association of teachers and scholars.

In *University Control*, protest against the anomalous condition of the American university faculty reflected a wide variety of more specific concerns. Jastrow, for example, looked back on the 1880s and 1890s as decades when "everything grew, enlarged, expanded—grounds, buildings, plans, facilities, positions, students, and duties." But because change had "come with a rush and was hurried to its consummation" (317), he wrote, it had left the American general public with little understanding of the primary purpose of the university. Along a different line, Stratton wondered why, in an allegedly democratic nation, university governance had "assumed a form that we might have expected to see in a land accustomed to kings. European universities have a constitution that might have come from some American political theorist; America universities are as though founded and fostered in the bourne of aristocracy" (426). Along the same line, Chapman wondered why America had created a university system in which professors were so "timid" in defending their interests and speculated that "too great specialization in their own education" had left them "helpless as all-around fighters" (460).

Not all of these concerns were generally shared. While Jastrow and Stratton decried the rapid expansion of the American university system, for example, Cattell welcomed it. Unlike them, he believed that the "patriotism and civic pride" of ordinary American people would lead them to "increase the wealth of their universities as rapidly as it can wisely be used" (422). Taken in its entirety, however, the "bill of particulars" drawn up by the contributors to *University Control* reflected

24. Joseph Jastrow, "The Academic Career as Affected by Administration," *Science* (Apr. 13, 1906), 569.

an overarching fear that all shared: namely, *that the corporate business model of governance did not simply obstruct the American university in realizing its ideal as a cultural institution, it actually established and maintained values and practices that were incompatible with those of any true university.* Contributors to *University Control* never minced language in making this point. The American university was governed "from without," Stratton declared, ruled by a board of governors that "belongs neither to those who study nor those who teach, and is in consequence disjoined from the real life of the institution" (427). Control of the American university, John Jay Chapman wrote, rested in the hands of "men whose ideals were as remote from scholarship as the ideal of New York theatrical managers are from poetry" (427). Jacob Schurman put the same point more directly: American university professors criticized presidents and boards of trustees because they governed the American university in pursuit of "an alien ideal, the ideal of a business corporation" (476).

In *University Control*, the common claim that the major disorders of the American university were defects that could be traced directly to an "alien" or incompatible system of governance—a claim the historian Walter Metzger aptly labeled "the thesis of cultural incompatibility"[25]—had its most forceful articulation in Joseph Jastrow's article "The Administrative Peril in Education." Jastrow began by declaring as unequivocally as possible that the "one paramount danger, the most comprehensively unfavorable factor affecting ominously the prospects of higher education . . . is *the undue dominance of administration*: in policy, in measures, in personal relations, in all the distinctive interests of education, and the welfare of ideas and ideals" (318). On one level, he worried that the American university's autocratic system of governance was discouraging strong personalities from joining the academic profession. He shared this worry with many of the other contributors to *University Control*, and Veblen would voice it again in *The Higher Learning in America*. But Jastrow worried even more that well-entrenched "external" forces were directing the American university in ways that did "not validly or adequately express" the "real intentions, demands, and ideals" of a true university (333). Above all, Jastrow condemned the corporate business model of university governance for undercutting the faculty's responsibility for, as well as its interest in, guiding the affairs of the university as a whole. The familiar response that "educational questions are decided by the faculty and financial ones by the board" he dismissed as "absolutely specious" (335). In the abstract, one could speak of "a group of plainly financial and a group of plainly educational questions."

25. Richard Hofstadter and Walter P. Metzger, *The Development of Academic Freedom in the United States* (New York: Columbia University Press, 1955), 452.

In reality, the work of addressing the two questions usually overlapped since university boards routinely exercised their fiscal authority by launching initiatives that either encroached on work already undertaken by the faculty or prevented expansion of faculty work that might otherwise occur.[26] Real power in the American university, Jastrow argued, was the university board's power over the budget, because it was the board's budget decisions that determined who was hired and who was not, what salaries were paid, and what programs were encouraged or shut off from further support.

The same disapproving view of lay board governance is fully endorsed and extended by Veblen in *The Higher Learning in America*. "Plato's classic scheme of folly, which would have the philosophers take over the management of affairs, has been turned on its head," he wrote, "the men of affairs have taken over the direction of the pursuit of knowledge" (88).[27] This is a waggishly clever précis of the "thesis of cultural incompatibility." It also is the book's great take-way sentence, though only, I think, for those who manage to ignore important twists and turns of Veblen's thinking about this matter. Like Stratton and Chapman before him, Veblen certainly scoffed at the notion that worldly success gave trustees the understanding or broad fund of knowledge needed to run a university. But he never said that in his day "men of affairs" had achieved complete dominance within the American university. Indeed, Veblen acknowledged that business practices had their place in the university's "fiscal affairs and the office-work incident to the care of its material equipment." With regard to these items, he conceded, the university is in fact "a business concern" (103). He also noted that university trustees and presidents were constrained in their decision making by the need for universities to cultivate their prestige by employing prominent scholars, as well as by the force of certain long-standing academic traditions that made for "forms of divided responsibility" (100) in a university's day-to-day operations.

And yet, while Veblen suggested that "forms of divided responsibility" would ensure that the scholarly purpose of the American university would never fade from sight, he also insisted they did not hide the underlying reality of the faculty's unequal position of power in governing the university. Echoing Jastrow, Veblen observed that the obvious problem with the view that power was sensibly divided

26. The example Jastrow gives in a long footnote explores the implications of an unnamed university's decision to build a new football stadium, a decision "reached without consulting the faculty who, it was assumed, if indeed they were considered at all, would delightedly approve this expenditure of funds even though other cherished purposes would thereby be deferred,—a common occurrence" (335, note 5).

27. In *The Republic* (380 BCE), the ancient Greek philosopher Plato (428–7 BCE–348–7 BCE) argued that the survival of a just city-state required rule by philosophers trained to be kings.

within the American university was that power was not divided when it came to decisions regarding the university's budget, which in turn meant that the larger political and financial determinants of academic life were well beyond the reach of the faculty. Or as Veblen put it, a "complaisant" view of university governance underestimates the extent to which "much effective surveillance of the academic work is exercised through the board's control of the budget. The academic staff can do little else than the specifications of the budget provide for," and without the money the board chooses to supply them, "they are as helpless as might be expected" (89). And it was precisely at this level, Veblen, continued, that business practices and values most deeply undermined the university's primary commitments to the claims of science and scholarship. Lay boards invariably prefer short-term returns over "those intangible, immaterial uses for which the university is established," he wrote, because such "uses leave no physical, tangible residue in the way of durable goods, such as will justify the expenditure in terms of vendible property acquired; therefore they are *prima facie imbecile*,[28] and correspondingly distasteful to men whose habitual occupation is with the acquisition of property" (90).

In *University Control*, the belief that an "alien" power, wielded by "men whose habitual occupation is with the acquisition of property," lurked at the center of the American university also informed discussions of what the principal contributors to the book saw as the most menacing of all the practices they associated with corporate system of "university control": the concentration of administrative power in the office of the American university president. At the outset of the twentieth century, there was no office in the British or German university systems that had the same authority as the office of the American university president, and nothing troubled these figures' conceptions of themselves as university professors more than the sweeping power exercised by a typical American university president. Some contributors acknowledged in passing that a few unnamed American university presidents did manage in hidden ways to act as representatives of the faculty. All recognized, however, that the existing American system of university governance compelled faculty to regard the president as essentially a member of the university's governing board and only incidentally a member of the faculty.

Contributors to *University Control* had various misgivings about this chain of command. Chapman, for example, decried it for rendering American university presidents in-house agents of wealthy businessmen who had used their money

28. Latin: stupid at first glance.

to found new universities or to reorganize old ones. Stevenson condemned university boards for appointing presidents "not to elevate the institution as an educational power, but to make of it a 'big thing.'" Jastrow took umbrage with a system that "so often uncritically" rendered the president "the recipient of praise as the visible embodiment of the source from whom all blessings flow" (325). So too did Stratton, who wrote that many faculty felt "that the presidency in our universities is like that oak in the Finnish tale, which sprang up late, and yet in the end shut out the light of day and must be felled, lest all other life should fail" (431).

Stratton's light-blocking oak metaphor captured the deepest of all the concerns voiced by contributors to *University Control*: the power of the American university president to appoint, to promote, and to dismiss the faculty. This concern was highly visible throughout the book, beginning with Cattell's introductory essay in which he employed a more ominous metaphor—in the American "academic jungle," he wrote, "the president is my black beast" (31)—to sound a warning chorused by almost all other contributors to *University Control*. Ladd declared the chief harm of giving the American university president such a free hand was "the degradation of the professional office." He wrote that, after completing graduate training, a typical candidate for an appointment at an American university would discover he was now poised to enter into a profession where his "whole career, and the reputation which he has won by a life of self-sacrificing labor, may at any moment be in peril through the caprice, or the cowardice, or ill-will of a single man, or a little group of men who have influence with that single man" (362–63). Stratton echoed Ladd's sentiments, adding that while American university faculty seemed to retain "the important power to define the requirements for admission to the university and its degrees," these activities too were in "a fundamental way directed by the president, since by his word comes growth to this department and atrophy to that" (427–28). The essence of the problem was that, while the authority of the American university president was "subject to a constitution, and he cannot quite justly be called an autocrat, nevertheless the charter brings to him perhaps less serious restrictions than those which often in the larger world bind men who bear the name of emperor" (428). Or, as Cattell put it more bluntly, "The trouble in the case of the university president is that he is not a leader, but a boss" (32).

Essentially, the same disapproving view of the office of the American university president is again repeated and extended in *The Higher Learning in America*. Veblen too portrayed American university presidents as dangerously far removed in power and public distinction from university professors. Half in jest, he put them on stage as "captains of erudition," academic equivalents of the "captains of industry" who had just built the nation's first large business corporations and now struggled among themselves to make good as leaders of competitive business concerns. Within the walls of the university, presidents functioned as preeminently powerful, and sometimes threatening, "executive heads" to whom boards of trustees gave "full command of the means entrusted" to them as well as "free power to appoint and dismiss, and to reward and punish" all those who work under their direction, subject only to the formal ratification of their decisions by boards "who will be careful not to interfere or inquire unduly in these matters— so long as their strong man shows results" (97–93). Veblen provided many illustrations of the ways in which the new American "captains of erudition" kept their ships in order. They appointed deans and department chairs who showed them unwavering loyalty. They bullied or fired professors who disagreed with their policies. They kept and shared "black lists" of professors with controversial views. Veblen never named names along the way. He did, however, make several veiled references to University of Chicago president William Rainey Harper and Columbia University president Nicholas Murray Butler (1862–1947) that would have been unmistakable for informed readers in his time.

Veblen also recognized that showing results involved a good deal more than just directing the university's internal affairs in ways that gained the board's approval. Academic strong men also had to keep their institutions "constantly in the public eye, with such 'pomp and circumstance' of untiring urgency and expedition as will carry the conviction abroad that the university under his management is a highly successful going concern." As a consequence, captains of erudition were public figures whose interests and influence extended into local, state, and national affairs. As public figures, they also regularly put their supposed erudition on display in a steady stream of addresses made before "popular audiences, at commencements, inaugurations, dedications, club meetings, church festivals, and the like." Public speaking, in fact, became such a pressing obligation, Veblen observed, that any American university president who aspired "to do his whole duty in these premises will become in some sort an itinerant dispensary of salutary verbiage," and thus a figure "conventionally indispensable for the effusion of graceful speech at all gatherings of the well-to-do for convivial deliberation of the state of mankind at large" (213).[29] The English language, in fact, wanted "a com-

29. Elsewhere in the book Veblen wrote that the American university president's craving for public distinction could be understood as the predictable outcome of viewing the university as a business concern whose quality could be measured in part by "the prestige of its executive." He also observed that the prestige that surrounded America's new captains of erudition could be understood "in very much the same way as the like will hold true, e.g., for any company of public amusement, itinerant or

petent designation" for all the public-minded activities undertaken by the American university president, Veblen remarked. But the new word *"philandropist"* might capture it, he suggested, and perhaps even gain quick public acceptance because it was "not a large innovation" and had the additional merit of "being self-explanatory" (213, note g).

This is Veblen ridiculing the office of the American university president in the final chapter of *The Higher Learning in America*, which he does at such great length it tends to obscure the book's guiding argument. But Veblen was usually serious when he was humorous. The book's second and third chapters advance essentially the same "thesis of cultural incompatibility" that informed similar criticism of the office voiced by contributors to *University Control*. In the second chapter, Veblen lays it down as an axiom, that where the power of appointing a university president rests entirely in the hands of a board composed largely of businessmen, the board "will create an academic head in its own image." He concedes that the board's choice at times may not fall on "a competent businessman," but this will not be "due to its inclining too far on the side of scholarship." University boards invariably select new presidents "primarily with a view to give the academic administration more of a businesslike character." So even when boards happen to select scholars they usually manage to pass them quickly "from the ranks of learning to those of business enterprise" and thereby delegate power "to one of their own kind" (90–93). Veblen also devotes part of his closing chapter to repeating the same argument. To understand the prestige-minded character of the typical American university president, he observed, one need only to look at the "characteristics of those boards who chose university presidents." Because university boards "are made up of well-to-do businessmen, with a penchant for popular notability," it follows that "the qualifications necessary to be put in evidence by aspirants for executive office are such as will convince such a board of their serviceability" (206).

What Set Veblen Apart? Why Read Veblen Today?

Readers who have followed my discussion to this point will have acquired, I hope, a new appreciation of how *The Higher Learning in America* reflects the time in which it was written. Veblen was by no means an isolated critic of the American university. Nor was he the first to warn that the American university put its inde-

---

sedentary, such as a circus, a theatrical or operatic enterprise, which all compete for the acclamation of those to whom these matters appeal" (109).

pendence at risk by adopting the methods and serving the needs of the larger business community. But other like-minded and once prominent early twentieth-century critics of the American university have long since faded from view. What set Veblen apart? And why read Veblen today?

The short answer to the first question is that tracing the presence of the main themes of the professors' literature of protest in *The Higher Learning in America* is not the same as actually reading the book page by page. The longer answer is that if we want to say that Veblen found his guiding themes in the professors' literature of protest, we also must say that his engagement with them so complicated and deepened the genre that it became something else.

It takes no more than a glance at the opening pages of *The Higher Learning in America* to see that Veblen's book has a complexity of prose and thinking not to be found in any examples of the professors' literature of protest that James McKeen Cattell gathered in *University Control. The Higher Learning in America* ultimately is a hybrid text that mutates from one generic category to another: part an essay in cultural history; part a thinly disguised autobiography; part a scathing criticism of the American university's anomalous system of governance; part a clear-eyed analysis of how American university governance actually works; and part a call to action (added at the last minute). Along the way, Veblen employed a vocabulary that was routine for anthropologists, economists, and philosophers of his day but in places made for prose whose intricacy seemed calculated to baffle and amuse at the same time. He almost never called things by their proper names and usually was content to make his case by allusion and indirection. Veblen also wrote in a voice that often changed its tone, one that was by turns critical, self-parodying, sarcastic, hyperbolic, combative, and conciliatory. Finally, he could not resist putting his literary erudition on display, peppering his text and footnotes with an array of phrases and quotations drawn from works that range in time from the Bible and *Kojiki* (the oldest survey book of Japanese myths and stories assembled by an anonymous eighth-century Japanese poet) to the essays of Matthew Arnold and the poetry of Rudyard Kipling. More than likely Veblen did not quite know what he had created with *The Higher Learning in America*. Doubtless he knew that his book makes many demands on a reader.

So what does Veblen have to offer in return? Or, more precisely, if we want to imagine him transported into the early twenty-first century, what does he have to offer to students of the American university in our time? The answer resists simplification, partly because American higher education has expanded and has been reshaped in ways that Veblen did not anticipate. *The Higher Learning in America* focuses on what in 1918 was a small number of mostly private American research universities.[30] In the 1920s, public institutions of higher education began to grow substantially in size and numbers. They also underwent a process of internal differentiation. More well-funded state research universities now began to rival elite private institutions. And new types of public colleges, especially access-oriented state colleges and two year colleges, were created to meet an increased postwar demand for more practically oriented education. World War II introduced federal support for scientific research, and in the postwar era, federal partnership would become a cornerstone of university-based research at both private and public institutions.

During the last third of the twentieth century, American higher education was reshaped in other ways. In the realms of teaching and scholarship, the power of American professors increased substantially during the 1960 and 1970s. The ideal of academic freedom and the practice of tenure spread from one institution to another. By the end of the century, university presidents no longer functioned as the primary gatekeepers of the faculty. Lay trustees also came to encompass a broader range of nonacademic professions. During the 1980s and 1990s, other economic developments further complicated the American academic landscape. The priorities of American universities were shaped by the increased power and temptations of big private philanthropy from wealthy individuals, especially from wealthy alumni. They also confronted other kinds of external economic pressures. Many of these were more subtle than those Veblen knew, exercised through direct monetary incentives as well as through more indirect forms of influence, and all of which some critics contend have made for an ongoing "corporatization" of the American university. Universities across the country today, for example, perform contract services for business corporations, ranging from drug testing for pharmaceutical companies to advertising for manufacturers of athletic apparel and shoes. They also have formed business partnerships with corporations and designed degree programs to serve corporate hiring needs. They accept corporate-funded professorships and fellowships. Corporations hire faculty as consultants and fund their research. Corporations also have penetrated American higher education more directly by creating universities explicitly run for profit.

Granted all that, we should not, I think, overdraw the distinction between the American university as Veblen knew it and the one we know today. University governance may be more widely shared in some academic arenas, but it is still

---

30. While the founding of the Association of American Universities (AAU) in 1900 signaled that the research university had come of age in the United States, it had only twelve charter members, eleven of which were private institutions. By 1918, membership had been expanded modestly to include seven public research universities. Still considered an association of the nation's preeminent private and public research universities, AAU membership today stands at sixty two.

divided essentially along the same lines as when Veblen began his career at the University of Chicago in 1892. Except perhaps at some of the nation's most elite universities, faculty as a group have little or no power in setting the overall academic and nonacademic agendas of their institutions. Boards of trustees still choose university presidents and have final authority in determining university budgets. They still also consist almost entirely of lay trustees, most of whom are financially successful nonacademics and whose primary employment is not in the university. From time to time, university trustees still engage in what Veblen called "bootless meddling" (80). But these days real power at almost all American universities rests where it did in Veblen's day: largely in the hands of presidents and other senior administrators, in no small part because boards composed of lay trustees still must rely almost entirely on them for information and plans regarding a university's current and future needs.

Yet if the impulse here is, understandably, to say that "Plato's scheme of folly" lives on, careful readers of *The Higher Learning in America* will notice that Veblen never expected things to be otherwise. He in fact saw little point in thinking about or promoting fundamental reform of American university governance. Ordinary Americans would be opposed to fundamental reform, he explained, because "popular sentiment" in his day "ran plainly to the effect that magnitude, arbitrary control, and businesslike administration is the only sane rule to be followed in any human enterprise" (202). No less important was the fact that any effort to reorganize university governance would come to nothing as long as the legal ground of the university remained a system of private ownership that granted boards of lay trustees "plenary discretion" in governing the university's affairs (88).

Neither the public's view nor the legal ground of American university governance has changed since 1918. If that is the case, it follows that the American university's ongoing corporatization probably would not prompt vigorous headshaking from Veblen either. Here again alert readers of *The Higher Learning in America* will notice that, as much as Veblen decried "the conduct of universities by businessmen," he never seriously envisaged the American university operating in an economic vacuum. Or put another way, Veblen was careful to separate his understanding of an ideal university from his sense of how it would be forced to operate in America. He understood that the priorities of the American university had been firmly set in economic context and almost certainly always would be. The more important point to note here, however, is that Veblen also steered away from the conclusion that the American university therefore was destined to be a mere tool of business. All "the graver issues of academic policy which now tax the discretion of the directive powers," he wrote, "reduce themselves in the main to a question between the claims of science and scholarship on the one hand and those of business principles and pecuniary gain on the other hand. *In one shape or another this problem of adjustment, reconciliation, or compromise between the needs of higher learning and the demands of business enterprise is forever present in the deliberations of the university directorate"* (68; italics added). So the question posed by the corporatization of the American university, Veblen might say, is not the corruption or decline of an ideal but rather the autonomy that a conflicted institution exercises in responding to economic contingencies and the principles it invokes in exercising that authority.[31] Can the American university maintain its core claims of "science and scholarship" in tension with the claims of the economic marketplace? How much "adjustment" and "compromise" can be achieved and by what means?

The Higher Learning in America summons us to ask these big questions perhaps as no other book has, partly because it goes out of its way to show us why they have no easy answers. Consider Veblen's discussion of faculty salaries. In American universities, faculty salaries have never been as uniform as they still remain in most British and European universities, where governments typically set a flat rate for everyone. By contrast, salaries of American university faculty are set by senior administrators and boards of trustees, and they observe what might be called the rule of "professional school exceptionalism," which allows faculty salaries to differ widely across academic fields. As Veblen described the rule, university-based professional schools—his examples were business and law schools, but the rule soon came to include medical schools—must offer higher salaries to attract "men of affairs" who otherwise would choose to practice their skills outside the university and bill for their services on the open market. The rule specifically dictates "the salaries paid these men of affairs" must be "some multiple of the salary assigned to men of comparable ability and attainments in the academic work proper" (183–84). The rule also extends to hiring administrative staff support for professional schools.

Veblen here is not talking about today's so-called star system, the related American university practice of hiring and favoring faculty who happen to become famous or popular regardless of field. He opens the window on a deeper and more long-standing problem: the willingness of American universities to tolerate salary differentials by field for faculty of equal merit and to let the magnitude of

31. My account of Veblen here and in the paragraphs that follow has him making several of the same points David Hollinger makes in "Money and Academic Freedom a Half-Century after McCarthyism: Universities amid the Force Fields of Capital," in *Cosmopolitanism and Solidarity: Studies in Ethnoracial, Religious, and Professional Affiliation in the United States* (Madison: University of Wisconsin Press, 2006), 77–105.

these field differences grow over time. "Professional school exceptionalism," as Veblen sees it, is not just an example of how American universities allow market values to guide their practices. It is also an index of the way in which their wide-ranging educational commitments work as a formidable obstacle to faculty solidarity, and which is in turn what makes it difficult for universities to preserve their autonomy as centers of "higher learning."

Veblen never disputed the need for the various kinds of advanced professional and vocational education that many today automatically assume are part of the province of a university. He was perhaps the first to recognize, however, two particularly fateful consequences of the American commitment to combine professional and vocational education and "higher learning" under the aegis of the university. The first was to make the American university appear to be from the start a site for careers defined in other arenas. The other was adoption of a salary policy that has undermined the notion that the American university might be a distinct cultural arena where faculty would all work together as a group in their capacity as professors on a single campus. Veblen recognized, in short, that what "professional school exceptionalism" would lead to is what the historian David Hollinger has argued we see almost everywhere today: American universities routinely paying the most money to faculty whose fields are least fully defined by the research and teaching mission of universities and paying the least to those faculty whose careers are the most fully defined by those missions, with the magnitudes of these field differences continuing to grow.[32]

The Higher Learning in America explores other more familiar examples of how the American university has embraced the ethos of the commercial marketplace. Because American universities were structured initially to operate as academic equivalents of large business enterprises, Veblen believed they had little choice but to behave as institutions driven to expand at the other's expense, with competition occurring across a variety of increasingly costly extra-scholastic fronts that included public relations, a broad array of student services, massive construction projects and monumental buildings, and public spectacles that range from grad-

32. See Hollinger, "Money and Academic Freedom a Half-Century after McCarthyism," 92–96, for a more extended discussion. Veblen thought that the formal incorporation of "technological and professional men" in the American university had another damaging consequence. It put such men in "a false position which unavoidably leads them to court the specious appearance of scholarship," and in the process gives university-based professional and technical schools "scientific and scholarly prestige." Veblen predicted that the professional schools' pursuit of 'scholarly prestige' would succeed, but only "to the extent that it produces desired conviction in the vulgar, who do not know the difference." However successfully staged, he argued, such "make-believe scholarship" (57) is not what professional schools were designed for. Many faculty at business, law, and medical schools today would take strong issue with this view.

uation ceremonies to intercollegiate athletic contests. But all these are examples of adjustments that have served to sustain what Veblen considered the internal contradictions of the American university. Why did he hold out hope that genuine compromises could be made between the needs of "higher learning" and the demands of the marketplace? The answer again resists simplification, partly because the truth is that Veblen sometimes wavered in that hope.

The Higher Learning in America contains sentences which seem to say, in effect, that the American university and its distinctive system of governance typically pull so strongly in opposite directions there is no hope of fixing things. "Seen from the point of view of the higher learning," Veblen wrote, the entire "run of events" that marked the incursion of business principles into the affairs of learning was "wholly untoward, not to say disastrous" (223). Indeed, the American university's governance structure had served to "defeat the end for which a university is maintained" (165). Such sentences make for what might be called Veblen's strong version of the "thesis of cultural incompatibility." But he has a weak version, too, evident in other sentences scattered throughout the book, and there are enough of them to suggest that he never really believed that the cause of "higher learning" in the American university was powerless. Or as Veblen put it, "The permeation of academic policy by business principles is a matter of more or less, not of absolute dominance. It appears to be a question of how wide a deviation from scholarly singleness of purpose the long-term common sense of the community will tolerate" (140–41).

How should we measure the relative weight of the "strong" and "weak" versions? Perhaps neither predominates. It is curious, however, that since *The Higher Learning in America* first appeared the book has found readers unable to see that both are present. Among the first was Brander Matthews (1852–1929), Columbia University professor of dramatic literature, who in his review for the *New York Times* declared that Veblen had launched a "gas attack" on the American university that completely misrepresented its actual organization. His "typical trustee, his typical president, his typical professor," Matthews wrote, could not "even be accepted as a caricature, because a caricature, however willfully distorted, must be drawn from an actual original."[33] And yet it was Veblen himself, who stated plainly enough that *The Higher Learning in America* did not describe "what has actually been accomplished in any concrete case," but instead showed "what should follow from the unrestrained dominion of business principles in academic policy"

33. Brander Matthews, "Mr. Veblen's Gas Attack on Our Colleges and Universities," *New York Times*, Mar. 16, 1919, 125, 127, 138.

(167). Veblen's own remarks about what he was up to are significant because they draw attention to what I suggest readers take not as his "weak" but rather as his considered position on the question of university governance.[34] By portraying extreme cases, one could say, Veblen's ultimate purpose was not just to show how the American university's system of corporate governance put its independence at risk but also to warn strongly against any additional sacrifices of the "claims of science and scholarship" to the demands of the marketplace.

Because Veblen never offers specific advice about how to act on this warning, it is fair to speculate that he doubted many would heed it. But he certainly did sound the warning, at the same time as he identified institutional actors and academic traditions he believed had power to impede further damaging adjustments with the marketplace. American academic tradition dictates, Veblen wrote, that "the faculty is the keeper of the academic interests of the university." It also dictates, "and commonly by explicit proviso," that while "the conduct of the university's affairs vest formally with the president," the president in turn must have "certain officially recognized advisors—the various deans, advisory committees, Academic Council, University Senate, and the like—with whom he shares responsibility." Veblen was quick to acknowledge that academic traditions and practices that make for shared responsibility are routinely circumvented. Presidents, after all, are free to surround themselves with staffs whose chief qualifications include "sympathy with their chief's ideals and methods and an unreserved subservience to his aims." And because the terms of American university governance in Veblen's day included providing presidents with the power to function as the primary gatekeepers of the faculty, they could open and shut the gate more or less as they pleased. Even so, Veblen also was clear in saying that he did not view such "reservations and abatements" as evidence that the organization of the American university in service of "business principles" had been fully accomplished. The "incursion of business principles," he wrote, was of "relatively recent date" and had not yet had time "to pervade the organization throughout and with full effect." What most troubled him in the end was that "the rate of advance along this line, and the present measure of achievement, are more considerable than even

34. The protracted composition of *The Higher Learning in America* may also help to explain the presence of strong and weak versions of the "thesis of cultural incompatibility" in the book. Detailed reconstruction of Veblen's additions and revisions are impossible because no notes survive, and all the early manuscript versions of the book have disappeared or have been destroyed. Even so, it seems fair to say that over the course of fourteen years, when Veblen sat down to expand or revise the paper he started in Chicago in 1904, at times he recognized a tendency to exaggerate any position he took up. Hence, on several occasions he flatly acknowledged that he was not repudiating the American system of university governance, nor was he giving serious thought to what if anything might replace it.

a very sanguine advocate of business principles could have dared to look for a couple of years ago" (99–101).

Where might Veblen say "the rate of advance along this line" is at the moment? The answer is open to debate. (Discussion might begin by asking what Veblen would make of the fact that in the early twenty-first century the United States is home to the largest, most independent, and most productive collection of universities in history.) But to gather in all that *The Higher Learning in America* has to say about the ways in which business principles have guided the conduct of the American university is to discover what perhaps was not obvious before. The Veblen who was a strident critic of the external governance structure of American university is also the Veblen who was simultaneously a clear-eyed analyst of how it must be made to operate. For all his criticism of that structure, he offered no plan for reorganizing or remaking it. He also recognized that the prevailing purpose of the American university has never been, and never will be, nurturing the life of the mind. In Veblen's view, it has no prevailing purpose. He labeled it an "enterprise in assorted education" (168). And as we work our way through *The Higher Learning in America*, what Veblen never allows us to forget is that the American university was created to pursue several ideas of what a university is for and so it has always made itself adaptable to a broad range of cultural, economic, and political needs. What follows from this recognition is a sobering but not despairing message: the American university must serve the dominant social order and yet continue to serve ideals and maintain practices that keep it apart from that order. In *The Higher Learning in America*, Veblen explains the origins and the earliest configurations of this conflicted role. More often than not, he also holds fast to the conviction that the American university can find ways of being subordinate without being servile, of being responsive to without being defined by the needs of the market. In doing so, he provides direction and measured hope to those who share his belief that the American university remains in a position to achieve its highest purpose, which is to provide a partial but substantive alternative to the market.

The Higher Learning in America

Preface

It is something more than a dozen years since the following observations on American academic life were first assembled in written form. In the meantime changes of one kind and another have occurred, although not such as to alter the course of policy which has guided American universities. Lines of policy which were once considered to be tentative and provisional have since then passed into settled usage. This altered and more stable state of the subject matter has permitted a revision to avoid detailed documentation of matters that have become commonplace, with some resulting economy of space and argument. But, unhappily, revision and abridgment carries its own penalties, in the way of a more fragmentary presentation and a more repetitious conduct of the argument; so that it becomes necessary to bespeak a degree of indulgence on that ground.

Unhappily, this is not all that seems necessary to plead in extenuation of recurrent infirmities. Circumstances, chiefly of a personal incidence, have repeatedly delayed publication beyond what the run of events at large would have indicated as a propitious date; and the same circumstances have also enjoined a severer and more repressive curtailment in the available data. It may not be out of place, therefore, to indicate in the most summary fashion what has been the nature of these fortuitous hindrances.

In its earlier formulation, the argument necessarily drew largely on first-hand observation of the conduct of affairs at Chicago, under the administration of its first president.[1] As is well known, the first president's share in the management of the university was intimate, masterful and pervasive, in a very high degree; so much so that no secure line of demarcation could be drawn between the administration's policy and the president's personal ruling. It is true, salient features of academic policy which many observers at that time were inclined to credit to the proclivities of Chicago's first president, have in the later course of things proved to belong to the impersonal essence of the case; having been approved by the

1. William Rainey Harper (1856–1906) was the first president of the University of Chicago. All subsequent numbered footnotes are provided by the editor. They identify events, institutions, persons, and publications that Veblen either alludes to or mentions in the text. Veblen's own originally numbered footnotes have been alphabetized to facilitate annotation.

members of the craft, and so having passed into general usage without abatement. Yet, at the time, the share of the Great Pioneer in reshaping American academic policy could scarcely have been handled in a detached way, as an impersonal phenomenon of the unfolding historical sequence. The personal note was, in fact, very greatly in evidence.

And just then, presently, that Strong Man's life was brought to a close.[2] So that it would unavoidably have seemed a breach of decorum to let these observations seek a hearing at that time, even after any practicable revision and excision which filial piety would enjoin. Under the rule of *Nihil nisi bonum*,[3] there seemed nothing for it but a large reticence.

But swiftly, with the passage of years, events proved that much of what had appeared to be personal to the Great Pioneer was in reality intrinsic to the historical movement; so that the innovations presently lost their personal color, and so went impersonally to augment the grand total of human achievement at large. Meanwhile general interest in the topic had nowise abated. Indeed, discussion of the academic situation was running high and in large volume, and much of it was taking such a turn—controversial, reproachful, hortatory, acrimonious—that anything in the way of a temperate survey should presumably have been altogether timely.

But fortuitous circumstances again intervened, such as made it seem the part of insight and sobriety again to defer publication, until the color of an irrelevant personal equation should again have had time to fade into the background. With the further passage of time, it is hoped that no fortuitous shadow will now cloud the issue in any such degree as to detract at all sensibly from whatever value this account of events and their causes may have.[4]

This allusion to incidents which have no material bearing on the inquiry may tolerantly be allowed, as going to account for a sparing use of local information and, it is hoped, to extenuate a degree of reserve and reticence touching divers intimate details of executive policy.

It goes without saying that the many books, papers and addresses brought out on the academic situation have had their share in shaping the essay. More particularly have these various expressions of opinion and concern made it possible to

2. A "strong man" is a leader or politician who uses threats and violence. It also can mean a man who performs in a circus and is strong. Veblen uses the term in both senses throughout the book, sometimes seriously, sometimes facetiously. William Rainey Harper died on January 10, 1906.

3. Abbreviation of Latin saying *De Mortuis Nil Nisi Bonum:* "Of the dead (say) nothing but good." Attributed to Chilon of Sparta (ca. 600 BCE).

4. On the composition of the Veblen manuscript, see "Introduction," 4–7.

take many things for granted, as matter of common notoriety, that would have appeared to require documentation a dozen or fifteen years ago, as lying at that time still in the field of surmise and forecast. Much, perhaps the greater bulk, of the printed matter issued on this head in the interval has, it is true, been of a hortatory or eloquently optimistic nature, and may therefore be left on one side. But the academic situation has also been receiving some considerable attention with a view to getting an insight into what is going forward. One and another of these writers to whom the present essay is in debt will be found referred to by name in the pages which more particularly lean on their support; and the like is true for various utterances by men in authority that have been drawn on for illustrative expressions. But a narrow scrutiny would doubtless make it appear that the unacknowledged indebtedness greatly exceeds what so is accredited and accounted for. That such is the case must not be taken as showing intentional neglect of the due courtesies.

March 1916

In the course of the past two years, while the manuscript has been lying in wait for the printer, a new situation[5] has been forcing itself on the attention of men who continue to take an interest in the universities. On this provocation a few paragraphs have been added, at the end of the introductory chapter. Otherwise there appears to be no call for a change in the general argument, and it has not been disturbed since the earlier date, which is accordingly left as it stands.

June 1918

5. The United States entered into World War I in April 1917. The armistice ending the war was signed in November 1918.

CHAPTER I

Introductory

The Place of the University in Modern Life

I

In any known civilization there will be found something in the way of esoteric knowledge.[1] This body of knowledge will vary characteristically from one culture to another, differing both in content and in respect of the canons of truth and reality relied on by its adepts. But there is this common trait running through all civilizations, as touches this range of esoteric knowledge, that it is in all cases held, more or less closely, in the keeping of a select body of adepts or specialists—scientists, scholars, savants, clerks, priests, shamans, medicine men—whatever designation may best fit the given case.

In the apprehension of the given society within which any such body of knowledge is found it will also be found that the knowledge in question is rated as an article of great intrinsic value, in some way a matter of more substantial consequence than any or all of the material achievements or possessions of the community. It may take shape as a system of magic or of religious beliefs, of mythology, theology, philosophy or science. But whatever shape it falls into in the given case, it makes up the substantial core of the civilization in which it is found, and it is felt to give character and distinction to that civilization.

In the apprehension of the group in whose life and esteem it lives and takes effect, this esoteric knowledge is taken to embody a systematization of fundamental and eternal truth; although it is evident to any outsider that it will take its character and its scope and method from the habits of life of the group, from the institutions with which it is bound in a web of give and take. Such is manifestly the case in all the historic phases of civilization, as well as in all those contemporary cultures that are sufficiently remote from our everyday interests to admit

1. In *The Theory of the Leisure Class: An Economic Study in the Evolution of Institutions* (New York: Macmillan, 1899), 367, Veblen defined "esoteric knowledge" as knowledge that is "primarily of no economic or industrial effect," as opposed to "exoteric knowledge," which is "knowledge of industrial processes and of natural phenomenon" that is "turned to account for the material purposes of life." This "line of demarcation," he added, "has in time become, at least in popular apprehension, the normal line between the higher learning and the lower."

of their being seen in adequate perspective. A passably dispassionate inquiry[2] into the place which modern learning holds in modern civilization will show that such is also the case of this latest, and in the mind of its keepers the most mature, system of knowledge. It should by no means be an insuperably difficult matter to show that this "higher learning" of the modern world, the current body of science and scholarship, also holds its place on such a tenure of use and wont, that it has grown and shifted in point of content, aims and methods in response to the changes in habits of life that have passed over the Western peoples during the period of its growth and ascendancy. Nor should it be embarrassingly difficult to reach the persuasion that this process of change and supersession in the scope and method of knowledge is still effectually at work, in a like response to institutional changes that still are incontinently going forward.[a]

To the adepts who are occupied with this esoteric knowledge, the scientists and scholars on whom its keeping devolves, the matter will of course not appear in just that light; more particularly so far as regards that special segment of the field of knowledge with the keeping and cultivation of which they may, each and several, be occupied. They are, each and several, engaged on the perfecting and conservation of a special line of inquiry, the objective end of which, in the view of its adepts, will necessarily be the final and irreducible truth as touches matters within its scope. But, seen in perspective, these adepts are themselves to be taken as creatures of habit, creatures of that particular manner of group life out of which their preconceptions in matters of knowledge, and the manner of their interest in the run of inquiry, have sprung. So that the terms of finality that will satisfy the adepts are also a consequence of habituation, and they are to be taken as conclusive only because and in so far as they are consonant with the discipline of habituation enforced by that manner of group life that has induced in these adepts their particular frame of mind.

Perhaps at a farther remove than many other current phenomena, but none the less effectually for that, the higher learning takes its character from the man-

---

a. An inquiry of this kind has been attempted elsewhere: cf. *The Instinct of Workmanship: And the State of the Industrial Arts* (1914), chapter vii, 321–340; "The Place of Science in Modern Civilization," *American Journal of Sociology*, Vol. XI (March, 1906), 585–609; "The Evolution of the Scientific Point of View," *University of California Chronicle* (1908), Vol. X, no. 4, 395–416.

2. Veblen crossed several disciplinary boundaries in the course of writing *The Higher Learning in American*. At the outset, his chief building block was late nineteenth- and early twentieth-century Anglo-American anthropology, with its practice of making very broad generalizations about "culture" and "civilization," two words then used interchangeably to group human beliefs, institutions, and practices under one comprehensive category of social life. Veblen also joined leading Anglo-American anthropologists of his time in believing that the explanation of all cultural phenomena lay in certain biologically transmitted predispositions or "instincts" deeply implanted in the human psyche in earlier stages of human evolution.

ner of life enforced on the group by the circumstances in which it is placed. These constraining circumstances that so condition the scope and method of learning are primarily, and perhaps most cogently, the conditions imposed by the state of the industrial arts, the technological situation; but in the second place, and scarcely less exacting in detail, the received scheme of use and wont in its other bearings has its effect in shaping the scheme of knowledge, both as to its content and as touches the norms and methods of its organization. Distinctive and dominant among the constituent factors of this current scheme of use and wont is the pursuit of business, with the outlook and predilections which that pursuit implies. Therefore any inquiry into the effect which recent institutional changes may have upon the pursuit of the higher learning will necessarily be taken up in a peculiar degree with the consequences which an habitual pursuit of business in modern times has had for the ideals, aims and methods of the scholars and schools devoted to the higher learning.

The Higher Learning as currently cultivated by the scholars and scientists of the Western civilization differs not generically from the esoteric knowledge purveyed by specialists in other civilizations, elsewhere and in other times. It engages the same general range of aptitudes and capacities, meets the same range of human wants, and grows out of the same impulsive propensities of human nature. Its scope and method are different from what has seemed good in other cultural situations, and its tenets and canons are so far peculiar as to give it a specific character different from these others; but in the main this specific character is due to a different distribution of emphasis among the same general range of native gifts that have always driven men to the pursuit of knowledge. The stress falls in a somewhat obviously different way among the canons of reality by recourse to which men systematize and verify the knowledge gained; which is in its turn due to the different habituation to which civilized men are subjected, as contrasted with the discipline exercised by other and earlier cultures.

In point of its genesis and growth any system of knowledge may confidently be run back, in the main, to the initiative and bias afforded by two certain impulsive traits of human nature: an Idle Curiosity, and the Instinct of Workmanship.[b]

In this generic trait the modern learning does not depart from the rule that

---

b. Cf. *The Instinct of Workmanship and the State of the Industrial Arts*, chap. i: 30–45, 52–62, 84–89. [Veblen considered this book his most important work because it provided what he considered his most systematic argument for the notion that instincts are the prime movers of human behavior. It also provided his most concise definition of "the instinct of idle curiosity." As opposed to "the instinct of workmanship," which refers to a human pre-disposition for tool-making and tool-using, Veblen believed, "the instinct of idle curiosity" makes us want to know things, to attain and increase knowledge for its own sake. –Ed.]

holds for the common run. Men instinctively seek knowledge, and value it. The fact of this proclivity is well summed up in saying that men are by native gift actuated with an idle curiosity—"idle" in the sense that a knowledge of things is sought, apart from any ulterior use of the knowledge so gained.[c] This, of course, does not imply that the knowledge so gained will not be turned to practical account. In point of fact, although the fact is not greatly relevant to the inquiry here in hand, the native proclivity here spoken of as the instinct of workmanship will unavoidably incline men to turn to account, in a system of ways and means, whatever knowledge so becomes available. But the instinct of workmanship has also another and more pertinent bearing in these premises, in that it affords the norms, or the scheme of criteria and canons of verity, according to which the ascertained facts will be construed and connected up in a body of systematic knowledge. Yet the sense of workmanship takes effect by recourse to diverse expedients and reaches its ends by recourse to varying principles, according as the habituation of workday life has enforced one or another scheme of interpretation for the facts with which it has to deal.

The habits of thought induced by workday life impose themselves as ruling principles that govern the quest of knowledge; it will therefore be the habits of thought enforced by the current technological scheme that will have most (or most immediately) to say in the current systematization of facts. The working logic of the current state of the industrial arts will necessarily insinuate itself as the logical scheme which must, of course, effectually govern the interpretation and generalizations of fact in all their commonplace relations. But the current state of the industrial arts is not all that conditions workmanship. Under any given institutional situation—and the modern scheme of use and wont, law and order, is no exception, workmanship is held to a more or less exacting conformity to several tests and standards that are not intrinsic to the state of the industrial arts, even if they are not alien to it; such as the requirements imposed by the current system of ownership and pecuniary values. These pecuniary conditions that impose themselves on the processes of industry and on the conduct of life, together with the pecuniary accountancy that goes with them—the price system— have much to say in the guidance and limitations of workmanship. And when

c. In the crude surmises of the pioneers in pragmatism this proposition was implicitly denied; in their later and more advisedly formulated positions the expositors of pragmatism have made peace with it. [The leading American "pioneers of pragmatism" were Charles Sanders Peirce (1839–1914) and William James (1842–1910). At the core of pragmatism is the belief that the validity of any idea or proposition lies in their observable consequences. By contrast, Veblen's belief in the instinct of idle curiosity assumes we seek knowledge only for its own sake. Veblen studied briefly with Peirce while he was a graduate student at Johns Hopkins in fall 1881. –Ed.]

and in so far as the habituation so enforced in the traffic of workday life goes into effect as a scheme of logic governing the quest of knowledge, such principles as have by habit found acceptance as being conventionally salutary and conclusive in the pecuniary conduct of affairs will necessarily leave their mark on the ideals, aims, methods and standards of science and those principles and scholarship. More particularly, standards of organization, control and achievement, that have been accepted as an habitual matter of course in the conduct of business will, by force of habit, in good part reassert themselves as indispensable and conclusive in the conduct of the affairs of learning. While it remains true that the bias of workmanship continues to guide the quest of knowledge, under the conditions imposed by modern institutions it will not be the naive conceptions of primitive workmanship that will shape the framework of the modern system of learning; but rather the preconceptions of that disciplined workmanship that has been instructed in the logic of the modern technology and sophisticated with much experience in a civilization in whose scheme of life pecuniary canons are definitive.

The modern technology is of an impersonal, matter-of-fact character in an unexampled degree, and the accountancy of modern business management is also of an extremely dispassionate and impartially exacting nature. It results that the modern learning is of a similarly matter-of-fact, mechanistic complexion, and that it similarly leans on statistically dispassionate tests and formulations. Whereas it may fairly be said that the personal equation once—in the days of scholastic learning—was the central and decisive factor in the systematization of knowledge, it is equally fair to say that in later time no effort is spared to eliminate all bias of personality from the technique or the results of science or scholarship. It is the "dry light of science" that is always in request, and great pains is taken to exclude all color of sentimentality.

Yet this highly sterilized, germ-proof system of knowledge, kept in a cool, dry place, commands the affection of modern civilized mankind no less unconditionally, with no more afterthought of an extraneous sanction, than once did the highly personalized mythological and philosophical constructions and interpretations that had the vogue in the days of the schoolmen.

Through all the mutations that have passed over this quest of knowledge, from its beginnings in puerile myth and magic to its (provisional) consummation in the "exact" sciences of the current fashion, any attentive scrutiny will find that the driving force has consistently been of the same kind, traceable to the same proclivity of human nature. In so far as it may fairly be accounted esoteric knowledge, or a "higher learning," all this enterprise is actuated by an idle curiosity, a disinterested proclivity to gain a knowledge of things and to reduce this knowledge to a comprehensible system. The objective end is a theoretical organization, a logical articulation of things known, the lines of which must not be deflected by any consideration of expediency or convenience, but must run true to the canons of reality accepted at the time. These canons of reality, or of verity, have varied from time to time, have in fact varied incontinently with the passage of time and the mutations of experience. As the fashions of modern time have come on, particularly the later phases of modern life, the experience that so has shaped and reshaped the canons of verity for the use of inquiring minds has fallen more and more into the lines of mechanical articulation and has expressed itself ever more unreservedly in terms of mechanical stress. Concomitantly the canons of reality have taken on a mechanistic complexion, to the neglect and progressive disuse of all tests and standards of a more genial sort; until in the off-hand apprehension of modern men, "reality" comes near being identified with mechanical fact, and "verification" is taken to mean a formulation in mechanical terms. But the final test of this reality about which the inquiries of modern men so turn is not the test of mechanical serviceability for human use, but only of mechanistically effectual matter-of-fact.

So it has come about that modern civilization is in a very special degree a culture of the intellectual powers, in the narrower sense of the term, as contrasted with the emotional traits of human nature. Its achievements and chief merits are found in this field of learning, and its chief defects elsewhere. And it is on its achievements in this domain of detached and dispassionate knowledge that modern civilized mankind most ingenuously plumes itself and confidently rests its hopes. The more emotional and spiritual virtues that once held the first place have been overshadowed by the increasing consideration given to proficiency in matter-of-fact knowledge. As prime movers in the tide of civilized life, these sentimental movements of the human spirit belong in the past—at least such is the self-complacent avowal of the modern spokesmen of culture. The modern technology, and the mechanistic conception of things that goes with that technology, are alien to the spirit of the "Old Order." The Church, the court, the camp, the drawing-room, where these elder and perhaps nobler virtues had their laboratory and playground, have grown weedy and gone to seed. Much of the apparatus of the old order, with the good old way, still stands over in a state of decent repair, and the sentimentally reminiscent endeavors of certain spiritual "hold-overs" still lend this apparatus of archaism something of a galvanic life. But that power of aspiration that once surged full and hot in the cults of faith, fashion, sentiment, exploit, and honor, now at its best comes to such a head as it may in the concerted adulation of matter-of-fact.

This esoteric knowledge of matter-of-fact has come to be accepted as something worthwhile in its own right, a self-legitimating end of endeavor in itself, apart from any bearing it may have on the glory of God or the good of man. Men have, no doubt, always been possessed of a more or less urgent propensity to inquire into the nature of things, beyond the serviceability of any knowledge so gained, and have always been given to seeking curious explanations of things at large. The idle curiosity is a native trait of the race. But in past times such a disinterested pursuit of unprofitable knowledge has, by and large, not been freely avowed as a legitimate end of endeavor; or such has at any rate been the state of the case through that later segment of history which students commonly take account of. A quest of knowledge has overtly been rated as meritorious, or even blameless, only in so far as it has appeared to serve the ends of one or another of the practical interests that have from time to time occupied men's attention. But latterly, during the past few generations, this learning has so far become an avowed "end in itself" that "the increase and diffusion of knowledge among men" is now freely rated as the most humane and meritorious work to be taken care of by any enlightened community or any public-spirited friend of civilization.

The expediency of such "increase and diffusion" is no longer held in doubt, because it has ceased to be a question of expediency among the enlightened nations, being itself the consummation upon which, in the apprehension of civilized men, the advance of culture must converge. Such has come to be the long-term common-sense judgment of enlightened public opinion. A settled presumption to some such effect has found lodgment as a commonplace conviction in the popular mind, in much the same measure and in much the same period of time as the current body of systematic knowledge has taken on the character of matter-of-fact. For good or ill, civilized men have come to hold that this matter-of-fact knowledge of things is the only end in life that indubitably justifies itself. So that nothing more irretrievably shameful could overtake modern civilization than the miscarriage of this modern learning, which is the most valued spiritual asset of civilized mankind.

The truth of this view is borne out by the professions even of those lieutenants of the powers of darkness who are straining to lay waste and debauch the peoples of Christendom.[3] In high-pitched concert they all swear by the name of a "culture"

---

3. No longer widely used term meaning that part of the world where most people are Christian.

whose sole inalienable asset is this same intellectual mastery of matters of fact. At the same time it is only by drawing on the resources of this matter-of-fact knowledge that the protagonists of reaction are able to carry on their campaign of debauchery and desolation.

Other interests that have once been held in higher esteem appear by comparison to have fallen into abeyance—religious devotion, political prestige, fighting capacity, gentility, pecuniary distinction, profuse consumption of goods. But it is only by comparison with the higher value given to this enterprise of the intellect that such other interests appear to have lost ground. These and the like have fallen into relative disesteem, as being sordid and insubstantial by comparison. Not that these "lower" human interests, answering to the "lower" ranges of human intellect, have fallen into neglect; it is only that they have come to be accounted "lower," as contrasted with the quest of knowledge; and it is only on sober second thought, and perhaps only for the ephemeral present, that they are so accounted by the common run of civilized mankind. Men still are in sufficiently hot pursuit of all these time-worn amenities, and each for himself is, in point of fact, more than likely to make the pursuit of such self-seeking ends the burden of his life; but on a dispassionate rating, and under the corrective of deliberate avowal, it will appear that none of these commend themselves as intrinsically worthwhile at large. At the best they are rated as expedient concessions to human infirmity or as measures of defense against human perversity and the outrages of fortune. The last resort of the apologists for these more sordid endeavors is the plea that only by this means can the ulterior ends of a civilization of intelligence be served. The argument may fairly be paraphrased to the effect that in order to serve God in the end, we must all be ready to serve the Devil in the meantime.

It is always possible, of course, that this pre-eminence of intellectual enterprise in the civilization of the Western peoples is a transient episode; that it may eventually—perhaps even precipitately, with the next impending turn in the fortunes of this civilization—again be relegated to a secondary place in the scheme of things and become only an instrumentality in the service of some dominant aim or impulse, such as a vainglorious patriotism, or dynastic politics, or the breeding of a commercial aristocracy. More than one of the nations of Europe have moved so far in this matter already as to place the primacy of science and scholarship in doubt as against warlike ambitions;[4] and the aspirations of the American com-

---

4. After the outbreak of the World War I in August 1914, Veblen was, like most American academics, appalled at the prostitution of academic standards among all the belligerent European powers. He fails

munity appear to be divided—between patriotism in the service of the captains of war, and commerce in the service of the captains of finance. But hitherto the spokesmen of any such cultural reversion are careful to declare a perfunctory faith in that civilization of disinterested intellectual achievement which they are endeavoring to suborn to their several ends. That such *pro forma* declarations are found necessary argues that the faith in a civilization of intelligence is still so far intact as to require all reactionaries to make their peace with it.

Meantime the easy matter-of-course presumption that such a civilization of intelligence justifies itself goes to argue that the current bias which so comes to expression will be the outcome of a secure and protracted experience. What underlies and has brought on this bent in the temper of the civilized peoples is a somewhat intricate question of institutional growth, and cannot be gone into here; but the gradual shifting of this matter-of-fact outlook into the primacy among the ideals of modern Christendom is sufficiently evident in point of fact, to any attentive student of modern times. Conceivably, there may come an abrupt term to its paramount vogue, through some precipitate sweep of circumstances; but it did not come in by anything like the sudden intrusion of a new invention in ideals—after the fashion of a religious conversion nor by the incursion of a hitherto alien element into the current scheme of life, but rather by force of a gradual and unintended, scarcely perceptible, shifting of emphasis between the several cultural factors that conjointly go to make up the working scheme of things.

Along with this shifting of matter-of-fact knowledge into the foreground among the ideals of civilized life, there has also gone on a similarly unpremeditated change in the attitude of those persons and establishments that have to do with this learning, as well as in the rating accorded them by the community at large. Again it is a matter of institutional growth, of self-wrought changes in the scheme of use and wont; and here as in other cases of institutional growth and displacement, the changes have gone forward for the most part blindly, by impulse, without much foreknowledge of any ulterior consequences to which such a sequence of change might be said to tend. It is only after the new growth of use and wont has taken effect in an altered range of principles and standards, that its direction and ulterior consequences can be appreciated with any degree of confidence. But this development that has thrown up matter-of-fact knowledge into its

---

to mention, however, that roughly three years later, after the American declaration of war on Germany in April 1917, doubts about the Allied cause all but disappeared within the ranks of the American professoriate. He also does not mention that in February 1918, more than 140,000 undergraduates from 516 American colleges and universities became "student soldiers" in newly created Student Army Training Corps. Virtually every college and university in the country quickly incorporated a series of government-sponsored courses into its curriculum, all of which were taught by US military officers.

place of paramount value for modern culture has in a peculiar degree been unintended and unforeseen; the like applies to the case of the schools and the personnel involved; and in a peculiar degree the drift and bearing of these changes have also not been appreciated while they have been going forward, doubtless because it has all been a peculiarly unprecedented phenomenon and a wholly undesigned drift of habituation. History records nothing that is fairly comparable. No era in the historic past has set a pattern for guidance in this matter, and the experience of none of the peoples of history affords a clue by which to have judged beforehand of the probable course and outcome of this specifically modern and occidental phase of culture.

Some slight beginnings and excursions in the way of a cultivation of matter-of-fact learning there may have been, now and again, among the many shifting systems of esoteric lore that have claimed attention here and there, early and late; and these need by no means be accounted negligible. But they have on the whole come to nothing much better than broken excursions, as seen from the point of view of the latter-day higher learning, and they have brought into bearing nothing appreciable in the way of establishments designed without afterthought to further the advance of disinterested knowledge. Anything like a cultural era that avowedly takes such a quest of knowledge as its chief and distinctive characteristic is not known to history. From this isolated state of the case it follows, unfortunately, that this modern phase is to be studied only in its own light; and since the sequence of development has hitherto reached no secure consummation or conclusion, there is also much room for conflicting opinions as to its presumptive or legitimate outcome, or even as to its present drift.

II

But notorious facts make this much plain, that civilized mankind looks to this quest of matter-of-fact knowledge as its most substantial asset and its most valued achievement—in so far as any consensus of appreciation or of aspirations is to be found among civilized mankind; and there is no similar consensus bearing on any other feature of that scheme of life that characterizes modern civilization. It is similarly beyond dispute that men look to the modern system of schools and related establishments of learning for the furtherance and conservation of this intellectual enterprise. And among the various items of this equipment the modern university is, by tradition, more closely identified with the quest of knowledge than any other. It stands in a unique and peculiarly intimate relation to this intellectual enterprise. At least such is the current apprehension of the university's work. The university is the only accepted institution of the modern culture on which the quest of knowledge unquestionably devolves; and the visible drift of circumstances as well as of public sentiment runs also to making this the only unquestioned duty incumbent on the university.

It is true, many other lines of work, and of endeavor that may not fairly be called work, are undertaken by schools of university grade; and also, many other schools that call themselves "universities" will have substantially nothing to do with the higher learning. But each and several of these other lines of endeavor, into which the universities allow themselves to be drawn, are open to question. Their legitimacy remains an open question in spite of the interested arguments of their spokesmen, who advocate the partial submergence of the university in such enterprises as professional training, undergraduate instruction, supervision and guidance of the secondary school system, edification of the unlearned by "university extension" and similar excursions into the field of public amusement, training of secondary school teachers, encouragement of amateurs by "correspondence," etc.[5] What and how much of these extraneous activities the university should allow itself is a matter on which there is no general agreement even among those whose inclinations go far in that direction; but what is taken for granted throughout all this advocacy of outlying detail is the secure premise that the university is in the first place a seminary of the higher learning, and that no school can make good its pretensions to university standing except by proving its fitness in this respect.[d]

The conservation and advancement of the higher learning involves two lines of work, distinct but closely bound together: (a) scientific and scholarly inquiry,

d. "The essential function of the university is to bring together, for the transmission of experience and impulse, the sages of the passing and the picked youths of the coming generation. By the extent and fullness with which they establish these social contacts, and thus transmit the wave of cumulative experience and idealist impulse—the real sources of moral and intellectual progress—the universities are to be judged."—Victor Branford (1863–1930), *Interpretations and Forecasts: A Study of Social Inheritance and Spiritual Development* (1914), chap. vi: "The Present as a Transition," 288. [Branford was a central figure in the institutional development of British sociology in the early twentieth century. –Ed.]

5. Allusion to William Rainey Harper's master plan for the University of Chicago, whose capacious goals were to encompass all sectors of American society, including adult students and nontraditional learners. During Harper's fourteen years in office, the work of the university proper came to include "affiliated" high schools and preparatory academies across the country; several undergraduate colleges; graduate schools (in both the arts and sciences and divinity); a law school; a business school; as well as schools of education, fine arts, and medicine. Chicago's "University Extension" sponsored various external programs that included regular courses of lectures in and around Chicago, evening course on college and university subjects (also in and around Chicago), and correspondence courses in all parts of the country. Chicago's "University Extension," Harper explained, was created to "assist teachers, students, businessmen, and women, and particularly those whom circumstances have deprived of educational opportunities once eagerly sought." Between 1892 and 1902, 87 percent of students enrolled in Chicago's correspondence courses were classified as educators.

and (b) the instruction of students.[e] The former of these is primary and indispensable. It is this work of intellectual enterprise that gives its character to the university and marks it off from the lower schools. The work of teaching properly belongs in the university only because and in so far as it incites and facilitates the university man's work of inquiry—and the extent to which such teaching furthers the work of inquiry is scarcely to be appreciated without a somewhat extended experience. By and large, there are but few and inconsequential exceptions to the rule that teaching, as a concomitant of investigation, is distinctly advantageous to the investigator; particularly in so far as his work is of the nature of theoretical inquiry. The instruction necessarily involved in university work, therefore, is only such as can readily be combined with the work of inquiry, at the same time that it goes directly to further the higher learning in that it trains the incoming generation of scholars and scientists for the further pursuit of knowledge. Training for other purposes is necessarily of a different kind and is best done elsewhere; and it does not become university work by calling it so and imposing its burden on the men and equipment whose only concern should be the higher learning.

University teaching, having a particular and special purpose—the pursuit of knowledge—it has also a particular and special character, such as to differentiate it from other teaching and at the same time leave it relatively ineffective for other purposes. Its aim is to equip the student for the work of inquiry, not to give him facility in that conduct of affairs that turns such knowledge to "practical account." Hence the instruction that falls legitimately under the hand of the university man is necessarily subsidiary and incidental to the work of inquiry, and it can effectually be carried on only by such a teacher as is himself occupied with the scrutiny of what knowledge is already in hand and with pushing the inquiry to further gains. And it can be carried on by such a teacher only by drawing his students into his own work of inquiry. The student's relation to his teacher necessarily becomes that of an apprentice to his master, rather than that of a pupil to his schoolmaster.

A university is a body of mature scholars and scientists, the "faculty,"—with whatever plant and other equipment may incidentally serve as appliances for their work in any given case. The necessary material equipment may under modern conditions be very considerable, as may also the number of care-takers, assis-

---

e. Cf. George T. Ladd (1842–1921), "The Need of Administrative Changes in the American University," in *University Control*, ed. James McKeen Cattell (1860–1944) (1913), 349. [Ladd was an American philosopher who taught Veblen during his years as a graduate student at Yale; Cattell was an American psychologist who taught at the University of Pennsylvania and Columbia. On Cattell's career, see "Introduction," 11, note 18. –Ed.]

tants, etc.; but all that is not the university, but merely its equipment. And the university man's work is the pursuit of knowledge, together with whatever advisory surveillance and guidance he may consistently afford such students as are entering on the career of learning at a point where his outlook and methods of work may be of effect for them. No man whose energies are not habitually bent on increasing and proving up the domain of learning belongs legitimately on the university staff. The university man is, properly, a student, not a schoolmaster. Such is the unmistakable drift of sentiment and professed endeavor, in so far as it is guided by the cultural aspirations of civilized mankind rather than by the emulative strategy of individuals seeking their own preferment.[f]

All this, of course, implies no undervaluing of the work of those men who aim to prepare the youth for citizenship and a practical career. It is only a question of distinguishing between things that belong apart. The scientist and the scholar on the one hand, and the schoolmaster on the other hand, both belong within the later growth of civilization; but a differentiation of the two classes, and a division of their work, is indispensable if they are to do their work as it should be done, and as the modern community thoughtfully intends that it should be done. And while such a division of labor has hitherto not been carried through with any degree of consistency, it is at least under way, and there is nothing but the presumption of outworn usage that continues to hold the two lines of work together, to the detriment of both; backed, it is true, by ambitions of self-aggrandizement on the part of many schools and many of their directorates.

The schoolmaster and his work may be equally, or more, valuable to the community at large—presumably more rather than less—but in so far as his chief interest is of the pedagogical sort his place is not in the university. Exposition, instruction and drill belong in the secondary and professional schools. The consistent aim there is, and should be, to instruct, to inculcate a knowledge of results, and to give the pupil a working facility in applying it. On the university level such information and training is (should be) incidental to the work of research. The university man is almost unavoidably a teacher, by precept and example, but

---

f. Cf., e. g., James McKeen Cattell, "Concerning the American University," *University Control* (1913), part III, chap. v. "The university is those who teach and those who learn and the work they do." "The university is its men and their work. But certain externals are necessary or at least usual—buildings and equipment, a president and trustees."

The papers by other writers associated with Mr. Cattell in this volume run to the same effect whenever they touch the same topic; and, indeed, it would be difficult to find a deliberate expression to the contrary among men entitled to speak in these premises.

It may be in place to add here that the volume referred to, on *University Control*, has been had in mind throughout the following analysis and has served as ground and material for much of the argument. [On Veblen's debts to contributors to *University Control*, see "Introduction," 13–21. –Ed.]

he cannot without detriment to his work as scientist or scholar serve as a task-master or a vehicle of indoctrination. The student who comes up to the university for the pursuit of knowledge is expected to know what he wants and to want it, without compulsion. If he falls short in these respects, if he has not the requisite interest and initiative, it is his own misfortune, not the fault of his teacher. What he has a legitimate claim to is an opportunity for such personal contact and guidance as will give him familiarity with the ways and means of the higher learning—any information imparted to him being incidental to this main work of habituation. He gets a chance to make himself a scholar, and what he will do with his opportunities in this way lies in his own discretion.

The difference between the modern university and the lower and professional schools is broad and simple; not so much a difference of degree as of kind. There is no difficulty about apprehending or appreciating this difference; the dispute turns not on the practicability of distinguishing between the two, but on the desirability of letting such a distinction go into effect. It is a controversy between those who wish to hold fast that which once was good and those who look to make use of the means in hand for new ends and meet new exigencies.

The lower schools (including the professional schools) are, in the ideal scheme, designed to fit the incoming generation for civil life; they are therefore occupied with instilling such knowledge and habits as will make their pupils fit citizens of the world in whatever position in the fabric of workday life they may fall. The university on the other hand is specialized to fit men for a life of science and scholarship; and it is accordingly concerned with such discipline only as will give efficiency in the pursuit of knowledge and fit its students for the increase and diffusion of learning. It follows that while the lower schools necessarily take over the surveillance of their pupils' everyday life, and exercise a large measure of authority and responsible interference in that behalf, the university assumes (or should assume) no responsibility for its students' fortunes in the moral, religious, pecuniary, domestic, or hygienic respect.

Doubtless the larger and more serious responsibility in the educational system belongs not to the university but to the lower and professional schools. Citizenship is a larger and more substantial category than scholarship; and the furtherance of civilized life is a larger and more serious interest than the pursuit of knowledge for its own idle sake. But the proportions which the quest of knowledge is latterly assuming in the scheme of civilized life require that the establishments to which this interest is committed should not be charged with extraneous duties; particularly not with extraneous matters themselves of such grave consequence as this training for citizenship and practical affairs. These are too serious a range of duties to be taken care of as a side-issue, by a seminary of learning, the members of whose faculty, if they are fit for their own special work, are not men of affairs or adepts in worldly wisdom.

III

In point of historical pedigree the American universities are of another derivation than their European counterpart; although the difference in this respect is not so sharp a matter of contrast as might be assumed at first sight. The European (Continental) universities appear to have been founded, originally, to meet the needs of professional training, more particularly theological (and philosophical) training in the earlier times. The American universities are, historically, an outgrowth of the American college; and the latter was installed, in its beginnings, largely as a means of professional training; chiefly training for Divinity, secondarily for the calling of the schoolmaster. But in neither case, neither in that of the European university nor in that of the American College, was this early vocational aim of the schools allowed to decide their character in the long run, nor to circumscribe the lines of their later growth. In both cases, somewhat alike, the two groups of schools came to their mature development, in the nineteenth century, as establishments occupied with disinterested learning, given over to the pursuit of intellectual enterprise, rather than as seminaries for training of a vocational kind. They still had a vocational value, no doubt, and the vocational needs of their students need not have been absent from the considerations that guided their directorates. It would particularly be found that the (clerical) directorates of the American colleges had more than half an eye to the needs of Divinity even at so late a date as when, in the third quarter of the century, the complexion of the American college situation began seriously to change. It is from this period—from the era of the Civil War and the Reconstruction—that the changes set in which have reshaped the academic situation in America.

At this era, some half a century ago, the American college was, or was at least pressed to be, given over to disinterested instruction, not specialized with a vocational, or even a denominational, bias. It was coming to take its place as the superior or crowning member, a sort of capstone, of the system of public instruction. The life history of any one of the state universities whose early period of growth runs across this era will readily show the effectual guidance of such an ideal of a college, as a superior and definitive member in a school system designed to afford an extended course of instruction looking to an unbiased increase and diffusion of knowledge. Other interests, of a professional or vocational kind, were also entrusted to the keeping of these new-found schools; but with a conclusive generality the rule holds that in these academic creations a college establishment of a disinterested, non-vocational character is counted in as the indispensable nucleus—that much was at that time a matter of course.

The further development shows two marked features: The American university has come into being; and the college has become an intermediate rather than a terminal link in the conventional scheme of education. Under the names "undergraduate" and "graduate," the college and the university are still commonly coupled together as subdivisions of a complex whole; but this holding together of the two disparate schools is at the best a freak of aimless survival. At the worst, and more commonly, it is the result of a gross ambition for magnitude on the part of the joint directorate. Whether the college lives by itself as an independent establishment on a foundation of its own, or is in point of legal formality a subdivision of the university establishment, it takes its place in the educational scheme as senior member of the secondary school system, and it bears no peculiarly close relation to the university as a seat of learning. At the closest it stands to the university in the relation of a fitting school; more commonly its relations are closer with the ordinary professional and vocational schools; and for the most part it stands in no relation, beyond that of juxtaposition, with the one or the other.

The attempt to hold the college and the university together in bonds of ostensible solidarity is by no means an advisedly concerted adjustment to the needs of scholarship as they run today. By historical accident the older American universities have grown into being on the ground of an underlying college, and the external connection so inherited has not usually been severed; and by ill-advised, or perhaps unadvised, imitation the younger universities have blundered into encumbering themselves with an undergraduate department to simulate this presumptively honorable pedigree, to the detriment both of the university and of the college so bound up with it. By this arrangement the college—undergraduate department—falls into the position of an appendage, a side issue, to be taken care of by afterthought on the part of a body of men whose chief legitimate interest runs—should run—on other things than the efficient management of such an undergraduate training-school—provided always that they are a *bona fide*[6] university faculty, and not a body of secondary-school teachers masquerading under the assumed name of a university.

The motive to this inclusion of an undergraduate department in the newer universities appears commonly to have been a headlong eagerness on the part of

6. Latin: real or genuine.

the corporate authorities to show a complete establishment of the conventionally accepted pattern, and to enroll as many students as possible.

Whatever may have been true for the earlier time, when the American college first grew up and flourished, it is beyond question that the undergraduate depart-ment which takes the place of the college today cannot be rated as an institution of the higher learning. At the best it is now a school for preliminary training, preparatory to entering on the career of learning, or in preparation for the further training required for the professions; but it is also, and chiefly, an establishment designed to give the concluding touches to the education of young men who have no designs on learning, beyond the close of the college curriculum. It aims to afford a rounded discipline to those whose goal is the life of fashion or of affairs. How well, or how ill, the college may combine these two unrelated purposes is a question that does not immediately concern the present inquiry. It is touched on here only to point the contrast between the American college and the university.[7]

It follows from the character of their work that while the university should offer no set curriculum, the college has, properly, nothing else to offer. But the retention or inclusion of the college and its aims within the university corpora-tion has necessarily led to the retention of college standards and methods of control even in what is or purports to be university work; so that it is by no means unusual to find university (graduate) work scheduled in the form of a curricu-lum, with all that boarding-school circumstance and apparatus that is so unavoid-able an evil in all undergraduate training. In effect, the outcome of these short-sighted attempts to take care of the higher learning by the means and method of the boys' school, commonly is to eliminate the higher learning from the case and substitute the aims and results of a boys' training-school.

Undergraduate work being task work, it is possible, without fatal effect, to re-duce it to standard units of time and volume, and so control and enforce it by a system of accountancy and surveillance; the methods of control,[8] accountancy and coercion that so come to be worked out have all that convincing appearance of tangible efficiency that belongs to any mechanically defined and statistically accountable routine, such as will always commend itself to the spirit of the school-master; the temptation to apply such methods of standardized routine wherever

7. In drawing a sharp contrast between the four-year undergraduate college and the university, Veblen echoed sentiments of American university architects such as Johns Hopkins University presi-dent Daniel Coit Gilman (1831–1907) and Clark University president G. Stanley Hall (1844–1924), both of whom would have preferred to organize their new institutions without an undergraduate college. Elsewhere, Columbia University president Nicholas Murray Butler (1862–1947) and Harvard Univer-sity president Charles W. Eliot (1834–1926) seriously considered paring their undergraduate colleges down to two or three years.

8. "Control" is short for governance and administration.

it is at all feasible is always present, and it is cogently spoken for by all those to whom drill is a more intelligible conception than scholarship. The work of learning, which distinctively belongs in the university, on the other hand, is a matter of personal contact and co-operation between teacher and student, and is not measurable in statistical units or amenable to mechanical tests; the men engaged in this work can accordingly offer nothing of the same definite character in place of the rigid routine and accountancy advocated by the schoolmasters; and the outcome in nearly all cases where the control of both departments vests in one composite corporate body, as it usually does, is the gradual insinuation of undergraduate methods and standards in the graduate school; until what is nominally university work settles down, in effect, into nothing more than an extension of the undergraduate curriculum. This effect is had partly by reducing such of the graduate courses as are found amenable to the formalities of the undergraduate routine, and partly by dispensing with such graduate work as will not lend itself, even ostensibly, to the schoolmaster's methods.

What has been said of the college in this connection holds true in the main also of the professional and technical schools.[9] In their aims, methods and achievements these schools are, in the nature of the case, foreign to the higher learning. This is, of course, not said in disparagement of their work; rather the contrary. As is the case with the college, so these schools also are often included in the university corporation by ties of an external and factitious kind, frequently by terms of the charter. But this formal inclusion of them under the corporate charter does not set aside the substantial discrepancy between their purpose, work and animus and those of the university proper. It can only serve to trouble the single-mindedness of both. It leaves both the pursuit of learning and the work of preparation for the professions somewhat at loose ends, confused with the bootless illusion that they are, in some recondite way, parallel variants of a single line of work.

In aim and animus the technical and professional schools are "practical," in the most thoroughgoing manner; while the pursuit of knowledge that occupies the scientists and scholars is not "practical" in the slightest degree. The divergent lines of interest to be taken care of by the professional schools and the university, respectively, are as widely out of touch as may well be within the general field of

9. Veblen follows the then traditional practice of reserving the word *professional* for just three non-academic occupations that long had required formal study and instruction: divinity, law, and medicine. He considered all other occupations—including business—"vocations" of a lesser nature. Newly established "technical institutions" such as Pratt Institute(1887), Drexel Institute (1891), and Carnegie Technical School of Pittsburgh functioned as continuing schools for students with previous work experience. Typically, teachers in technical institutes possessed industrial experience.

human knowledge. The one is animated wholly by considerations of material expediency, and the range of its interest and efforts is strictly limited by consideration of the useful effect to which the proficiency that it gives is to be turned; the other knows nothing of expediency, and is influenced by no consideration of utility or disutility, in its appreciation of the knowledge to be sought. The animus of the one is worldly wisdom; of the other, idle curiosity. The two are incommensurably at variance so far as regards their purpose, and in great measure also as regards their methods of work, and necessarily so.

But with all this divergence of purpose and animus there is after all a broad and very substantial bond of community between the technical schools, on the one hand, and the proper work of the university, on the other hand, in that the two are, in great measure, occupied with the same general range of materials and employ somewhat the same logical methods in handling these materials. But the relation that results from this community of material is almost wholly external and mechanical. Nor does it set up any presumption that the two should expediently be included in the same corporate establishment, or even that they need be near neighbors or need maintain peculiarly close relations of personnel. The technical schools, and in a less degree the professional schools not properly classed as technical, depend in large measure on results worked out by the scientists, who properly belong in the universities. But the material so made use of for technical ends are taken over and turned to account without afterthought. The technologist's work is related to that of the scientists very much as the work of the designer is related to that of the inventor. To a considerable extent the scientists similarly depend on the work of the technical men for information, and for correction and verification of their own theoretical work. But there is, on this account, nothing to gain by associating any given technical school with any given university establishment; incorporation in any given university does not in any degree facilitate the utilization of the results of the sciences by the technical men; nor is it found in practice to further the work of the sciences. The schools in question do not in any peculiar degree draw on the work of the scientists attached to their particular university, nor do these scientists, on the other hand, have any special use for the work of their associated technical schools. In either case the source drawn on is the general literature of the subject, the body of materials available at large, not the work of particular men attached to particular schools. The generalizations of science are indispensable to the technical men; but what they draw on is the body of science at large, regardless of what any given university establishment may have had to do with the work out of which the particular items of scientific information have emerged. Nor is this scientific material useful

to the technologists for the further pursuit of science; to them the scientific results are data, raw material to be turned to practical use, not means by which to
carry scientific inquiry out to further results.

Similarly, the professions and the technical schools afford valuable data for the
use of the professed scholars and scientists, information that serves as material
of investigation, or that will at least be useful as a means of extending correcting, verifying and correlating lines of inquiry on which they are engaged. But the
further bearing of these facts upon the affairs of life, their expediency or futility,
is of no interest or consequence. The affairs of life, except the affairs of learning,
do not touch the interest of the university man as a scholar or scientist. What is
of importance to him in all these matters with which the professions and technologists are busy is their bearing on those matters of fact into which his scientific interest leads him to inquire. The tests and experiments carried out at these
technical schools, as well as the experience gathered by the members of their
staff, will occasionally afford him material for further inquiry or means whereby
to check results already arrived at; but for such material he does not by preference
resort to any one of the technical schools as contrasted with any other, and it is
quite an idle question whether the source of any such serviceable information is
a school attached to his own university. The investigator finds his material where
he can; which comes to saying that he draws on the general body of technical
knowledge, with no afterthought as to what particular technical school may have
stood in some relation or other to the information which he finds useful.

Neither to the man engaged in university work nor to the technical schools
that may serve him as occasional sources of material is there any advantage to be
derived from their inclusion in the university establishment. Indeed, it is a detriment to both parties, as has already been remarked, but more decidedly to the
university men. By including the technical and professional schools in the university corporation the technologists and professional men attached to these schools
are necessarily included among the academic staff, and so they come to take their
part in the direction of academic affairs at large. In what they so do toward shaping the academic policy they will not only count for all they are worth, but they
are likely to count for something more than their due share in this respect; for
they are to some extent trained to the conduct of affairs, and so come in for something of that deference that is currently paid to men of affairs, at the same time
that this practical training gives them an advantage over their purely academic
colleagues, in the greater assurance and adroitness with which they are able to
present their contentions. By virtue of this same training, as well as by force of

current practical interest, the technologist and the professional man are, like other men of affairs, necessarily and habitually impatient of any scientific or scholarly work that does not obviously lend itself to some practical use. The technologist appreciates what is mechanically serviceable; the professional man, as, for instance, the lawyer, appreciates what promises pecuniary gain; and the two unite with the business-man at large in repudiating whatever does not look directly to such a utilitarian outcome. So that as members of the academic staff these men are likely to count at their full weight toward the diversion of the university's forces from disinterested science and scholarship to such palpably utilitarian ends.

But the active measures so taken by the academic authorities at the instance of the schoolmasters and "practical" men are by no means the only line along which their presence in the academic corporation affects the case. Intimate association with these "utilitarians" unavoidably has its corrupting effect on the scientists and scholars, and induces in them also something of the same bias toward "practical" results in their work; so that they no longer pursue the higher learning with undivided interest, but with more or less of an eye to the utilitarian main chance; whereby the advantages of specialization, which are the reason for these schools, are lost, and the pride of the modern community is wounded in its most sensitive spot—the efficiency of its specialists.

So also, on the other hand, the formal incorporation of these technological and professional men in the academic body, with its professedly single-minded interest in learning, has its effect on their frame of mind. They are, without intending it, placed in a false position, which unavoidably leads them to court a specious appearance of scholarship, and so to invest their technological discipline with a degree of pedantry and sophistication; whereby it is hoped to give these schools and their work some scientific and scholarly prestige, and so lift it to that dignity that is pressed to attach to a non-utilitarian pursuit of learning. Doubtless this pursuit of scholarly prestige is commonly successful, to the extent that it produces the desired conviction of awe in the vulgar, who do not know the difference; but all this make-believe scholarship, however successfully staged, is not what these schools are designed for; or at least it is not what is expected of them, nor is it what they can do best and most efficiently.

To the substantial gain of both parties, though with some lesion of the vanity of both, the separation between the university and the professional and technical schools should be carried through and made absolute. Only on such conditions can either the one or the other do its own work in a workmanlike manner. Within the university precincts any aim or interest other than those of irresponsible science and scholarship—pursuit of matter-of-fact knowledge—are to be rated as interlopers.[10]

IV

To all this there is the ready objection of the schoolmasters and utilitarians that such a project is fantastic and unpractical, useless and undesirable; that such has not been the mission of the university in the past, nor its accepted place and use in the educational system of today and yesterday, that the universities of Christendom have from their first foundation been occupied with professional training and useful knowledge; that they have been founded for utilitarian purposes and their work has been guided mainly or altogether by utilitarian considerations;— all of which is conceded without argument. The historical argument amounts to saying that the universities were founded before modern civilization took on its modern character, before the disinterested pursuit of knowledge had come to take the first place among the ideals of civilized mankind, and that they were established to take care of those interests which were then accounted of first importance, and that this intellectual enterprise in pursuit of disinterested knowledge consequently was not at that time confided to the care of any special establishment or freely avowed as a legitimate interest in its own right.

It is true that, by historical accident, the university at large has grown out of professional training-schools—primarily schools for training in theology, secondarily in law and medicine. It is also true, in likewise and in like degree, that modern science and scholarship have grown out of the technology of handicraft and the theological philosophy of the schoolmen.[g] But just as it would be a bootless enterprise to cut modern science back into handicraft technology, so would it be a gratuitous imbecility to prune back the modern university to that inchoate phase of its life-history and make it again a corporation for the training of theologians, jurists and doctors of medicine. The historical argument does not enjoin a return to the beginning of things, but rather an intelligent appreciation of what things are coming to.

The genesis of the university at large, taken as an institution of civilized life, is an incident of the transition from the barbarian culture[11] of the middle ages to

g. Cf. *The Instinct of Workmanship: And the State of the Industrial Arts*, chaps. vi and vii.

10. People who interfere with the affairs of others.

11. This is the first of several references to "barbarian culture," a phrase that Veblen uses in the technical anthropological sense first developed by Lewis H. Morgan (1818–81) in *Ancient Society: Research in the Lines of Human Progress from Savagery through Barbarism to Civilization* (1877). Building

modern times, and its later growth and acquirement of character is an incident of the further growth of modern civilization; and the character of this later growth of the university reflects the bent of modern civilization, as contrasted with the barbarian spirit of things in the mediaeval spiritual world.

In a general way, the place of the university in the culture of Christendom is still substantially the same as it has been from the beginning. Ideally, and in the popular apprehension, it is, as it has always been, a corporation for the cultivation and care of the community's highest aspirations and ideals. But these ideals and aspirations have changed somewhat with the changing scheme of the Western civilization; and so the university has also concomitantly so changed in character, aims and ideals as to leave it still the corporate organ of the community's dominant intellectual interest. At the same time, it is true, these changes in the purpose and spirit of the university have always been, and are always being, made only tardily, reluctantly, concessively, against the protests of those who are zealous for the commonplaces of the day before yesterday. Such is the character of institutional growth and change; and in its adaptation to the altered requirements of an altered scheme of culture the university has in this matter been subject to the conditions of institutional growth at large. An institution is, after all, a prevalent habit of thought, and as such it is subject to the conditions and limitations that surround any change in the habitual frame of mind prevalent in the community.

The university of medieval and early modern times, that is to say the barbarian university, was necessarily given over to the pragmatic, utilitarian disciplines, since that is the nature of barbarism; and the barbarian university is but another, somewhat sublimated, expression of the same barbarian frame of mind. The barbarian culture is pragmatic, utilitarian, worldly wise, and its learning partakes of the same complexion. The barbarian, late or early, is typically an unmitigated pragmatist; that is the spiritual trait that most profoundly marks him off from the savage on the one hand and from the civilized man on the other hand. "He turns a keen, untroubled face home to the instant need of things."[12]

The high era of barbarism in Europe, the Dark and Middle Ages, is marked off from what went before and from what has followed in the cultural sequence, by a hard and fast utilitarian animus. The all-dominating spiritual trait of those

on Morgan's highly speculative anthropology, Veblen assigned great significance to an evolving scheme of three historical stages. The first ("savage") corresponded roughly to the Neolithic period and was characterized by a sedentary subsistence economy, communal solidarity, and peace. The second ("barbaric," or "predatory" stage) corresponded roughly to feudalism, was devoted to hunting and plundering, and saw the emergence of property and a "leisure" class. The third ("civilization") began as an era of handicraft that had recently given way to modern machinery.

12. Quoted from Rudyard Kipling's (1865–1925) "An American."

times is that men then made the means of life its end. It is perhaps needless to call to mind that much of this animus still survives in later civilized life, especially in so far as the scheme of civilized life is embodied in the competitive system. In that earlier time, practical sagacity and the serviceability of any knowledge acquired, its bearing on individual advantage, spiritual or temporal, was the ruling consideration, as never before or since. The best of men in that world were not ashamed to avow that a boundless solicitude for their own salvation was their worthiest motive of conduct, and it is plain in all their speculations that they were unable to accept any other motive or sanction as final in any bearing. Saint and sinner alike knew no higher rule than expediency, for this world and the next. And, for that matter, so it still stands with the saint and the sinner—who make up much of the commonplace human material in the modern community; although both the saint and the sinner in the modern community carry, largely by shame-faced subreption, an ever increasing side-line of other and more genial interests that have no merit in point of expediency whether for this world or the next.

Under the rule of such a cultural ideal the corporation of learning could not well take any avowed stand except as an establishment for utilitarian instruction, the practical expediency of whose work was the sole overt test of its competency. And such it still should continue to be according to the avowed aspirations of the staler commonplace elements in the community today. By subreption,[13] and by a sophisticated subsumption under some ostensibly practical line of interest and inquiry, it is true, the university men of the earlier time spent much of their best endeavor on matters of disinterested scholarship that had no bearing on any human want more to the point than an idle curiosity; and by a similar turn of subreption and sophistication the later spokesmen of the barbarian ideal take much complacent credit for the "triumphs of modern science" that have nothing but an ostensible bearing on any matter of practical expediency, and they look to the universities to continue this work of the idle curiosity under some plausible pretext of practicality.

So the university of that era unavoidably came to be organized as a more or less comprehensive federation of professional schools or faculties devoted to such branches of practical knowledge as the ruling utilitarian interests of the time demanded. Under this overshadowing barbarian tradition the universities of early modern times started out as an avowed contrivance for indoctrination in the ways and means of salvation, spiritual and temporal, individual and collective— in some sort a school of engineering, primarily in divinity, secondarily in law and

---

13. Deliberate misrepresentation. *Subreption* is among the most frequently used words in the book.

politics, and presently in medicine and also in the other professions that serve a recognized utilitarian interest. After that fashion of a university that answered to this manner of ideals and aspirations had once been installed and gained a secure footing, its pattern acquired a degree of authenticity and prescription, so that later seminaries of learning came unquestioningly to be organized on the same lines; and further changes of academic policy and practice, such as are demanded by the later growth of cultural interests and ideals, have been made only reluctantly and with a suspicious reserve, gradually and by a circuitous sophistication; so that much of the non-utilitarian scientific and scholarly work indispensable to the university's survival under modern conditions is still scheduled under the faculties of law or medicine, or even of divinity.

But the human propensity for inquiry into things, irrespective of use or expediency, insinuated itself among the expositors of worldly wisdom from the outset; and from the first this quest of idle learning has sought shelter in the university as the only establishment in which it could find a domicile, even on sufferance, and so could achieve that footing of consecutive intellectual enterprise running through successive generations of scholars which is above all else indispensable to the advancement of knowledge. Under the régime of unmitigated pragmatic aims that ruled the earlier days of the European universities, this pursuit of knowledge for its own sake was carried on as a work of scholarly supererogation by men whose ostensibly sole occupation was the promulgation of some accredited line of salutary information. Frequently it had to be carried on under some colorable masquerade of practicality. And yet so persistent has the spirit of idle curiosity proved to be, and so consonant with the long-term demands even of the laity, that the dissimulation and smuggling-in of disinterested learning has gone on ever more openly and at an ever increasing rate of gain; until in the end, the attention given to scholarship and the non-utilitarian sciences in these establishments has come far to exceed that given to the practical disciplines for which the several faculties were originally installed. As time has passed and as successive cultural mutations have passed over the community, shifting the center of interest and bringing new ideals of scholarship, and bringing the whole cultural fabric nearer to its modern complexion, those purposes of crass expediency that were of such great moment and were so much a matter of course in earlier academic policy, have insensibly fallen to the rank of incidentals. And what had once been incidental, or even an object of surreptitious tolerance in the university, remains today as the only unequivocal duty of the corporation of learning, and stands out as the one characteristic trait without which no establishment can claim rank as a university.

Philosophy—the avowed body of theoretical science in the late medieval time—had grown out of the schoolmen's speculations in theology, being in point of derivation a body of refinements on the divine scheme of salvation; and with a view to quiet title, and to make manifest their devotion to the greater good of eschatological expediency, those ingenious speculators were content to proclaim that their philosophy is the handmaid of theology—*Philosophia theologiae ancillans.*[14] But their philosophy has fallen into the alembic of the idle curiosity and has given rise to a body of modern science, godless and unpractical, that has no intended or even ostensible bearing on the religious fortunes of mankind; and their sanctimonious maxim would today be better accepted as the subject of a limerick than of a homily. Except in degree, the fortunes of the temporal pragmatic disciplines, in Law and Medicine, have been much the same as that of their elder sister, Theology. Professionalism and practical serviceability have been gradually crowded into the background of academic interests and overlaid with quasi-utilitarian research—such as the history of jurisprudence, comparative physiology, and the like. They have in fact largely been eliminated.[h]

And changes running to this effect have gone farthest and have taken most consistent effect in those communities that are most fully imbued with the spirit of the modern peaceable civilization. It is in the more backward communities and schools that the barbarian animus of utilitarianism still maintains itself most nearly intact, whether it touches matters of temporal or of spiritual interest. With the later advance of culture, as the intellectual interest has gradually displaced the older ideals in men's esteem, and barring a reactionary episode here and there, the university has progressively come to take its place as a seat of the higher learning, a corporation for the pursuit of knowledge; and barring accidental reversions, it has increasingly asserted itself as an imperative necessity, more and more consistently, that the spirit of disinterested inquiry must have free play in these seminaries of the higher learning, without afterthought as to the practical or utilitarian consequences which this free inquiry may conceivably have for the professional training or for the social, civil or religious temper of the students or

h. With the current reactionary trend of things political and civil toward mediaeval-barbarian policies and habits of thought in the Fatherland, something of a correlative change has also latterly come in evidence in the German universities; so that what is substantially "cameralistic science"—training and information for prospective civil servants and police magistrates is in some appreciable measure displacing disinterested inquiry in the field of economics and political theory. This is peculiarly true of those corporations of learning that come closely in touch with the *Cultus Ministerium*. ["Cameralistic science": originally used to describe the thinking of early-modern German civil servants who advocated economic policies designed to strengthen the position of states. *Cultus Ministerium*: Latin for Ministry of Culture or Education. –Ed.]

14. Latin, usually *Philosophia ancilla theologiae*: philosophy is the servant or handmaiden of theology.

the rest of the community. Nothing is felt to be so irremediably vicious in academic policy as a coercive bias, religious, political, conventional or professional, in so far as it touches that quest of knowledge that constitutes the main interest of the university.

Professional training and technological work at large have of course not lost ground, either in the volume and the rigor of their requirements or in the application bestowed in their pursuit; but as within the circle of academic interests, these utilitarian disciplines have lost their preferential place and have been pushed to one side; so that the professional and technical schools are now in fact rated as adjuncts rather than as integral constituents of the university corporation. Such is the unmistakable sense of this matter among academic men. At the same time these vocational schools have, one with another, progressively taken on more of a distinctive, independent and close-knit structure; an individual corporate existence, autonomous and academically self-sufficient, even in those cases where they most tenaciously hold to their formal connection with the university corporation. They have reached a mature phase of organization, developed a type of personnel and control peculiar to themselves and their special needs, and have in effect come out from under the tutelage of the comprehensive academic organization of which they once in their early days were the substantial core. These schools have more in common among themselves as a class than their class have with the academic aims and methods that characterize the university proper. They are in fact ready and competent to go on their own recognizances—indeed they commonly resent any effective interference or surveillance from the side of the academic corporation of which they nominally continue to be members, and insist on going their own way and arranging their own affairs as they know best. Their connection with the university is superficial and formal at the best, so far as regards any substantial control of their affairs and policy by the university authorities at large; it is only in their interference with academic policy, and in injecting their own peculiar bias into university affairs, that they count substantially as corporate members of the academic body. And in these respects, what is said of the professional and technical schools holds true also of the undergraduate departments.

It is quite feasible to have a university without professional schools and without an undergraduate department; but it is not possible to have one without due provision for that non-utilitarian higher learning about which as a nucleus these utilitarian disciplines cluster. And this in spite of the solicitous endeavors of the professional schools to make good their footing as the substantial core of the corporation.

V

As intimated above, there are two main reasons for the continued and tenacious connection between these schools and the universities: (a) ancient tradition, fortified by the solicitous ambition of the university directorate to make a brave show of magnitude, and (b) the anxiety of these schools to secure some degree of scholarly authentication through such a formal connection with a seat of learning. These two motives have now and again pushed matters fairly to an extreme in the reactionary direction. So, for instance, the chances of intrigue and extra-academic clamor have latterly thrown up certain men of untempered "practicality" as directive heads of certain universities, and some of these have gone so far as to avow a reactionary intention to make the modern university a cluster of professional schools or faculties, after the ancient barbarian fashion.[i] But such a policy of return to the lost crudities is unworkable in the long run under modern conditions. It may serve excellently as a transient expedient in a campaign of popularity, and such appears to have been its chief purpose where a move of this kind has been advocated, but it runs on superficial grounds and can afford neither hope nor fear of a permanent diversion in the direction so spoken for.

In the modern community, under the strain of the price system and the necessities of competitive earning and spending, many men and women are driven by an habitual bias in favour of a higher "practical" efficiency in all matters of education; that is to say, a more single-minded devotion to the needs of earning and spending. There is, indeed, much of this spirit abroad in the community, and any candidate for popular favor and prestige may find his own advantage in conciliating popular sentiment of this kind. But there is at the same time equally prevalent through the community a long-term bias of another kind, such as will not enduringly tolerate the sordid effects of pursuing an educational policy that looks mainly to the main chance, and unreservedly makes the means of life its chief end. By virtue of this long-term idealistic drift, any seminary of learning that plays fast and loose in this way with the cultural interests entrusted to its keeping loses caste and falls out of the running. The universities that are subjected in this fashion to an experimental reversion to vocationalism, it appears, will unavoidably return presently to something of the non-professional type, on pain of falling

i. Cf. "Some Considerations on the Function of the State University." (Inaugural Address of Edmund Janes James (1855–1920), Ph.D., LL.D., in *Science* (November 17, 1905). [President of the University of Illinois from 1904 to 1920, James also was the first dean of the University of Chicago's University Extension from 1893 to 1902. –Ed.]

into hopeless discredit. There have been some striking instances, but current notions of delicacy will scarcely admit a citation of names and dates. And while the long-term drift of the modern idealistic bias may not permit the universities permanently to be diverted to the service of Mammon in this fashion, yet the unremitting endeavors of "educators" seeking prestige for worldly wisdom results at the best in a fluctuating state of compromise, in which the ill effects of such bids for popularity are continually being outworn by the drift of academic usage.

The point is illustrated by the American state universities as a class, although the illustration is by no means uniformly convincing. The greater number of these state schools are not, or are not yet, universities except in name.[15] These establishments have been founded, commonly, with a professed utilitarian purpose, and have started out with professional training as their chief avowed aim. The purpose made most of in their establishment has commonly been to train young men for proficiency in some gainful occupation; along with this have gone many half-articulate professions of solicitude for cultural interests to be taken care of by the same means. They have been installed by politicians looking for popular acclaim, rather than by men of scholarly or scientific insight, and their management has not infrequently been entrusted to political masters of intrigue, with scant academic qualifications; their foundations have been the work of practical politicians with a view to conciliate the good will of a lay constituency clamoring for things tangibly "useful"—that is to say, pecuniarily gainful. So these experts in short-term political prestige have made provision for schools of a "practical" character; but they have named these establishments "universities" because the name carries an air of scholarly repute, of a higher, more substantial kind than any naked avowal of material practicality would give. Yet, in those instances where the passage of time has allowed the readjustment to take place, these quasi-"universities," installed by men of affairs, of a crass "practicality," and in response to the utilitarian demands of an unlearned political constituency, have in the long run taken on more and more of an academic, non-utilitarian character, and have been gradually falling into line as universities claiming a place among the seminaries of the higher learning. The long-term drift of modern cultural ideals leaves these schools no final resting place short of the university type, however far short of such a consummation the greater number of them may still be found.

15. Some historians believe that, over time, state universities succeeded in hammering out the image of the university that today most closely approximates that held by most Americans: namely, a general purpose institution that pursues several ideas of what a university is, and as a result always stands ready to adapt to different economic and social needs.

What has just been said of the place which the university occupies in modern civilization, and more particularly of the manner in which it is to fill its place, may seem something of a fancy sketch. It is assuredly not a faithful description of any concrete case, by all means not of any given American university; nor does it faithfully describe the line of policy currently pursued by the directorate of any such establishment. Yet it is true to the facts, taken in a generalized way, and it describes the type to which the American schools unavoidably gravitate by force of the community's long-term idealistic impulse, in so far as their drift is not continually corrected and offset by vigilant authorities who, from motives of their own, seek to turn the universities to account in one way and another. It describes an institutional ideal; not necessarily an ideal nursed by any given individual, but the ideal logically involved in the scheme of modern civilization, and logically coming out of the historical development of Western civilization hitherto, and visible to any one who will dispassionately stand aside and look to the drift of latter-day events in so far as they bear on this matter of the higher learning, its advancement and conservation.

Many if not most of those men who are occupied with the guidance of university affairs would disown such a projected ideal, as being too narrow and too unpractical to fit into the modern scheme of things, which is above all else a culture of affairs; that it does not set forth what should be aimed at by any who have the good of mankind at heart, or who in any sensible degree appreciate the worth of real work as contrasted with the leisurely intellectual finesse of the confirmed scientist and man of letters. These and the like objections and strictures may be well taken, perhaps. The question of what, in any ulterior sense, ought to be sought after in the determination of academic policy and the conduct of academic affairs will, however, not coincide with the other question, as to what actually is being accomplished in these premises, on the one hand, nor as to what the long-term cultural aspirations of civilized men are setting toward, on the other hand.

Now, it is not intended here to argue the merits of the current cultural ideals as contrasted with what, in some ulterior sense, ought to be aimed at if the drift of current aspirations and impulse should conceivably permit a different ideal to be put into effect. It is intended only to set forth what place, in point of fact and for better or worse, the higher learning and the university hold in the current scheme of Western civilization, as determined by that body of instinctive aspirations and proclivities that holds this civilization to its course as it runs today; and further to show how and how far certain institutional factors comprised in this modern scheme of life go to help or hinder the realization of this ideal which men's aspirations and proclivities so make worthwhile to them. The sketch here offered in characterization of the university and its work, therefore, endeavors to take account of the community's consensus of impulses and desires touching the animus and aims that should move the seminaries of the higher learning, at the same time that it excludes those subsidiary or alien interests in whose favor no such consensus is found to prevail.

There are many of these workday interests, extraneous to the higher learning, each and several of which may be abundantly good and urgent in its own right; but, while they need not be at cross purposes with the higher learning, they are extraneous to that disinterested pursuit of knowledge in which the characteristic intellectual bent of modern civilization culminates. These others are patent, insistent and palpable, and there need be no apprehension of their going by default. The intellectual predilection—the idle curiosity—abides and asserts itself when other pursuits of a more temporal but more immediately urgent kind leave men free to take stock of the ulterior ends and values of life; whereas the transient interests, preoccupation with the ways and means of life, are urgent and immediate, and employ men's thought and energy through the greater share of their life. The question of material ways and means, and the detail requirements of the day's work, are forever at hand and forever contest the claims of any avowed ulterior end; and by force of unremitting habituation the current competitive system of acquisition and expenditure induces in all classes such a bias as leads them to overrate ways and means as contrasted with the ends which these ways and means are in some sense designed to serve.

So, one class and another, biased by the habitual preoccupation of the class, will aim to divert the academic equipment to some particular use which habit has led them to rate high; or to include in the academic discipline various lines of inquiry and training which are extraneous to the higher learning but which the class in question may specially have at heart; but taking them one with another, there is no general or abiding consensus among the various classes of the community in favor of diverting the academic establishment to any other specific uses, or of including in the peculiar work of the university anything beyond the pursuit of knowledge for its own sake.[16]

Now, it may be remarked by the way, that civilized mankind should have come so to set their heart on this chase after a fugitive knowledge of inconsequential

16. In the years following World War I, disagreements regarding "specific uses" of the university entered a new phase, partly as a result of the rise of the junior college, a new institution that for a time raised the realistic possibility of splitting the traditional four years of university-sponsored education in half.

facts may be little to the credit of the race or of that scheme of culture that so centers about this cult of the idle curiosity. And it is perhaps to their credit, as well as to the credit of the community whose creatures they are, that the spokesmen of some tangible ideal, some materially expedient aspiration, embodying more of worldly wisdom, are forever urging upon the institutions of the higher learning one or another course of action of a more palpably expedient kind. But, for better or worse, the passage of time brings out the fact that these sober and sensible courses of policy so advocated are after all essentially extraneous, if not alien, to those purposes for which a university can be maintained, on the ground afforded by the habits of thought prevalent in the modern civilized community.

One and another of these "practical" and expedient interests have transiently come to the front in academic policy, and have in their time given a particular bent to the pursuit of knowledge that has occupied the universities. Of these extraneous interests the two most notable have, as already indicated above, been the ecclesiastical and the political. But in the long run these various interests and ideals of expediency have, all and several, shown themselves to be only factional elements in the scheme of culture, and have lost their preferential voice in the shaping of academic life. The place in men's esteem once filled by church and state is now held by pecuniary traffic, business enterprise. So that the graver issues of academic policy which now tax the discretion of the directive powers, reduce themselves in the main to a question between the claims of science and scholarship on the one hand and those of business principles and pecuniary gain on the other hand. In one shape or another this problem of adjustment, reconciliation or compromise between the needs of the higher learning and the demands of business enterprise is forever present in the deliberations of the university directorate. This question gathers in its net all those perplexing details of expediency that now claim the attention of the ruling bodies.

VI[17]

Since the paragraphs that make up the foregoing chapter were written the American academic community has been thrown into a new and peculiar position by the fortunes of war. The progress and the further promise of the war hold in prospect new and untried responsibilities, as well as an unexampled opportunity.

17. This is the only section in the eight chapters in *The Higher Learning in America* whose composition we can date with any confidence. It is a revised and expanded version of Veblen's essay "The War and Higher Learning," published by the *Dial* magazine on July 18, 1918. Veblen inserted it into the final corrected typescript manuscript he sent to his publisher B. W. Huebsch in September 1918.

So that the outlook now (June 1918) would seem to be that the Americans are to be brought into a central place in the republic of learning; to take a position, not so much of dominance as of trust and guardianship; not so much by virtue of their own superior merit as by force of the insolvency of the European academic community.

Again, it is not that the war is expected to leave the lines of European scholars and scientists extinct; although there is no denying the serious inroads made by the war, both in the way of a high mortality among European men of learning, and in the way of a decimation of the new men on whom the hopes of the higher learning for the incoming generation should have rested. There is also a serious diversion of the young forces from learning to transiently urgent matters of a more material, and more ephemeral nature. But possibly more sinister than all these losses that are in a way amenable to statistical record and estimate, is the current and prospective loss of morale.

Naturally, it would be difficult and hazardous to offer an appraisal of this prospective loss of morale, with which it is to be expected that the disintegrated European community of learned men will come through the troubled times. But that there is much to be looked for on this score, that there is much to be written off in the way of lowered aggregate efficiency and loss of the spirit of team-work—that much there is no denying, and it is useless to blink the fact.

There has already a good deal of disillusionment taken effect throughout the nations of Christendom in respect of the temper and trustworthiness of German scholarship these past three or four years, and it is fairly beyond computation what further shift of sentiment in this respect is to be looked for in the course of a further possible period of years given over to the same line of experience. Doubtless, the German scholars, and therefore the German seats of learning whose creatures and whose custodians these German scholars are, have earned much of the distrust and dispraise that is falling to their share. There is no overlooking the fact that they have proved the frailty of their hold on those elementary principles of sobriety and single mind that underlie all sound work in the field of learning. To anyone who has the interest of the higher learning at heart, the spectacle of maudlin chauvinism and inflated scurrility unremittingly placed on view by the putative leaders of German science and scholarship cannot but be exceedingly disheartening.[18]

---

18. Allusion to the first and best-known instance of the widespread cooperation of European professors in wartime propaganda: "To the Civilized World," an open letter of October 1914 signed by some one hundred leading German intellectuals and university professors, which endorsed outrageously false German official assertions about the origins and conduct of the war.

It may be argued, and it may be true, of course, that much of this failure of intelligence and spiritual force among Germany's men of learning is of the nature of a transient eclipse of their powers; that with the return of settled conditions there is due to come a return of poise and insight. But when all due argument has been heard, it remains true that the distrust set afoot in the mind of their neighbors, by this highly remarkable exhibition of their personal equation, will long inure to the disability of Germany's men of learning as a force to be counted on in that teamwork that is of the essence of things for the advancement of learning. In effect, Germany, and Germany's associates in this warlike enterprise, will presumably be found bankrupt in this respect on the return of peace, even beyond the other nations.

These others have also not escaped the touch of the angel of decay, but the visible corruption of spiritual and intellectual values does not go the same length among them. Nor have these others suffered so heavy a toll on their prospective scholarly man power. It is all a matter of degree and of differential decline, coupled with a failure of corporate organization and of the usages and channels of communion and co-operation. Chauvinistic self-sufficiency and disesteem of their neighbors have apparently also not gone so deep and far among the other nations; although here again it is only a relative degree of immunity that they enjoy.

And all this holds true of the Americans in much the same way as of the rest; except that the Americans have, at least hitherto, not been exposed to the blight in anything like the same degree as any one of those other peoples with whom they come in comparison here. It is, of course, not easy to surmise what may yet overtake them, and the others with them; but judged on the course of things hitherto, and on the apparent promise of the calculable future, it is scarcely to be presumed that the Americans are due to suffer so extreme a degree of dilapidation as the European peoples—even apart from the accentuated evil case of the Germans. The strain has hitherto been lighter here, and it promises so to continue, whether the further duration of the war shall turn out to be longer or shorter. The Americans are, after all, somewhat sheltered from the impact; and so soon as the hysterical anxiety induced by the shock has had time to spend itself, it should reasonably be expected that this people will be able soberly to take stock of its assets and to find that its holdings in the domain of science and scholarship are, in the main, still intact.

Not that no loss has been incurred, nor that no material degree of derangement is to be looked for, but in comparison with what the experience of the war is bringing to the Europeans, the case of the Americans should still be the best there is to be looked for and the best is always good enough, perforce. So it becomes a question, what the Americans will do with the best opportunity which the circumstances offer. And on their conduct of their affairs in this bearing turns not only their own fortune in respect of the interests of science and scholarship, but in great measure the fortunes of their overseas friends and co-partners in the republic of learning as well.

The fortunes of war promise to leave the American men of learning in a strategic position, in the position of a strategic reserve, of a force to be held in readiness, equipped and organized to meet the emergency that so arises, and to retrieve so much as may be of those assets of scholarly equipment and personnel that make the substantial code of Western civilization. And so it becomes a question of what the Americans are minded to do about it. It is their opportunity, and at the same time it carries the gravest responsibility that has yet fallen on the nation; for the spiritual fortunes of Christendom are bound up with the line of policy which this surviving contingent of American men of learning shall see fit to pursue. They are not all that is to be left over when the powers of decay shall begin to retire, nor are they, perhaps, to be the best and most valuable contingent among these prospective survivors; but they occupy a strategic position, in that they are today justly to be credited with disinterested motives, beyond the rest, at the same time that they command those material resources without which the quest of knowledge can hope to achieve little along the modern lines of inquiry. By force of circumstances they are thrown into the position of keepers of the ways and means whereby the republic of learning is to retrieve its fortunes. By force of circumstances they are in a position, if they so choose, to shelter many of those masters of free inquiry whom the one-eyed forces of reaction and partisanship overseas will seek to suppress and undo; and they are also in a position, if they so choose, to install something in the way of an international clearing house and provisional headquarters for the academic community throughout that range of civilized peoples whose goodwill they now enjoy—a place of refuge and a place of meeting, confluence and dissemination for those views and ideas that live and move and have their being in the higher learning.

There is, therefore, a work of reconstruction to be taken care of in the realm of learning, no less than in the working scheme of economic and civil institutions. And as in this other work of reconstruction, so here; if it is to be done without undue confusion and blundering it is due to be set afoot before the final emergency is at hand. But there is the difference that, whereas the framework of civil institutions may still, with passable success, be drawn on national lines and confined within the national frontiers; and while the economic organization can also, without fatal loss, be confined in a similar fashion, in response to short-sighted patriotic preconceptions; the interests of science, and therefore of the academic community, do not run on national lines and cannot similarly be confined within geographical or political boundaries. In the nature of the case these interests are of an international character and cannot be taken care of except by unrestricted collusion and collaboration among the learned men of all those peoples whom it may concern. Yet there is no mistaking the fact that the spirit of invidious patriotism has invaded these premises, too, and promises to bungle the outcome; which makes the needed work of reconstruction all the more difficult and all the more imperative. Unhappily, the state of sentiment on both sides of the line of cleavage will presumably not admit a cordial understanding and co-operation between the German contingent and the rest of the civilized nations, for some time to come. But the others are in a frame of mind that should lend itself generously to a larger measure of co-operation in this respect now than ever before.

So it may not seem out of place to offer a suggestion, tentatively and under correction, looking to this end. A beginning may well be made by a joint enterprise among American scholars and universities for the installation of a freely endowed central establishment where teachers and students of all nationalities, including Americans with the rest, may pursue their chosen work as guests of the American academic community at large, or as guests of the American people in the character of a democracy of culture. There should also be nothing to hinder the installation of more than one of these academic houses of refuge and entertainment; nor should there be anything to hinder the enterprise being conducted on such terms of amity, impartiality and community interest as will make recourse to it an easy matter of course for any scholars whom its opportunities may attract. The same central would at the same time, and for the time being, take care of those channels of communication throughout the academic world that have been falling into enforced neglect under the strain of the war. So also should provision be made, perhaps best under the same auspices, for the (transient) taking-over of the many essential lines of publicity and publication on which the men engaged in scholarly and scientific inquiry have learned to depend, and which have also been falling into something of a decline during the war.

Measures looking to this end might well be made, at the same time, to serve no less useful a purpose within the American Academic community. As is well known, there prevails today an extensive and wasteful competitive duplication of plant, organization and personnel among the American universities, as regards both publications and courses of instruction. Particularly is this true in respect of that advanced work of the universities that has to do with the higher learning. At the same time, these universities are now pinched for funds, due to the current inflation of prices. So that any proposal of this nature, which might be taken advantage of as an occasion for the pooling of common issues among the universities, might hopefully be expected to be welcomed as a measure of present relief from some part of the pecuniary strain under which they are now working.

But competition is well ingrained in the habitual outlook of the American schools. To take the issue to neutral ground, therefore, where this competitive animus may hopefully be counted on to find some salutary abatement, it may be suggested that a practicable nucleus for this proposed joint enterprise can well be found in one or another—perhaps in one and another—of those extra-academic foundations for research of which there already are several in existence—as, e. g., the Carnegie Institution.[19] With somewhat enlarged powers, or perhaps rather with some abatement of restrictions, and with such additional funds as may be required, the necessary work and organization should readily be taken care of by such an institution. Further growth and ramification would be left to future counsel and advisement.

The contemplated enterprise would necessarily require a certain planning and organization of work and something in the way of an administrative and clerical staff, a setting up of something in the way of "organization tables"; but there can be no question of offering detailed proposals on that head here. Yet the caution may well be entered here that few specifications are better than many, in these premises, and that the larger the latitude allowed from the outset, the fewer the seeds of eventual defeat—as is abundantly illustrated by contraries.

It is also evident that such an enterprise will involve provision for some expenditure of funds; presumably a somewhat generous expenditure; which comes near implying that recourse should be had to the public revenues, or to resources that may legitimately be taken over by the public authorities from private hands where they now serve no useful purpose. There are many items of material resources in the country that come legitimately under this head. At the same time it is well in this connection to call to mind that there is no prospect of the country's being in any degree impoverished in the course of the war; so that there need be no apprehension of a shortage of means for the carrying on of such an enterprise, if only the available sources are drawn on without prejudice. In the mind of any disinterested student of the American economic situation, there can be no serious apprehension that the American people, collectively, will be at all worse

19. The Carnegie Institution of Washington (1901) and the Rockefeller Institute for Medical Research (1902) were the most important and well-endowed of America's freestanding research institutes.

off in point of disposable means at the close of the war than they were at its beginning; quite the contrary in fact. To anyone who will look to the facts it is evident that the experience of the war, and the measures taken and to be taken, are
leading to a heightened industrial productiveness and a concomitant elimination
of waste. The resulting net gain in productive efficiency has not gone at all far,
and there need be no apprehension of its going to great lengths; but, for more or
less, it is going so far as safely to promise a larger net annual production of useful
goods in the immediate future than in the immediate past; and the disposable
means of any people is always a matter of the net annual production, and it need
be a question of nothing else. The manner in which this net product is, and is to
be, shared among the classes and individuals of the community is another question, which does not belong here.

A question of graver weight and of greater perplexity touches the presumptive
attitude of the several universities and their discretionary authorities in the face
of any proposed measure of this kind; where the scope of the enterprise is so far
beyond their habitual range of interest. When one calls to mind the habitual pa-
rochialism of the governing boards of these seminaries of the higher learning,
and the meticulous maneuvers of their executives seeking each to enhance his
own prestige and the prestige of his own establishment, there is not much of an
evident outlook for large and generous measures looking to the common good.
And yet it is also to be called to mind that these governing boards and executives
are, after all, drawn from the common stock of humanity, picked men as they
may be; and that they are subject, after all, to somewhat the same impulses and
infirmities as the common run, picked though they may be with a view to paro-
chialism and blameless futility. Now, what is overtaking the temper of the common run under the strain of the war situation should be instructive as to what may
be also looked for at the bands of these men in whose discretion rest the fortunes
of the American universities. There should be at least a fighting chance that, with
something larger, manlier, more substantial, to occupy their attention and to
shape the day's work for them, these seminaries of learning may, under instant
pressure, turn their best efforts to their ostensible purpose, "the increase and
diffusion of knowledge among men," and to forego their habitual preoccupation
with petty intrigue and bombastic publicity, until the return of idler days.

CHAPTER II

The Governing Boards

In the working theory of the modern civilized community—that is to say in the current common-sense[1] apprehension of what is right and good, as it works out in the long run—the university is a corporation of learning, disinterested and dispassionate. To its keeping is entrusted the community's joint interest in esoteric knowledge. It is given over to the single-minded pursuit of science and scholarship, without afterthought and without a view to interests subsidiary or extraneous to the higher learning. It is, indeed, the one great institution of modern times that works to no ulterior end and is controlled by no consideration of expediency beyond its own work. Typically, normally, in point of popular theory, the university is moved by no consideration other than "the increase and diffusion of knowledge among men."[2] This is so because this profitless quest of knowledge has come to be the highest and ulterior aim of modern culture.

Such has been the case, increasingly, for some generations past; but it is not until quite recently that such a statement would hold true unequivocally and with an unqualified generality. That the case stands so today is due to the failure of theoretical interests of a different kind; directly and immediately it is due to the fact that in the immediate present the cult of knowledge has, by default, taken over that primacy among human interests which an eschatologically thrifty religious sentiment once held in the esteem of Christendom. So long as the fear of God still continued to move the generality of civilized men in sufficient measure,

1. Veblen uses the phrase "common sense" repeatedly, and it usually carries a technical meaning that came out of the eighteenth-century Scottish common-sense school of philosophy, especially Thomas Reid's (1710–1796), *An Inquiry into the Human Mind, on the Principles of Common Sense* (1764). Reid taught that all human beings are born with certain ultimate and unexplainable principles that are intuitively recognized as true and taken for granted by common sense without need for logical proof. In the absence of such common-sense principles, Reid and his followers argued, we would have no starting points for conduct and thought. During his years as a Yale graduate student, Veblen almost certainly studied common-sense philosophy with Noah Porter (1811–1922), whose work sought to fashion a new synthesis of Scottish common-sense philosophy and nineteenth-century German idealism.

2. The phrase English scientist James Smithsonian (1765–1829) used in his will when stipulating that his remaining assets pass to the United States and be used to found the Smithsonian Institution. Veblen uses the phrase repeatedly.

their theoretical knowledge was organized for "the glory of God and the good of man"—the latter phrase being taken in the eschatological sense; and so long the resulting scheme of learning was laid out and cultivated with an eye to the main chance in a hereafter given over, in the main and for its major effect, to pains and penalties. With the latter-day dissipation of this fear of God, the scheme of knowledge handed down out of a devout past and further amplified in the (theoretically) Godless present, has, by atrophy of disuse, lost its ulterior view to such spiritual expediency, and has come to stand over as an output of intellectual enterprise working under the impulsion and guidance of an idle curiosity simply. All this may not be much to the credit of civilized mankind, but dispassionate reflection will not leave the fact in doubt. And the outcome for the university, considered as an institution of this modern culture, is such as this conjuncture of circumstances will require.

But while such is the dispassionate working theory, the long-term drift of modern common sense as touches the work of the university, it is also a matter of course that this ideally single-minded course of action has never been realized in any concrete case. While it holds true, by and large, that modern Christendom has outlived the fear of God—that is to say of "the Pope, the Turk, and the Devil,"[3]—it does not therefore follow that men take a less instant interest in the affairs of life, or carry on the traffic of their lives with a less alert eye to the main chance, than they once did under the habitual shadow of that barbarian[4] fear. The difference is, for the purpose in hand, that the same solicitous attention that once converged on such an avoidance of ulterior consequences now centers on questions of present ways and means. Worldly wisdom has not fallen into decay or abeyance, but it has become a wisdom of ways and means that lead to nothing beyond further ways and means. Expediency and practical considerations have come to mean considerations of a pecuniary kind; good, on the whole, for pecuniary purposes only; that is to say, gain and expenditure for the sake of further gain and expenditure, with nothing that will stand scrutiny as a final term to this traffic in ways and means—except only this cult of the idle curiosity to which the seats of learning are, in theory, dedicate. But unremitting habituation to the competitive pursuit of ways and means has determined that "practical" interests of this complexion rule workday life in the modern community throughout, and they are therefore so intimately and ubiquitously bound up with current habits of thought, and have so strong and immediate a hold on current workday sen-

---

3. The three members of what German Protestant theologian Martin Luther (1483–1546) dubbed "the unholy trinity."

4. Cf. chapter I, "Introductory," note 11.

timent, that, hitherto, in no case have the seats of learning been able to pursue their quest of knowledge with anything like that single-mindedness which academic men are moved to profess in their moments of academic elation.

Some one vital interest of this practical sort, some variant of the quest of gain, is always at hand and strenuously effective in the community's life, and therefore dominates their everyday habits of thought for the time being. This tone-giving dominance of such a workday interest may be transient or relatively enduring; it may be more or less urgently important and consequential under the circumstances in which the community is placed, or the clamor of its spokesmen and beneficiaries may be more or less ubiquitous and pertinacious; but in any case it will have its effect in the counsels of the "Educators," and so it will infect the university as well as the lower levels of the educational system. So that, while the higher learning still remains as the enduring purpose and substantial interest of the university establishment, the dominant practical interests of the day will, transiently but effectually, govern the detail lines of academic policy, the range of instruction offered, and the character of the personnel; and more particularly and immediately will the character of the governing boards and the academic administration so be determined by the current run of popular sentiment touching the community's practical needs and aims; since these ruling bodies stand, in one way or another, under the critical surveillance of a lay[5] constituency.

The older American universities have grown out of underlying colleges—undergraduate schools. Within the memory of men still living it was a nearly unbroken rule that the governing boards of these higher American schools were drawn largely from the clergy and were also guided mainly by ecclesiastical, or at least by devotional, notions of what was right and needful in matters of learning. This state of things reflected the ingrained devoutness of that portion of the American community to which the higher schools then were of much significance. At the same time it reflected the historical fact that the colleges of the early days had been established primarily as training schools for ministers of the church. In their later growth, in the recent past, while the chief purpose of these seminaries has no longer been religious, yet ecclesiastical prepossessions long continued to

5. Short for *layman*: a person who is not a member of a particular profession. The essence of lay governance, as the historian Richard Hofstadter explained it, is that boards of laymen, not the faculty, "are, in law, the college or university, and that legally they can hire and fire faculty and make almost all the decisions governing the institution." Almost nowhere outside the United States and Canada are colleges or universities governed by laymen. In Europe, the traditional model of university governance is based on a strong interplay of state regulation and academic self-regulation. See Richard Hofstadter and Walter P. Metzger, *The Development of Academic Freedom in the United States* (New York: Columbia University Press, 1955), 120.

mark the permissible limits of the learning which they cultivated, and continued also to guard the curriculum and discipline of the schools.

That phase of academic policy is past. Due regard at least is, of course, still had to the religious proprieties—the American community, by and large, is still the most devout of civilized countries—but such regard on the part of the academic authorities now proceeds on grounds of businesslike expediency rather than on religious conviction or on an ecclesiastical or priestly bias in the ruling bodies. It is a concessive precaution on the part of a worldly-wise directorate, in view of the devout prejudices of those who know no better.

The rule of the clergy belongs virtually to the prehistory of the American universities. While that rule held there were few if any schools that should properly be rated as of university grade. Even now, it is true, much of the secondary school system, including the greater part, though a diminishing number, of the smaller colleges, is under the tutelage of the clergy;[6] and the academic heads of these schools are almost universally men of ecclesiastical standing and bias rather than of scholarly attainments. But that fact does not call for particular notice here, since these schools lie outside the university field, and so outside the scope of this inquiry.

For a generation past, while the American universities have been coming into line as seminaries of the higher learning, there has gone on a wide-reaching substitution of laymen in the place of clergymen on the governing boards. This progressive secularization is sufficiently notorious, even though there are some among the older establishments the terms of whose charters require a large proportion of clergymen on their boards. This secularization is entirely consonant with the prevailing drift of sentiment in the community at large, as is shown by the uniform and uncritical approval with which it is regarded. The substitution is a substitution of businessmen and politicians; which amounts to saying that it is a substitution of businessmen. So that the discretionary control in matters of university policy now rests finally in the hands of businessmen.[7]

6. In 1918, more than half of American institutions of higher education enrolled fewer than three hundred students. Only 37 of 672 universities, colleges, and professional schools enrolled over two thousand students. Just eight enrolled more than five thousand students. A gradually diminishing majority of the colleges were religiously affiliated.

7. A modern scholarly study tracing the displacement of Protestant clergymen from governing boards at major Northeastern private universities and technical institutes during 1861–1929 has shown that Protestant clergymen were still the largest interest group (22.5 percent) represented on governing boards of these institutions as late as a decade after the Civil War. By 1920, however, their number had shrunk to 4.5 percent, and sizeable numbers of businessmen (44.5 percent) and lawyers (16.7 percent) now appeared on boards. See Clyde Barrow, *Universities and the Capitalist State: Corporate Liberalism and the Reconstruction of American Higher Education, 1894–1928* (Madison: University of Wisconsin Press, 1990), 37–46. Of the twenty-one trustees on the University of Chicago's first board of

The reason which men prefer to allege for this state of things is the sensible need of experienced men of affairs to take care of the fiscal concerns of these university corporations; for the typical modern university is a corporation possessed of large property and disposing of large aggregate expenditures, so that it will necessarily have many and often delicate pecuniary interests to be looked after. It is at the same time held to be expedient in case of emergency to have several wealthy men identified with the governing board, and such men of wealth are also commonly businessmen. It is apparently believed, though on just what ground this sanguine belief rests does not appear, that in case of emergency the wealthy members of the boards may be counted on to spend their substance in behalf of the university. In point of fact, at any rate, poor men and men without large experience in business affairs are felt to have no place in these bodies. If by any chance such men, without the due pecuniary qualifications, should come to make up a majority, or even an appreciable minority of such a governing board, the situation would be viewed with some apprehension by all persons interested in the case and cognizant of the facts. The only exception might be cases where, by tradition, the board habitually includes a considerable proportion of clergymen:

"Such great regard is always lent

By men to ancient precedent."[8]

The reasons alleged are no doubt convincing to those who are ready to be so convinced, but they are after all more plausible at first sight than on reflection. In point of fact these businesslike governing boards commonly exercise little if any current surveillance of the corporate affairs of the university, beyond a directive oversight of the distribution of expenditures among the several academic purposes for which the corporate income is to be used; that is to say, they control the budget of expenditures; which comes to saying that they exercise a pecuniary discretion in the case mainly in the way of deciding what the body of academic men that constitutes the university may or may not do with the means in hand; that is to say, their pecuniary surveillance comes in the main to an interference with the academic work, the merits of which these men of affairs on the governing board are in no special degree qualified to judge. Beyond this, as touches the actual running administration of the corporation's investments, income and expenditures—all that is taken care of by permanent officials who have, as they necessarily must, sole and responsible charge of those matters. Even the auditing of the corporation's accounts is commonly vested in such officers of the corporation, who have

---

trustees, only one was an ordained minister; the others were mostly Chicago-based bankers, businessmen, lawyers, and editors.

8. Proverbial expression apparently coined by Veblen.

none but a formal, if any, direct connection with the governing board. The governing board, or more commonly a committee of the board, on the other hand, will then formally review the balance sheets and bundles of vouchers duly submitted by the corporation's fiscal officers and their clerical force—with such effect of complaisant oversight as will best be appreciated by any person who has had the fortune to look into the accounts of a large corporation.

So far as regards its pecuniary affairs and their due administration, the typical modern university is in a position, without loss or detriment, to dispense with the services of any board of trustees, regents, curators, or what not. Except for the insuperable difficulty of getting a hearing for such an extraordinary proposal, it should be no difficult matter to show that these governing boards of business-men commonly are quite useless to the university for any businesslike purpose. Indeed, except for a stubborn prejudice to the contrary, the fact should readily be seen that the boards are of no material use in any connection; their sole effectual function being to interfere with the academic management in matters that are not of the nature of business, and that lie outside their competence and outside the range of their habitual interest.

The governing boards—trustees, regents, curators, fellows, whatever their style and title—are an aimless survival from the days of clerical rule, when they were presumably of some effect in enforcing conformity to orthodox opinions and observances, among the academic staff. At that time, when means for maintenance of the denominational colleges commonly had to be procured by an appeal to impecunious congregations, it fell to these bodies of churchmen to do service as sturdy beggars for funds with which to meet current expenses. So that as long as the boards were made up chiefly of clergymen they served a pecuniary purpose; whereas, since their complexion has been changed by the substitution of busi-nessmen in the place of ecclesiastics, they have ceased to exercise any function other than a bootless meddling with academic matters which they do not under-stand. The sole ground of their retention appears to be an unreflecting deferen-tial concession to the usages of corporate organization and control, such as have been found advantageous for the pursuit of private gain by businessmen banded together in the exploitation of joint-stock companies with limited liability.[a]

a. An instance showing something of the measure and incidence of fiscal service rendered by such a businesslike board may be suggestive, even though it is scarcely to be taken as faithfully illustrating current practice, in that the particular board in question has exercised an uncommon measure of surveillance over its university's pecuniary concerns.

A university corporation endowed with a large estate (appraised at something over $30,000,000) has been governed by a board of the usual form, with plenary discretion, established on a basis of co-

The fact remains, the modern civilized community is reluctant to trust its serious interests to others than men of pecuniary substance, who have proved their fitness for the direction of academic affairs by acquiring, or by otherwise being possessed of, considerable wealth.[b] It is not simply that experienced businessmen are, on mature reflection, judged to be the safest and most competent trustees of the university's fiscal interests. The preference appears to be almost wholly impulsive, and a matter of habitual bias. It is due for the greater part to the high esteem currently accorded to men of wealth at large, and especially to wealthy men who have succeeded in business, quite apart from any special capacity shown by

---

optation. In point of practical effect, the board, or rather that fraction of the board which takes an active interest in the university's affairs, has been made up of a group of local business men engaged in diverse enterprises of the kind familiar to men of relatively large means, with somewhat extensive interests of the nature of banking and underwriting, where large extensions of credit and the temporary use of large funds are of substantial consequence. By terms of the corporate charter the board was required to render to the governor of the state a yearly report of all the pecuniary affairs of the university; but no penalty was attached to their eventual failure to render such report, though some legal remedy could doubtless have been had on due application by the parties in interest, as e. g., by the academic head of the university. No such report has been rendered, however, and no steps appear to have been taken to procure such a report, or any equivalent accounting. But on persistent urging from the side of his faculty, and after some courteous delay, the academic head pushed an inquiry into the corporation's finances so far as to bring out facts somewhat to the following effect:

The board, or the group of local business men who constituted the habitual working majority of the board, appear to have kept a fairly close and active oversight of the corporate funds entrusted to them, and to have seen to their investment and disposal somewhat in detail—and, it has been suggested, somewhat to their own pecuniary advantage. With the result that the investments were found to yield a current income of some three percent. (rather under than over)—in a state where investment on good security in the open market commonly yielded from six per cent to eight per cent. Of this income approximately one-half (apparently some forty-five per cent) practically accrued to the possible current use of the university establishment. Just what disposal was made of the remainder is not altogether clear; though it is loosely presumed to have been kept in hand with an eventual view to the erection and repair of buildings. Something like one-half of what so made up the currently disposable income was further set aside in the character of a sinking fund, to accumulate for future use and to meet contingencies; so that what effectually accrued to the university establishment for current use to meet necessary academic expenditures would amount to something like one per cent (or less) on the total investment. But of this finally disposable fraction of the income, again, an appreciable sum was set aside as a special sinking fund to accumulate for the eventual use of the university library—which, it may be remarked, was in the meantime seriously handicapped for want of funds with which to provide for current needs. So also the academic establishment at large was perforce managed on a basis of penurious economy, to the present inefficiency and the lasting damage of the university.

The figures and percentages given above are not claimed to be exact; it is known that a more accurate specification of details would result in a less favorable showing.

At the time when these matters were disclosed (to a small number of the uneasy persons interested) there was an ugly suggestion afloat touching the pecuniary integrity of the board's management, but this is doubtless to be dismissed as being merely a loose expression of ill-will; and the like is also doubtless to be said as regards the suggestion that there may have been an interested collusion between the academic head and the active members of the board. These were "all honorable men," of great repute in the community and well known as sagacious and successful men in their private business ventures. [Nothing more is known about this episode than what Veblen relates in his note. In 1919, only three American universities—Columbia, Harvard, and Stanford—had endowments valued at more than $30 million. The quoted phrase is from William Shakespeare, *Julius Caesar*, III, ii: "For Brutus is an honorable man; / So are they all honorable men." –Ed.]

b. Cf. *The Instinct of Workmanship: And the State of Industrial Arts* (1914), ch. vii, 343–352.

such success for the guardianship of any institution of learning. Business success is by common consent, and quite uncritically, taken to be conclusive evidence of wisdom even in matters that have no relation to business affairs. So that it stands as a matter of course that businessmen must be preferred for the guardianship and control of that intellectual enterprise for the pursuit of which the university is established, as well as to take care of the pecuniary welfare of the university corporation. And, full of the same naive faith that business success "answereth all things,"[9] these businessmen into whose hands this trust falls are content to accept the responsibility and confident to exercise full discretion in these matters with which they have no special familiarity. Such is the outcome, to the present date, of the recent and current secularization of the governing boards. The final discretion in the affairs of the seats of learning is entrusted to men who have proved their capacity for work that has nothing in common with the higher learning.[c]

As bearing on the case of the American universities, it should be called to mind that the businessmen of this country, as a class, are of a notably conservative habit of mind. In a degree scarcely equaled in any community that can lay claim to a modicum of intelligence and enterprise, the spirit of American business is a spirit of quietism, caution, compromise, collusion, and chicane.[10] It is not that the spirit of enterprise or of unrest is wanting in this community, but only that, by selective effect of the conditioning circumstances, persons affected with that spirit are excluded from the management of business, and so do not come into the class of successful businessmen from which the governing boards are drawn. American inventors are bold and resourceful, perhaps beyond the common run of their class elsewhere, but it has become a commonplace that Amer-

c. A subsidiary reason of some weight should not be overlooked in seeking the cause of this secularization of the boards, and of the peculiar color which the secularization has given them. In any community where wealth and business enterprise are held in such high esteem, men of wealth and of affairs are not only deferred to, but their countenance is sought from one motive and another. At the same time election to one of these boards has come to have a high value as an honorable distinction. Such election or appointment therefore is often sought from motives of vanity, and it is at the same time a convenient means of conciliating the good will of the wealthy incumbent.

It may be added that now and again the discretionary control of large funds which so falls to the members of the board may come to be pecuniarily profitable to them, so that the office may come to be attractive as a business proposition as well as in point of prestige. Instances of the kind are not wholly unknown, though presumably exceptional.

9. Quoted phrase from Ecclesiastes 10:19: "A feast is made for laughter, and wine maketh merry, but money answereth all things."

10. Variant of *chicanery*: use of deception or trickery; actions or statement designed to trick people into believing something that is not true. By characterizing the spirit of American business as he does, Veblen mocked the heroic status of businessmen in his time. In *The Theory of Business Enterprise* (1904), he observed that businessmen often used the language of gambling, referring to their transactions as "deals" involving an element of "bluff." For Veblen, success in poker and success in business required the similar skills of deception and disguise.

ican inventors habitually die poor; and one does not find them represented on the boards in question. American engineers and technologists are as good and efficient as their kind in other countries; but they do not as a class accumulate wealth enough to entitle them to sit on the directive board of any self-respecting university, nor can they claim even a moderate rank as "safe and sane" men of business. American explorers, prospectors and pioneers cannot be said to fall short of the common measure in hardihood, insight, temerity or tenacity; but wealth does not accumulate in their hands, and it is a common saying, of them as of the inventors, that they are not fit to conduct their own (pecuniary) affairs; and the reminder is scarcely needed that neither they nor their qualities are drawn into the counsels of these governing boards. The wealth and the serviceable results that come of the endeavors of these enterprising and temerarious Americans habitually inure to the benefit of such of their compatriots as are endowed with a "safe and sane" spirit of "watchful waiting,"—of caution, collusion and chicane. There is a homely but well-accepted American colloquialism which says that "The silent hog eats the swill."

As elsewhere, but in a higher degree and a more cogent sense than elsewhere, success in business affairs, in such measure as to command the requisite deference, comes only by getting something for nothing. And, barring accidents and within the law, it is only the waiting game and the defensive tactics that will bring gains of that kind, unless it be strategy of the nature of finesse and chicane. Now it happens that American conditions during the past one hundred years have been peculiarly favorable to the patient and circumspect man who will rather wait than work; and it is also during these hundred years that the current traditions and standards of business conduct and of businesslike talent have taken shape and been incorporated in the community's common sense. America has been a land of free and abounding resources; which is to say, when converted into terms of economic theory, that it is the land of the unearned increment. In all directions, wherever enterprise and industry have gone, the opportunity was wide and large for such as had the patience or astuteness to place themselves in the way of this multifarious flow of the unearned increment, and were endowed with the retentive grasp. Putting aside the illusions of public spirit and diligent serviceability, sedulously cultivated by the apologists of business, it will readily be seen that the great mass of reputably large fortunes in this country are of such an origin; nor will it cost anything beyond a similar lesion to the affections to confirm the view that such is the origin and line of derivation of the American propertied business community and its canons of right and honest living.

It is a common saying that the modern taste has been unduly commercialized by the unremitting attention necessarily given to matters of price and of profit and loss in an industrial community organized on business principles; that pecuniary standards of excellence are habitually accepted and applied with undue freedom and finality. But what is scarcely appreciated at its full value is the fact that these pecuniary standards of merit and efficiency are habitually applied to men as well as to things, and with little less freedom and finality. The man who applies himself undeviatingly to pecuniary affairs with a view to his own gain, and who is habitually and cautiously alert to the main chance, is not only esteemed for and in respect of his pecuniary success, but he is also habitually rated high at large, as a particularly wise and sane person. He is deferred to as being wise and sane not only in pecuniary matters but also in any other matters on which he may express an opinion.

A very few generations ago, before the present pecuniary era of civilization[11] had made such headway, and before the common man in these civilized communities had lost the fear of God, the like wide-sweeping and obsequious veneration and deference was given to the clergy and their opinions; for the churchmen were then, in the popular apprehension, proficient in all those matters that were of most substantial interest to the common man of that time. Indeed, the salvation of men's souls was then a matter of as grave and untiring solicitude as their commercial solvency has now become. And the trained efficiency of the successful clergyman of that time for the conduct of spiritual and ecclesiastical affairs lent him a prestige with his fellow men such as to give his opinions, decisions and preconceptions great and unquestioned weight in temporal matters as well; he was then accepted as the type of wise, sane and benevolent humanity, in his own esteem as well as in the esteem of his fellows. In like manner also, in other times and under other cultural conditions the fighting-man has held the first place in men's esteem and has been deferred to in matters that concerned his trade and in matters that did not.

Now, in that hard and fast body of aphoristic wisdom that commands the faith of the business community there is comprised the conviction that learning is of no use in business. This conviction is, further, backed up and colored with the

11. Veblen viewed his era as one in which modern industry and its products were no longer controlled by worker-owners but by a new and separate class of owners driven entirely by "pecuniary" motives. The control of advanced industrial economies by profit-driven business organizations had several negative consequences in his view. As he listed them in *Engineers and the Theory of the Price System* (1921), they included underutilization of manpower, overvaluing "salesmanship", and producing and marketing superfluous and spurious goods. Business control of the American university, in Veblen's view, brought roughly the same set of negative consequences.

tenet, held somewhat doubtfully, but also, and therefore, somewhat doggedly, by the common run of businessmen, that what is of no use in business is not worthwhile. More than one of the greater businessmen have spoken, advisedly and with emphasis, to the effect that the higher learning is rather a hindrance than a help to any aspirant for business success;[d] more particularly to any man whose lot is cast in the field of business enterprise of a middling scale and commonplace circumstances. And notoriously, the like view of the matter prevails throughout the business community at large. What these men are likely to have in mind in passing this verdict, as shown by various expressions on this head, is not so much the higher learning in the proper sense, but rather that slight preliminary modicum that is to be found embodied in the curriculum of the colleges—for the common run of businessmen are not sufficiently conversant with these matters to know the difference, or that there is a difference, between the college and the university. They are busy with other things.

It is true, men whose construction of the facts is colored by their wish to commend the schools to the good will of the business community profess to find ground for the belief that university training, or rather the training of the undergraduate school, gives added fitness for a business career, particularly for the larger business enterprise. But they commonly speak apologetically and offer extenuating considerations, such as virtually to concede the case, at the same time that they are very prone to evade the issue by dwelling on accessory and subsidiary considerations that do not substantially touch the question of trained capacity for the conduct of business affairs.[e] The apologists commonly shift from the undebatable ground of the higher learning as related to business success, to the more defensible ground of the undergraduate curriculum, considered as introductory to those social amenities that devolve on the successful man of business; and in so far as they confine themselves to the topic of education and business they commonly spend their efforts in arguing for the business utility of the train-

d. Cf., e. g., Richard T. Crane (1832–1912), *The Futility of All Kinds of Higher Schooling* (1911), especially part I, chap. iv. [Crane was a wealthy Chicago-based manufacturer of brass goods and plumbing. As it happened, he also was the nephew of another Chicago businessman, Martin Ryerson (1818–87), whose son the younger Martin Ryerson (1856–1932) was the first president of the University of Chicago's board of trustees. –Ed.]

e. Cf. Crane, *The Futility of All Kinds of Higher Schooling*, especially part I, chaps. ii, iii, and vi. Cf. also Harry Pratt Judson (1849–1927), *The Higher Education as a Training for Business* (1911), where the case is argued in a typically commonplace and matter-of-fact spirit, but where "The Higher Education" is taken to mean the undergraduate curriculum simply; also "*A Symposium* on the value of humanistic, particularly classical, studies as a training for men of affairs," in *Proceedings of the Classical Conference* at Ann Arbor, Michigan, April 3, 1909. [Judson was the second president of the University of Chicago, 1907–23. During the year he served as interim president following William Rainey Harper's death in January 1906, it was Judson who accepted Veblen's resignation in April. –Ed.]

ing afforded by the professional and technical schools, included within the university corporation or otherwise. There is ground for their contention in so far as "university training" is (by subreption[12] taken to mean training in those "practical" branches of knowledge (Law, Politics, Accountancy, etc.) that have a place within the university precincts only by force of a *non sequitur*.[13] And the spokesmen for these views are commonly also, and significantly, eager to make good their contention by advocating the introduction of an increased proportion of these "practical" subjects into the schedule of instruction.

The facts are notorious and leave little room for cavil on the merits of the case. Particularly is the award of the facts unequivocal in America—the native ground of the self-made businessman, and at the same time the most admirably thorough-paced business community extant. The American business community is well enough as it is, without the higher learning, and it is fully sensible that the higher learning is not a business proposition.

But a good rule works both ways. If scholarly and scientific training, such as may without shame be included under the caption of the higher learning, unfits men for business efficiency, then the training that comes of experience in business must also be held to unfit men for scholarly and scientific pursuits, and even more pronouncedly for the surveillance of such pursuits. The circumstantial evidence for the latter proposition is neither less abundant nor less unequivocal than for the former. If the higher learning is incompatible with business shrewdness, business enterprise is, by the same token, incompatible with the spirit of the higher learning. Indeed, within the ordinary range of lawful occupations these two lines of endeavor, and the animus that belongs to each, are as widely out of touch as may be. They are the two extreme terms of the modern cultural scheme; although at the same time each is intrinsic and indispensable to the scheme of modern civilization as it runs. With the excision or serious crippling of either, Western Civilization would suffer a dislocation amounting to a revolutionary change.

On the other hand, the higher learning and the spirit of scientific inquiry have much in common with modern industry and its technological discipline. More particularly is there a close bond of sympathy and relationship between the spirit of scientific inquiry and the habit of mind enforced by the mechanical industries of the modern kind. In both of these lines of activity men are occupied with impersonal facts and deal with them in a matter-of-fact way. In both, as far as may be, the personal equation is sought to be eliminated, discounted and avoided, so

12. Cf. chapter I, "Introductory," note 13.
13. Latin: a statement not connected in a clear or logical way with anything said before.

as to leave no chance for discrepancies due to personal infirmity or predilection. But it is only on its mechanical side that the industrial organization so comes in touch with modern science and the pursuit of matter-of-fact knowledge; and it is only in so far as their habits of thought are shaped by the discipline of the mechanical industries that there is induced in the industrial population the same bent as goes to further or to appreciate the work of modern science. But it would be quite nugatory[14] to suggest that the governing boards of the universities should be made up of, or should comprise, impecunious technologists and engineers.

There is no similar bond of consanguinity between the business occupations and the scientific spirit; except so far as regards those clerical and subaltern employments that lie wholly within the mechanical routine of business traffic; and even as regards these employments and the persons so occupied it is, at the most, doubtful whether their training does not after all partake more of that astute and invidious character of cunning that belongs to the conduct of business affairs than of the dispassionate animus of scientific inquiry.

These extenuating considerations do not touch the case of that body of businessmen, in the proper sense of the term, from which the membership of the governing boards is drawn. The principles that rule business enterprise of that larger and pecuniarily effectual sort are a matter of usage, appraisement, contractual arrangement and strategic maneuvers. They are the principles of a game of competitive guessing and pecuniary coercion, a game carried on wholly within the limits of the personal equation, and depending for its movement and effect on personal discrepancies of judgment. Science has to do with the opaquely veracious sequence of cause and effect, and it deals with the facts of this sequence without mental reservation or ulterior purposes of expediency. Business enterprise proceeds on ulterior purposes and calculations of expediency; it depends on shrewd expedients and lives on the margin of error, on the fluctuating margin of human miscalculation. The training given by these two lines of endeavor—science and business—is wholly divergent; with the notorious result that for the purposes of business enterprise the scientists are the most ignorant, gullible and incompetent class in the community. They are not only passively out of touch with the business spirit, out of training by neglect, but they are also positively trained out of the habit of mind indispensable to business enterprise. The converse is true of the men of business affairs.[f]

f. Cf. Francis Bacon (1561–1626), *Essays*: "Of Cunning" and "Of Wisdom for a Man's Self." [Bacon published three editions of essays over the course of his lifetime. The final edition, titled *Essays or Counsels, Civil and Morals*, was published in 1625. "Knowledge is power" is an axiom commonly attributed to Bacon. –Ed.]

14. Of little or no importance; trifling.

Plato's classic scheme of folly,[15] which would have the philosophers take over the management of affairs, has been turned on its head; the men of affairs have taken over the direction of the pursuit of knowledge. To anyone who will take a dispassionate look at this modern arrangement it looks foolish, of course— ingeniously foolish; but, also, of course, there is no help for it and no prospect of its abatement in the calculable future.

It is a fact of the current state of things, grounded in the institutional fabric of Christendom; and it will avail little to speculate on remedial corrections for this state of academic affairs so long as the institutional ground of this perversion remains intact. Its institutional ground is the current system of private ownership. It claims the attention of students as a feature of the latter-day cultural growth, as an outcome of the pecuniary organization of modern society, and it is to be taken as a base-line in any inquiry into the policy that controls modern academic life and work—just as any inquiry into the circumstances and establishments of learning in the days of scholasticism must take account of the ecclesiastical rule of that time as one of the main controlling facts in the case. The fact is that businessmen hold the plenary discretion,[16] and that business principles guide them in their management of the affairs of the higher learning; and such must continue to be the case so long as the community's workday material interests continue to be organized on a basis of business enterprise. All this does not promise well for the future of science and scholarship in the universities, but the current effects of this method of university control are sufficiently patent[17] to all academic men— and the whole situation should perhaps trouble the mind of no one who will be at pains to free himself from the (possibly transient) preconception that "the increase and diffusion of knowledge among men" is, in the end, more to be de-sired than the acquisition and expenditure of riches by the astuter men in the community.

Many of those who fancy themselves conversant with the circumstances of Amer-ican academic life would question the view set forth above, and they would par-ticularly deny that business principles do or can pervade the corporate manage-ment of the universities in anything like the degree here implied. They would contend that while the boards of control are commonly gifted with all the dis-

15. Allusion to Plato's (428–7 BCE to 348–7 BCE) *Republic* (380 BCE), where the ancient Greek philosopher argued that the survival of a just city-state required rule by philosophers trained to be kings.

16. Plenary discretion: unqualified or absolute right to choose what is to be done in a particular situation.

17. Readily visible or intelligible; obvious.

abilities described—that much being not open to dispute—yet these boards do not, on the whole, in practice, extend the exercise of their plenary discretion to the directive control of what are properly speaking academic matters; that they habitually confine their work of directorship to the pecuniary affairs of the corporation; and that in so far as they may at times interfere in the university's scholarly and scientific work, they do so in their capacity as men of culture, not as men of property or of enterprise. This latter would also be the view to which the men of property on the boards would themselves particularly incline. So it will be held by the spokesmen of content that virtually full discretion in all matters of academic policy is delegated to the academic head of the university, fortified by the advice and consent of the senior members of his faculty; by the free choice of the governing boards, in practice drawn out from under the control of these businessmen in question and placed in the hands of the scholars. And such, commonly, is at least ostensibly the case, in point of form; more particularly as regards those older establishments that are burdened with academic traditions running back beyond the date when their governing boards were taken over by the businessmen, and more particularly in the recent past than in the immediate present or for the establishments of a more recent date.

This complaisant[18] view overlooks the fact that much effective surveillance of the academic work is exercised through the board's control of the budget. The academic staff can do little else than what the specifications of the budget provide for; without the means with which the corporate income should supply them they are as helpless as might be expected.

Imbued with an alert sense of those tangible pecuniary values which they are by habit and temperament in a position to appreciate, a sagacious governing board may, for instance, determine to expend the greater proportion of the available income of the university in improving and decorating its real estate, and they may with businesslike thrift set aside an appreciable proportion of the remainder for a sinking fund to meet vaguely unforeseen contingencies, while the academic staff remains (notoriously) underpaid and so scantily filled as seriously to curtail their working capacity. Or the board may, again, as has also happened, take a thrifty resolution to "concede" only a fraction—say ten or fifteen per-cent—of the demands of the staff for books and similar working materials for current use; while setting aside a good share of the funds assigned for such use, to accumulate until at some future date such materials may be purchased at more reasonable prices than those now ruling. These illustrations are not supplied by fancy. There

18. Willing or eager to please other people.

is, indeed, a visible reluctance on the part of these businesslike boards to expend the corporation's income for those intangible, immaterial uses for which the university is established. These uses leave no physical, tangible residue, in the way of durable goods, such as will justify the expenditure in terms of vendible property acquired; therefore they are *prima facie imbecile*,[19] and correspondingly distasteful, to men whose habitual occupation is with the acquisition of property. By force of the same businesslike bias the boards unavoidably incline to apportion the funds assigned for current expenses in such a way as to favor those "practical" or quasi-practical lines of instruction and academic propaganda that are presumed to heighten the business acumen of the students or to yield immediate returns in the way of a creditable publicity.

As to the delegation of powers to the academic head. There is always the reservation to be kept in mind, that the academic head is limited in his discretion by the specifications of the budget. The permissible deviations in that respect are commonly neither wide nor of a substantial character; though the instances of a university president exercising large powers are also not extremely rare. But in common practice, it is to be noted, the academic head is vested with somewhat autocratic powers, within the lines effectually laid down in the budget; he is in effect responsible to the governing board alone, and his responsibility in that direction chiefly touches his observance of the pecuniary specifications of the budget.

But it is more to the point to note that the academic head commonly holds office by choice of the governing board. Where the power of appointment lies freely in the discretion of such a board, the board will create an academic head in its own image. In point of notorious fact, the academic head of the university is selected chiefly on grounds of his business qualifications, taking that expression in a somewhat special sense. There is at present an increasingly broad and strenuous insistence on such qualifications in the men selected as heads of the universities; and the common sense of the community at large bears out the predilections of the businesslike board of control in this respect. The new incumbents are selected primarily with a view to give the direction of academic policy and administration more of a businesslike character. The choice may not always fall on a competent business man, but that is not due to its inclining too far to the side of scholarship. It is not an easy matter even for the most astute body of busi-

19. Latin: imbecile or stupid person at first glance.

nessmen to select a candidate who shall measure up to their standard of business-like efficiency in a field of activity that has substantially nothing in common with that business traffic in which their preconceptions of efficiency have been formed.

In many cases the alumni have much to say in the choice of a new academic head, whether by courtesy or by express provision; and the results under these circumstances are not substantially different. It follows as an inevitable consequence of the current state of popular sentiment that the successful business-men among the alumni will have the deciding voice, in so far as the matter rests with the alumni; for the successful men of affairs assert themselves with easy confidence, and they are looked up to, in any community whose standards of esteem are business standards, so that their word carries weight beyond that of any other class or order of men. The community at large, or at least that portion of the community that habitually makes itself heard, speaks to the same effect and on the same ground—viz., a sentimental conviction that pecuniary success is the final test of manhood. Business principles are the sacred articles of the secular creed, and business methods make up the ritual of the secular cult.

The one clear note of acclaim that goes up, from the avowed adepts of culture and from those without the pale, when a new head has, as recently been called to one of the greater universities, is in commendation of his business capacity, "commercial sense," executive ability, financiering tact; and the effectual canvass of his qualifications does not commonly range much outside of these prime requisites. The modicum of scholarship and scholarly ideals and insight concessively deemed indispensable in such a case is somewhat of the nature of a perquisite, and is easily found. It is not required that the incumbent meet the prepossessions of the contingent of learned men in the community in this respect; the choice does not rest with that element, nor does its ratification, but rather at the other end of the scale, with that extreme wing of the laity that is taken up with "practical," that is to say pecuniary, affairs.

As to the requirements of scholarly or scientific competency, a plausible speaker with a large gift of assurance, a businesslike "educator" or clergyman, some urbane pillar of society, some astute veteran of the scientific demimonde, will meet all reasonable requirements. Scholarship is not barred, of course, though it is commonly the quasi-scholarship of the popular *raconteur* that comes in evidence in these premises; and the fact that these incumbents of executive office show so much of scholarly animus and attainments as they do is in great measure a fortuitous circumstance. It is, indeed, a safe generalization that in point of fact the average of university presidents fall short of the average of their academic staff in

Figure 3. David Starr Jordan, 1908. Stanford University Archives

scholarly or scientific attainments, even when all persons employed as instructors are counted as members of the staff.[20] It may also be remarked by the way that when, as may happen, a scholar or scientist takes office as directive head of a university, he is commonly lost to the republic of learning; he has in effect passed from the ranks of learning to those of business enterprise.

The upshot of it all should be that when and in so far as a businesslike governing board delegates powers to the university's academic head, it delegates these powers to one of their own kind, who is somewhat peremptorily expected to live

20. This "safe generalization" arguably would not apply to two of the three American university presidents who appointed Veblen to their faculties. Before his appointment as University of Chicago's first president, William Rainey Harper was a nationally recognized scholar of the Bible, and remained an active scholar to the end of his life. David Starr Jordan (1851–1931), Stanford's first president, was a zoologist who attained national eminence in the field of ichthyology (a branch of zoology that deals with fishes), and remained an active scholar during his years as president (see figure 3).

up to the aspirations that animate the board. What such a man, so placed, will do with the powers and opportunities that so devolve on him is a difficult question that can be answered only in terms of the compulsion of the circumstances in which he is placed and of the moral wear and tear that comes of arbitrary powers exercised in a tangle of ambiguities.[g]

g. Cf. chapter viii, "Summary and Trial Balance," 204–22.

CHAPTER III

The Academic Administration and Policy

Men dilate on the high necessity of a businesslike organization and control of the university, its equipment, personnel and routine. What is had in mind in this insistence on an efficient system is that these corporations of learning shall set their affairs in order after the pattern of a well-conducted business concern. In this view the university is conceived as a business house dealing in merchantable knowledge, placed under the governing hand of a captain of erudition,[1] whose office it is to turn the means in hand to account in the largest feasible output. It is a corporation with large funds, and for men biased by their workday training in business affairs it comes as a matter of course to rate the university in terms of investment and turnover. Hence the insistence on business capacity in the executive heads of the universities, and hence also the extensive range of businesslike duties and powers that devolve on them.

Yet when all these sophistications of practical wisdom are duly allowed for, the fact remains that the university is, in usage, precedent, and common-sense preconception, an establishment for the conservation and advancement of the higher learning, devoted to a disinterested pursuit of knowledge. As such, it consists of a body of scholars and scientists, each and several of whom necessarily goes to his work on his own initiative and pursues it in his own way. This work necessarily follows an orderly sequence and procedure, and so takes on a systematic form, of an organic kind. But the system and order that so govern the work, and that come into view in its procedure and results, are the logical system and order of intellectual enterprise, not the mechanical or statistical systematization that goes into effect in the management of an industrial plant or the financiering of a business corporation.

Those items of human intelligence and initiative that go to make up the pursuit of knowledge, and that are embodied in systematic form in its conclusions,

1. Famous phrase coined by Veblen to suggest a mocking equivalence between the first generation of American university presidents and the so-called captains of industry who headed America's new industrial corporations.

do not lend themselves to quantitative statement, and cannot be made to appear on a balance sheet. Neither can that intellectual initiative and proclivity that goes in as the indispensable motive force in the pursuit of learning be reduced to any known terms of subordination, obedience, or authoritative direction. No scholar or scientist can become an employee in respect of his scholarly or scientific work. Mechanical systematization and authoritative control can in these premises not reach beyond the material circumstances that condition the work in hand, nor can it in these external matters with good effect go farther than is necessary to supply the material ways and means requisite to the work, and to adapt them to the peculiar needs of any given line of inquiry or group of scholars. In order to their best efficiency, and indeed in the degree in which efficiency in this field of activity is to be attained at all, the executive officers of the university must stand in the relation of assistants serving the needs and catering to the idiosyncrasies of the body of scholars and scientists that make up the university;[a] in the degree in which the converse relation is allowed to take effect, the unavoidable consequence is wasteful defeat. A free hand is the first and abiding requisite of scholarly and scientific work.

Now, in accepting office as executive head of a university, the incumbent necessarily accepts all the conditions that attach to the administration of his office, whether by usage and common-sense expectation, by express arrangement, or by patent understanding with the board to which he owes his elevation to this post of dignity and command. By usage and precedent it is incumbent on him to govern the academic personnel and equipment with an eye single to the pursuit of knowledge, and so to conduct its affairs as will most effectually compass that end. That is to say he must so administer his office as best to serve the scholarly needs of the academic staff, due regard being scrupulously had to the idiosyncrasies, and even to the vagaries, of the men whose work he is called on to further. But by patent understanding, if not by explicit stipulation, from the side of the governing board, fortified by the preconceptions of the laity at large to the same effect, he is held to such a conspicuously efficient employment of the means in hand as will gratify those who look for a voluminous turnover. To this end he must keep the academic administration and its activity constantly in the public eye, with such "pomp and circumstance"[2] of untiring urgency and expedition as will carry the conviction abroad that the university under his management is a highly successful going concern, and he must be able to show by itemized accounts

a. Cf. George T. Ladd, "The Need of Administrative Changes in the American University," in *University Control*, 352–353.
2. Elaborate ceremonies.

that the volume of output is such as to warrant the investment. So the equipment and personnel must be organized into a facile and orderly working force, held under the directive control of the captain of erudition at every point, and so articulated and standardized that its rate of speed and the volume of its current output can be exhibited to full statistical effect as it runs.

The university is to make good both as a corporation of learning and as a business concern dealing in standardized erudition, and the executive head necessarily assumes the responsibility of making it count wholly and unreservedly in each of these divergent, if not incompatible lines.[b] Humanly speaking, it follows by necessary consequence that he will first and always take care of those duties that are most jealously insisted on by the powers to whom he is accountable, and the due performance of which will at the same time yield some sufficiently tangible evidence of his efficiency. That other, more recondite side of the university's work that has substantially to do with the higher learning is not readily set out in the form of statistical exhibits, at the best, and can ordinarily come to appraisal and popular appreciation only in the long run. The need of a businesslike showing is instant and imperative, particularly in a business era of large turnover and quick returns, and to meet this need the uneventful scholastic life that counts toward the higher learning in the long run is of little use; so it can wait, and it readily becomes a habit with the busy executive to let it wait.

It should be kept in mind also that the incumbent of executive office is presumably a man of businesslike qualifications, rather than of scholarly insight— the method of selecting the executive heads under the present régime makes that nearly a matter of course.[3] As such he will in his own right more readily appreciate those results of his own management that show up with something of the glare of publicity, as contrasted with the slow-moving and often obscure working of inquiry that lies (commonly) somewhat beyond his intellectual horizon. So that with slight misgivings, if any, he takes to the methods of organization and control that have commended themselves in that current business enterprise to which it is his ambition to assimilate the corporation of learning.

These precedents of business practice that are to afford guidance to the captain of erudition are, of course, the precedents of competitive business. It is one

b. Ladd, "The Need of Administrative Changes," 351–352.

3. In 1920, the American Association of University Professors (AAUP) published the results of a survey of governance practices at 110 leading American colleges and universities. Among the 47 institutions that replied, only 7 reported that they allowed for formal faculty participation in the nominating process of the president by their boards of trustees. See "Report of Committee T on the Place and Function of Faculties in University Government and Administration," in *AAUP Bulletin*, 6, no. 3 (March 1920), 110.

of the unwritten, and commonly unspoken, commonplaces lying at the root of modern academic policy that the various universities are competitors for the traffic in merchantable instruction, in much the same fashion as rival establishments in the retail trade compete for custom. Indeed, the modern department store offers a felicitous analogy, that has already been found serviceable in illustration of the American university's position in this respect, by those who speak for the present régime as well as by its critics. The fact that the universities are assumed to be irreconcilable competitors, both in the popular apprehension and as evidenced by the maneuvers of their several directors, is too notorious to be denied by any but the interested parties. Now and again it is formally denied by one and another among the competing captains of erudition, but the reason for such denial is the need of it.[c]

Now, the duties of the executive head of a competitive business concern are of a strategic nature, the object of his management being to get the better of rival concerns and to engross the trade. To this end it is indispensable that he should be a "strong man"[4] and should have a free hand—though perhaps under the general and tolerant surveillance of his board of directors. Any wise board of directors, and in the degree in which they are endowed with the requisite wisdom, will be careful to give their general manager full discretion, and not to hamper him with too close an accounting of the details of his administration, so long as he shows gratifying results. He must be a strong man; that is to say, a capable man of affairs, tenacious and resourceful in turning the means at hand to account for this purpose, and easily content to let the end justify the means. He must be a man of scrupulous integrity, so far as may conduce to his success, but with a shrewd eye to the limits within which honesty is the best policy, for the purpose in hand. He must have full command of the means entrusted to him and full control of the force of employees and subordinates who are to work under his direction, and he must be able to rely on the instant and unwavering loyalty of his

c. Apart from the executive's need of satisfying the prejudices of the laity in this matter, there is no ground for this competition between the universities, either in the pecuniary circumstances of the several establishments or in the work they are to take care of. So much is admitted on all hands. But the fact remains that no other one motive has as much to do with shaping academic policy as this same competition for traffic. The cause of it appears to be very little if anything else than that the habits of thought induced by experience in business are uncritically carried over into academic affairs.

Critics of the present régime are inclined to admit that the colleges of the land are in great part so placed as to be thrown into competition by force of circumstances, both as to the acquisition of funds and as to the enrolment of students. The point may be conceded, though with doubt and reservation, as applies to the colleges; for the universities there is no visible ground of such rivalry, apart from unreflecting prejudice on the part of the laity, and an ambition for popular acclaim on the part of the university directorate.

4. Cf. "Preface," note 1.

staff in any line of policy on which he may decide to enter. He must therefore have free power to appoint and dismiss, and to reward and punish, limited only by the formal ratification of his decisions by the board of directors who will be careful not to interfere or inquire unduly in these matters—so long as their strong man shows results.

The details and objective of his strategy need not be known to the members of the staff; indeed, all that does not concern them except in the most general way. They are his creatures, and are responsible only to him and only for the due performance of the tasks assigned them; and they need know only so much as will enable them to give ready and intelligent support to the moves made by their chief from day to day. The members of the staff are his employees, and their first duty is a loyal obedience; and for the competitive good of the concern they must utter no expression of criticism or unfavorable comment on the policy, actions or personal characteristics of their chief, so long as they are in his employ. They have eaten his bread,[5] and it is for them to do his bidding.

Such is the object-lesson afforded by business practice as it bears on the duties incumbent on the academic head and on the powers of office delegated to him. It is needless to remark on what is a fact of common notoriety, that this rule drawn from the conduct of competitive business is commonly applied without substantial abatement in the conduct of academic affairs.[d]

Under this rule the academic staff becomes a body of graded subalterns,[6] who

d. An incumbent of executive office, recently appointed, in one of the greater universities was at pains a few years ago to speak his mind on this head, to the effect that the members of the academic staff are employees in the pay of the university and under the orders of its president, and as such they are bound to avoid all criticism of him and his administration so long as they continue on the pay-roll; and that if any member of the staff has any fault to find with the conduct of affairs he must first sever his connection with the university, before speaking his mind. These expressions were occasioned by the underhand dismissal of a scholar of high standing and long service, who had incurred the displeasure of the president then in charge, by overt criticism of the administration. As to its general features the case might well have been the one referred to by Professor Ladd (cf. *University Control*, 359), though the circumstances of the dismissal offer several details of a more discreditable character than Professor Ladd appears to have been aware of. [The "incumbent of executive office" in question here probably is Columbia University president Nicholas Murray Butler, who dismissed Joel Spingarn (1875–1931) from the faculty in January, 1911. Spingarn, then a well-known scholar of comparative literature, had openly challenged Butler's authority in opposing his decision to force the merger of Columbia's then separate departments of Comparative Literature and English. Butler was by far the most autocratic of any of the presidents who headed elite American colleges and universities during Veblen's time. After he took office, Butler ended the practice of Columbia University faculty electing their own deans so he could appoint them himself. In June 1917, he also announced that he would accept no dissent from the American war effort from the Columbia faculty. The American social critic and essayist Randolph Bourne (1886–1918) mockingly dubbed Butler "Dr. Alexander Mackintosh Butcher of Pluribus University." –Ed.]

5. Allusion to 1 Corinthians 11:23–26, where Jesus instructs his disciples to eat bread and drink wine when they remember his death.

6. People holding subordinate positions. During Veblen's years at Chicago, the gradation of the "academic staff" was particularly elaborate and hierarchical. The university's core of lecturers and

share confidence of the chief in varying degrees, but who no decisive voice in the policy or the conduct of affairs of the concern in whose pay they are held. The faculty is conceived as a body of employees, hired to render certain services and turn out certain scheduled vendible[7] results.

The chief may take advice; and, as is commonly the practice in analogous circumstances in commercial business, he will be likely to draw about him from among the faculty a conveniently small number of advisers who are in sympathy with his own ambitions, and who will in this way form an unofficial council, or cabinet, or "junta,"[8] to whom he can turn for informal, anonymous and irresponsible, advice and moral support at any juncture. He will also, in compliance with charter stipulations and parliamentary usage, have certain officially recognized advisers—the various deans, advisory committees, Academic Council, University Senate, and the like—with whom he shares responsibility, particularly for measures of doubtful popularity, and whose advice he formally takes *coram publico*;[9] but he cannot well share discretion with these, except on administrative matters of inconsequential detail. For reasons of practical efficiency, discretion must be undivided in any competitive enterprise. There is much fine-spun strategy to be taken care of under cover of night and cloud.

But the academic tradition, which still drags on the hands of the captains of erudition, has not left the ground prepared for such a clean-cut businesslike organization and such a campaign of competitive strategy. By tradition the faculty is the keeper of the academic interests of the university and makes up a body of loosely-bound noncompetitive co-partners, with no view to strategic team play and no collective ulterior ambition, least of all with a view to engrossing the trade. By tradition, and indeed commonly by explicit proviso, the conduct of the university's academic affairs vests formally in the president, with the advice and consent of the faculty, or of the general body of senior members of the faculty. In due observance of these traditions, and of the scholastic purposes notoriously underlying all university life, certain forms of disinterested zeal must be adhered to in all official pronouncements of the executive, as well as certain punctilios[10] of conference and advisement between the directive head and the academic staff.

---

teachers was divided into twelve classes: scholar, fellow, lecturer, reader, docent, tutor, instructor, assistant professor, associate professor, non-resident professor, professor, and head professor (the equivalent of a department chair today). Veblen was an assistant professor when he resigned from Chicago in April 1906.

7. Suitable or fit for sale.

8. Military faction controlling a government after taking it by force.

9. Latin: in the presence of the people; publicly.

10. Minute details of conduct.

All of which makes the work of the executive head less easy and ingenuous than it might be. The substantial demands of his position as chief of a competitive business are somewhat widely out of touch with these forms of divided responsibility that must (formally) be observed in administering his duties, and equally out of touch with the formal professions of disinterested zeal for the cause of learning that he is by tradition required to make from time to time. All that may reasonably be counted on under these trying circumstances is that he should do the best he can—to save the formalities and secure the substance. To compass these difficult incongruities, he will, as already remarked above, necessarily gather about him, within the general body of the academic personnel, a corps of trusted advisors and agents, whose qualifications for their peculiar work is an intelligent sympathy with their chief's ideals and methods and an unreserved subservience to his aims—unless it should come to pass, as may happen in case its members are men of force and ingenuity, that this unofficial cabinet should take over the direction of affairs and work out their own aims and purposes under cover of the chief's ostensibly autocratic rule.

Among these aids and advisers will be found at least a proportion of the higher administrative officials, and among the number it is fairly indispensable to include one or more adroit parliamentarians, competent to procure the necessary modicum of sanction for all arbitrary acts of the executive, from a distrustful faculty convened as a deliberative body. These men must be at least partially in the confidence of the executive head. From the circumstances of the case it also follows that they will commonly occupy an advanced academic rank, and so will take a high (putative) rank as scholars and scientists. High academic rank comes of necessity to these men who serve as coadjutors and vehicles of the executive policy, as does also the relatively high pay that goes with high rank; both are required as a reward of merit and an incitement to a zealous serviceability on the one hand, and to keep the administration in countenance on the other hand by giving the requisite dignity to its agents. They will be selected on the same general grounds of fitness as their chief—administrative facility, plausibility, proficiency as public speakers and parliamentarians, ready versatility of convictions, and a staunch loyalty to their bread. Experience teaches that scholarly or scientific capacity does not enter in any appreciable measure among the qualifications so required for responsible academic office, beyond what may thriftily serve to mask the conventional decencies of the case.

It is, further, of the essence of this scheme of academic control that the captain of erudition should freely exercise the power of academic life and death over the members of his staff,[11] to reward the good and faithful servant and to abase the recalcitrant. Otherwise discipline would be a difficult matter, and the formally requisite "advice and consent"[12] could be procured only tardily and grudgingly.

Admitting such reservations and abatement as may be due, it is to be said that the existing organization of academic control under business principles falls more or less nearly into the form outlined above. The perfected type, as sketched in the last paragraphs, has doubtless not been fully achieved in practice hitherto, unless it be in one or another of the newer establishments with large ambitions and endowment, and with few traditions to hamper the working out of the system. The incursion of business principles into the academic community is also of relatively recent date, and should not yet have had time to pervade the organization throughout and with full effect; so that the régime of competitive strategy should as yet be neither so far advanced nor so secure a matter of course as may fairly be expected in the near future. Yet the rate of advance along this line, and the measure of present achievement, are more considerable than even a very sanguine advocate of business principles could have dared to look for a couple of decades ago.

In so far as these matters are still in process of growth, rather than at their full fruition, it follows that any analysis of the effects of this régime must be in some degree speculative, and must at times deal with the drift of things as much as with accomplished fact. Yet such an inquiry must approach its subject as an episode of history, and must deal with the personal figures and the incidents of this growth objectively, as phenomena thrown up to view by the play of circumstances in the dispassionate give and take of institutional change. Such an impersonal attitude, it is perhaps needless to remark, is not always easy to maintain in dealing with facts of so personal, and often of so animated, a character. Particularly will an observer who has seen these incidents from the middle and in the making find it difficult uniformly to preserve that aloof perspective that will serve the ends of an historical appreciation. The difficulty is increased and complicated by the necessity of employing terms, descriptions and incidents that have been habitually employed in current controversy, often with a marked animus. Men have

---

11. In Veblen's time, faculty members of all ranks were subject to dismissal for inadequate performance of academic duties and personal misconduct. Legal authority to appoint and dismiss faculty belonged to boards of trustees, but the actual exercise of that authority usually was delegated to college and university presidents.

12. Phrase in the United States Constitution that allows the Senate to constrain the president's powers of appointment and treaty-making.

taken sides on these matters, and so are engaged in controversy on the merits of the current régime and on the question of possible relief and remedy for what are considered to be its iniquities. Under the shadow of this controversy, it is nearly unavoidable that any expression or citation of fact that will bear a partisan construction will habitually be so construed. The vehicle necessarily employed must almost unavoidably infuse the analysis with an unintended color of bias, to one side or the other of the presumed merits of the case. A degree of patient attention is therefore due at points where the facts cited, and the characterization of these facts and their bearing, would seem, on a superficial view, to bear construction as controversial matter.

In this episode of institutional growth, plainly, the executive head is the central figure. The light fails on him rather than on the forces that move him, and it comes as a matter of course to pass opinions on the resulting incidents and consequences, as the outcome of his free initiative rather than of the circumstances whose creature he is. No doubt, his initiative, if any, is a powerful factor in the case, but it is after all a factor of transmission and commutation rather than of genesis and self-direction; for he is chosen for the style and measure of initiative with which he is endowed, and unless he shall be found to measure up to expectations in kind and degree in this matter he will go in the discard, and his personal ideals and initiative will count as little more than a transient obstruction. He will hold his place, and will count as a creative force in his world, in much the same degree in which he responds with ready flexibility to the impact of those forces of popular sentiment and class conviction that have called him to be their servant. Only so can he be a "strong man"; only in so far as, by fortunate bent or by its absence, he is enabled to move resistlessly with the parallelogram[13] of forces.

The exigencies of a businesslike administration demand that there be no division of powers between the academic executive and the academic staff; but the exigencies of the higher learning require that the scholars and scientists must be left quite free to follow their own bent in conducting their own work. In the nature of things this work cannot be carried on effectually under coercive rule. Scientific inquiry cannot be pursued under direction of a layman in the person of a superior officer. Also, learning is, in the nature of things, not a competitive business[14] and can make no use of finesse, diplomatic equivocation and tactful

13. A four-sided flat shape made up of two pairs of straight parallel lines that are equal in length.
14. It should be said that in Veblen's day, as now, a university's adoption of "business principles" was not the only development that made for "competition" among university scholars. Other forces

regard for popular prejudices, such as are of the essence of the case in competitive business. It is, also, of no advantage to learning to engross the trade. Tradition and present necessity alike demand that the body of scholars and scientists who make up the university must be vested with full powers of self-direction, without ulterior consideration. A university can remain a corporation of learning, *de facto*, on no other basis.

As has already been remarked, business methods of course have their place in the corporation's fiscal affairs and in the office-work incident to the care of its material equipment. As regards these items the university is a business concern, and no discussion of these topics would be in place here. These things concern the university only in its externals, and they do not properly fall within the scope of academic policy or academic administration. They come into consideration here only in so far as a lively regard for them may, as it sometimes does, divert the forces of the establishment from its ostensible purpose.

Under the rule imposed by those businesslike preconceptions that decide his selection for office, the first duty of the executive head is to see to the organization of an administrative machinery for the direction of the university's internal affairs, and the establishment of a facile and rigorous system of accountancy for the control and exhibition of the academic work. In the same measure in which such a system goes into effect the principles of competitive business will permeate the administration in all directions; in the personnel of the academic staff, in the control and intercourse of teachers and students, in the schedule of instruction, in the disposition of the material equipment, in the public exhibits and ceremonial of the university, as well as in its pecuniary concerns.

Within the range of academic interests proper, these business principles primarily affect the personnel and the routine of instruction. Here their application immediately results in an administrative system of bureau or departments, a hierarchical gradation of the members of the staff, and a rigorous parcelment[15] and standardization of the instruction offered. Some such system is indispensable to any effective control of the work from above, such as is aimed at in the appointment of a discretionary head of the university—particularly in a large school; and the measure of control desired will decide the degree of thoroughness with which this bureaucratic organization is to be carried through. The need of a well-devised bureaucratic system is greater the more centralized and coercive the control to

---

included the ordinary progression of generations, naturally occurring differences of opinions, contests for preference and success, and the establishment of new universities of the kind in which Veblen was trained and made his living.

15. Rare: division into parcels.

which the academic work is to be subject; and the degree of control to be exercised will be greater the more urgent the felt need of a strict and large accountancy may be. All of which resolves itself into a question as to the purposes sought by the installation of such a system.

For the everyday work of the higher learning, as such, little of a hierarchical gradation, and less of bureaucratic subordination, is needful or serviceable; and very little of statistical uniformity, standard units of erudition, or detail accountancy, is at all feasible. This work is not of a mechanical character and does not lend itself, either in its methods or its results, to any mechanically standardized scheme of measurements or to a system of accounting percent per time unit. This range of instruction consists substantially in the facilitation of scholarly and scientific habits of thought, and the imposition of any appreciable measure of such standardization and accounting[16] must unavoidably weaken and vitiate the work of instruction, in just the degree in which the imposed system is effective.

It is not within the purpose of this inquiry to go into the bearing of all this on the collegiate (undergraduate) departments or on the professional and technical schools associated with the university proper in American practice. But something of a detailed discussion of the system and principles of control applied in these schools is necessary because of its incidental bearing on graduate work.

It is plain beyond need of specification that in the practical view of the public at large, and of the governing boards, the university is primarily an undergraduate school, with graduate and professional departments added to it. And it is similarly plain that the captains of erudition chosen as executive heads share the same preconceptions, and go to their work with a view primarily to the needs of their undergraduate departments. The businesslike order and system introduced into the universities, therefore, are designed primarily to meet the needs and exploit the possibilities of the undergraduate school; but, by force of habit, by a desire of uniformity, by a desire to control and exhibit the personnel and their work, by heedless imitation, or what not, it invariably happens that the same scheme of order and system is extended to cover the graduate work also.

16. The two targets of Veblen's criticism here were central features of what at its inception was a distinctly American structure of undergraduate education. "Standardization" means a degree curriculum divided into self-contained courses—or what the historian Sheldon Rothblatt calls teaching "modules"—with each course taught by a single instructor who also examines and assigns a final mark or grade. "Accounting" means degrees that are awarded on the basis of a certain number of courses distributed among numerous and different subject areas, typically with concentration on one subject during the last two years of the undergraduate years. "Accounting" also means grading viewed as a reliable measure of material learned and credit hours viewed as reliable testimony to the volume of instruction received. This remains the basic set-up today. See Sheldon Rothblatt, The Modern University and Its Discontents (Cambridge: Cambridge University Press, 1997), 30–31.

While it is the work of science and scholarship, roughly what is known in American usage as graduate work, that gives the university its rank as a seat of learning and keeps it in countenance as such with laymen and scholars, it is the undergraduate school, or college, that still continues to be the larger fact, and that still engages the greater and more immediate attention in university management. This is due in part to received American usage, in part to its more readily serving the ends of competitive ambition; and it is a fact in the current academic situation which must be counted in as a chronic discrepancy, not to be got clear of or to be appreciably mitigated so long as business principles continue to rule.

What counts toward the advancement of learning and the scholarly character of the university is the graduate work, but what gives statistically formidable results in the way of a numerous enrolment, many degrees conferred, public exhibitions, courses of instruction—in short what rolls up a large showing of turnover and output—is the perfunctory work of the undergraduate department, as well as the array of vocational schools latterly subjoined as auxiliaries to this end. Hence the needs and possibilities of the undergraduate and vocational schools are primarily, perhaps rather solely, had in view in the bureaucratic organization of the courses of instruction, in the selection of the personnel, in the divisions of the school year, as well as in the various accessory attractions offered, such as the athletic equipment, facilities for fraternity and other club life, debates, exhibitions and festivities, and the customary routine of devotional amenities under official sanction.

The undergraduate or collegiate schools, that now bulk so large in point of numbers as well as in the attention devoted to their welfare in academic management, have undergone certain notable changes in other respects than size, since the period of that shifting from clerical control to a business administration that marks the beginning of the current régime. Concomitant with their growth in numbers they have taken over an increasing volume of other functions than such as bear directly on matters of learning. At the same time the increase in numbers has brought a change in the scholastic complexion of this enlarged student body, of such a nature that a very appreciable proportion of these students no longer seek residence at the universities with a view to the pursuit of knowledge, even ostensibly. By force of conventional propriety a "college course"—the due term of residence at some reputable university, with the collegiate degree certifying honorable discharge—has become a requisite of gentility. So considerable is the resulting genteel contingent among the students, and so desirable is their enrolment and the countenance of their presence, in the apprehension of the university directorate, that the academic organization is in great part, and of strategic necessity, adapted primarily to their needs.

This contingent, and the general body of students in so far as this contingent from the leisure class[17] has leavened the lump, are not so seriously interested in their studies that they can in any degree be counted on to seek knowledge on their own initiative. At the same time they have other interests that must be taken care of by the school, on pain of losing their custom and their good will, to the detriment of the university's standing in genteel circles and to the serious decline in enrolment which their withdrawal would occasion. Hence college sports come in for an ever increasing attention and take an increasingly prominent and voluminous place in the university's life; as do also other politely blameless ways and means of dissipation, such as fraternities, clubs, exhibitions, and the extensive range of extra-scholastic traffic known as "student activities."

At the same time the usual and average age of the college students has been slowly falling farther back into the period of adolescence;[18] and the irregularities and uncertain temper of that uneasy period consequently are calling for more detailed surveillance and a more circumspect administration of college discipline. With a body of students whose everyday interest, as may be said without exaggeration, lies in the main elsewhere than in the pursuit of knowledge, and with an imperative tradition still standing over that requires the college to be (ostensibly at least) an establishment for the instruction of the youth, it becomes necessary to organize this instruction on a coercive plan, and hence to itemize the scholastic tasks of the inmates with great nicety of subdivision and with a meticulous regard to an exact equivalence as between the various courses and items of instruction to which they are to be subjected. Likewise as regards the limits of permissible irregularities of conduct and excursions into the field of sports and social amenities.

To meet the necessities of this difficult control, and to meet them always without jeopardizing the interests of the school as a competitive concern, a close-cut mechanical standardization, uniformity, surveillance and accountancy are indis-

17. Term made famous by Veblen in his book *Theory of the Leisure Class* (1899), where he defined the "leisure class" as a class of men whose occupations and wealth exempt them from actual production and allow them to compel others to work on their behalf. The leisure class, he argued, secured its status by flaunting signs of its avoidance of work—initially by engaging in nonproductive activity, such as warfare and sports, and subsequently in societies with advanced economies by ostentatious displays of accumulated and wasteful wealth that Veblen labeled "conspicuous consumption."

18. Veblen is mistaken here. Students at antebellum American colleges ranged in age from 14 to 25. After the Civil War, thanks in part to the introduction of new admissions policies, the age of student bodies began to range more narrowly between 17 and 22.

pensable. As regards the schedule of instruction, *bona fide*[19] students will require but little exacting surveillance in their work, and little in the way of an apparatus of control. But the collegiate school has to deal with a large body of students, many of whom have little abiding interest in their academic work, beyond the academic credits necessary to be accumulated for honorable discharge—indeed their scholastic interest may fairly be said to center in unearned credits.

For this reason, and also because of the difficulty of controlling a large volume of perfunctory labor, such as is involved in undergraduate instruction, the instruction offered must be reduced to standard units of time, grade and volume. Each unit of work required, or rather of credit allowed, in this mechanically drawn scheme of tasks must be the equivalent of all the other units; otherwise a comprehensive system of scholastic accountancy will not be practicable, and injustice and irritation will result both among the pupils and the schoolmasters. For the greater facility and accuracy in conducting this scholastic accountancy, as well as with a view to the greater impressiveness of the published schedule of courses offered, these mechanical units of academic bullion are increased in number and decreased in weight and volume; until the parcelment and mechanical balance of units reaches a point not easily credible to any outsider who might naively consider the requirements of scholarship to be an imperative factor in academic administration. There is a well-considered preference for semi-annual or quarterly periods of instruction, with a corresponding time limit on the courses offered; and the parcelment of credits is carried somewhat beyond the point which this segmentation of the school year would indicate. So also there prevails a system of grading the credits allowed for the performance of these units of task-work, by percentages (often carried out to decimals) or by some equivalent scheme of notation; and in the more solicitously perfected schemes of control of this task-work, the percentages so turned in will then be further digested and weighed by expert accountants, who revise and correct these returns by the help of statistically ascertained index numbers that express the mean average margin of error to be allowed for each individual student or instructor.

In point of formal protestation, the standards set up in this scholastic accountancy are high and rigorous; in application, the exactions of the credit system must not be enforced in so inflexible a spirit as to estrange that much-desired contingent of genteel students whose need of an honorable discharge is greater than their love of knowledge. Neither must its demands on the student's time

19. Latin: real or genuine.

and energy be allowed seriously to interfere with those sports and "student activities" that make up the chief attraction of college life for a large proportion of the university's young men, and that are, in the apprehension of many, so essential a part in the training of the modern gentleman.

Such a system of accountancy acts to break the continuity and consistency of the work of instruction and to divert the interest of the students from the work in hand to the making of a passable record in terms of the academic "miner's inch."[20] Typically, this miner's inch is measured in terms of standard text per time unit, and the immediate objective of teacher and student so becomes the compassing of a given volume of prescribed text, in print or lecture form—leading up to the broad principle: "*Nichts als was im Buche steht.*"[21] Which puts a premium on mediocrity and perfunctory work, and brings academic life to revolve about the office of the Keeper of the Tape and Sealing Wax.[22] Evidently this organization of departments, schedules of instruction, and scheme of scholastic accountancy, is a matter that calls for insight and sobriety on the part of the executive; and in point of fact there is much deliberation and solicitude spent on this behalf.

The installation of a rounded system of scholastic accountancy brings with it, if it does not presume, a painstaking distribution of the personnel and the courses of instruction into a series of bureaux[23] or departments. Such an organization of the forces of the establishment facilitates the oversight and control of the work, at the same time that it allows the array of scheduled means, appliances and personnel at its disposal to be statistically displayed to better effect. Under existing circumstances of rivalry among these institutions of learning, there is need of much shrewd management to make all the available forces of the establishment count toward the competitive end; and in this composition it is the part of worldly wisdom to see that appearances may often be of graver consequence than achievement—as is true in all competitive business that addresses its appeal to a large and scattered body of customers. The competition is for custom, and for such prestige as may procure custom, and these potential customers on whom it

20. Phrase used to describe a unit of water flow that varies with locality; originally intended for measuring small quantities of water flow.

21. German: "nothing else but what is [written] in the book."

22. *Sealing wax*, in the past, was wax used especially for making seals on documents and letters.

23. Plural of *bureau*: a specialized administrative unit; office for transaction of a particular business. Veblen's identification of academic departments simply as a "series of bureau" allows him to add the now characteristic departmental organization of the American university to his list of threats to "higher learning." The growing authority of academic departments in the day-to-day operations of the university, however, also reflected the growing authority of the professional academic disciplines they represented. Taken together, these two developments meant that, in Veblen's day, presidential appointments of junior faculty members at American research universities usually were made on recommendations of individual academic departments.

is desirable to produce an impression, especially as regards the undergraduate school, are commonly laymen who are expected to go on current rumor and the outward appearance of things academic.

The exigencies of competitive business, particularly of such retail trade as seems chiefly to have contributed to the principles of businesslike management in the competing schools, throw the stress on appearances. In such business, the "good will" of the concern has come to be (ordinarily) its most valued and most valuable asset. The visible success of the concern, or rather the sentiments of confidence and dependence inspired in potential customers by this visible success, is capitalized as the chief and most substantial element of the concern's intangible assets. And the accumulation of such intangible assets, to be gained by convincing appearances and well-devised pronouncements, has become the chief object of persistent endeavor on the part of sagacious business men engaged in such lines of traffic. This, that the substance must not be allowed to stand in the way of the shadow, is one of the fundamental principles of management which the universities, under the guidance of business ideals, have taken over from the wisdom of the business community.

Accepting the point of view of the captains of erudition, and so looking on the universities as competitive business concerns, and speaking in terms applicable to business concerns generally, the assets of these seminaries of learning are in an exceptional degree intangible assets. There is, of course, the large item of the good-will or prestige of the university as a whole, considered as a going concern. But this collective body of "immaterial capital" that pertains to the university at large is made up in great part of the prestige of diverse eminent persons included among its personnel and incorporated in the fabric of its bureaucratic departments, and not least the prestige of its executive head; in very much the same way as the like will hold true, e. g., for any company of public amusement, itinerant or sedentary, such as a circus, a theatrical or operatic enterprise, which all compete for the acclamation and custom of those to whom these matters appeal.

For the purposes of such competition the effectual prestige of the university as a whole, as well as the detail prestige of its personnel, is largely the prestige which it has with the laity rather than with the scholarly classes.[24] And it is safe

24. The question of what constitutes university "prestige" has become more complicated in our time. But Veblen provides an accurate description of where things stood in the early twentieth century, when at American colleges and universities across the country, the status of the president, the social standing of the board and students, and the significance of higher education in the sponsoring community, played considerably more important roles in determining an institution's "prestige" than the specific achievements of its faculty. In fact, before World War II, few American university professors were publishing scholars or scientists with national reputations.

to say that a somewhat more meretricious showing of magnitude and erudition will pass scrutiny, for the time being, with the laity than with the scholars. Which suggests the expediency for the university, as a going concern competing for the traffic, to take recourse to a somewhat more tawdry exhibition of quasi-scholarly feats, and a somewhat livelier parade of academic splendor and magnitude, than might otherwise be to the taste of such a body of scholars and scientists. As a business proposition, the meretricious[25] quality inherent in any given line of publicity should not consign it to neglect, so long as it is found effectual for the end in view.

Competitive business concerns that find it needful to commend themselves to a large and credulous body of customers, as, e. g., newspapers or department stores, also find it expedient somewhat to overstate their facilities for meeting all needs, as also to overstate the measure of success which they actually enjoy. Indeed, much talent and ingenuity is spent in that behalf, as well as a very appreciable outlay of funds. So also as touches the case of the competitive seminaries of learning. And even apart from the exigencies of intercollegiate rivalry, taken simply as a question of sentiment it is gratifying to any university directorate to know and to make known that the stock of merchantable knowledge on hand is abundant and comprehensive, and that the registration and graduation lists make a brave numerical showing, particularly in case the directive head is duly imbued with a businesslike penchant for tests of accountancy and large figures. It follows directly that many and diverse bureau or departments are to be erected, which will then announce courses of instruction covering all accessible ramifications of the field of learning, including subjects which the corps of instructors may not in any particular degree be fit to undertake. A further and unavoidable consequence of this policy, therefore, is perfunctory work.

For establishments that are substantially of secondary school character, including colleges and undergraduate departments, such a result may not be of extremely serious consequence; since much of the instruction in these schools is of a perfunctory kind anyway. But since the university and the college are, in point of formal status and of administrative machinery, divisions of the same establishment and subject to the same executive control; and since, under competitive business principles, the collegiate division is held to be of greater importance, and requires the greater share of attention; it comes about that the college in great measure sets the pace for the whole, and that the undergraduate scheme of credits, detailed accountancy, and mechanical segmentation of the work, is

25. Falsely attractive, or attractive in a vulgar manner.

carried over into the university work proper. Such a result follows more consistently and decisively, of course, in those establishments where the line of demarcation between undergraduate and graduate instruction is advisedly blurred or disregarded. It is not altogether unusual latterly, advisedly to efface the distinction between the undergraduate and the graduate division and endeavor to make a gradual transition from the one to the other.[e] This is done in the less conspicuous fashion of scheduling certain courses as Graduate and Senior, and allowing scholastic credits acquired in certain courses of the upper-class undergraduate curriculum to count toward the complement of graduate credits required of candidates for advanced degrees. More conspicuously and with fuller effect the same end is sought at other universities by classifying the two later years of the undergraduate curriculum as "Senior College"; with the avowed intention that these two concluding years of the usual four are scholastically to lie between the stricter undergraduate domain, now reduced to the freshman and sophomore years, on the one hand, and the graduate division as such on the other hand. This "Senior College" division so comes to be accounted in some sort a halfway graduate school; with the result that it is assimilated to the graduate work in the fashion of its accountancy and control; or rather, the essentially undergraduate methods that still continue to rule unabated in the machinery and management of this "senior college" are carried over by easy sophistication of expediency into the graduate work; which so takes on the usual, conventionally perfunctory, character that belongs by tradition and necessity to the undergraduate division; whereby in effect the instruction scheduled as "graduate" is, in so far, taken out of the domain of the higher learning and thrown back into the hands of the schoolmasters.[26] The rest of the current undergraduate standards and discipline tends strongly to follow the lead so given and to work over by insensible precession into the graduate school; until in the consummate end the free pursuit of learning should no longer find a standing-place in the university except by subreption and dissimu-

e. The strategic reason for this is the desire to retain for graduate registration any student who might otherwise prefer to look for graduate instruction elsewhere. The plan has not been found to work well, and it is still on trial. [Arrangements at the University of Chicago during Veblen's time were more complicated than he manages to suggest here. It is true that William Rainey Harper at first envisioned the last two years of college work—what he initially termed "university college"—as part of the larger graduate mission of the University of Chicago. However, Harper's early description of the first two years of undergraduate study at Chicago as "academic college" served to acknowledge a then well-established tradition of secondary education provided by nineteenth-century college preparatory academies. As Harper saw things, a student in his or her first two years at the University of Chicago was completing preparatory work begun in high school. Hence an undergraduate's second-term of two years logically became "university college"—what Harper later termed "Senior College"—signifying completion of all preparatory work and the development of the skills and maturity needed to do university-level work. –Ed.]

26. Cf. note c, *supra*.

lation; much after the fashion in which, in the days of ecclesiastical control and scholastic lore, the pursuit of disinterested knowledge was constrained to a shifty simulation of interest in theological speculations and a disingenuous formal conformity to the standards and methods that were approved for indoctrination in divinity.

Perfunctory work and mechanical accountancy may be sufficiently detrimental in the undergraduate curriculum, but it seems altogether and increasingly a matter of course in that section; but it is in the graduate division that it has its gravest consequences. Yet even in undergraduate work it remains true, as it does in all education in a degree, that the instruction can be carried on with best effect only on the ground of an absorbing interest on the part of the instructor; and he can do the work of a teacher as it should be done only so long as he continues to take an investigator's interest in the subject in which he is called on to teach. He must be actively engaged in an endeavor to extend the bounds of knowledge at the point where his work as teacher falls. He must be a specialist offering instruction in the specialty with which he is occupied; and the instruction offered can reach its best efficiency only in so far as it is incidental to an aggressive campaign of inquiry on the teacher's part.

But no one is a competent specialist in many lines; nor is any one competent to carry on an assorted parcel of special inquiries, cut to a standard unit of time and volume. One line, somewhat narrowly bounded as a specialty, measures the capacity of the common run of talented scientists and scholars for first-class work, whatever side-lines of subsidiary interest they may have in hand and may carry out with passably creditable results. The alternative is schoolmaster's task-work; or if the pretense of advanced learning must be kept up, the alternative which not unusually goes into effect is amateurish pedantry, with the charlatan ever in the near background. By and large, if the number of distinct lines of instruction offered by a given departmental corps appreciably exceeds the number of men on the staff, some of these lines or courses will of necessity be carried in a perfunctory fashion and can only give mediocre results, at the best. What practically happens at the worst is better left under the cover of a decent reticence.

Even those preferred lines of instruction which in their own right engage the serious interest of the instructors can get nothing better than superficial attention if the time and energy of the instructors are dissipated over a scattering variety of courses. Good work, that is to say sufficiently good work to be worthwhile, requires a free hand and a free margin of time and energy. If the number of distinct lines of instruction is relatively large, and if, as happens, they are distributed scatteringly among the members of the staff, with a relatively large assignment of hours to each man, so as to admit no assured and persistent concentration on any point, the run of instruction offered will necessarily be of this perfunctory character, and will therefore be of such amateurish and pedantic quality. Such an outcome is by no means unusual where regard is had primarily to covering a given inclusive range of subjects, rather than to the special aptitudes of the departmental corps; as indeed commonly happens, and as happens particularly where the school or the department in question is sufficiently imbued with a businesslike spirit of academic rivalry. It follows necessarily and in due measure on the introduction of the principles, methods, and tests of competitive business into the work of instruction.[f]

Under these principles of accountancy and hierarchical control, each of the several bureau of erudition—commonly called departments—is a competitor with all its fellow bureau in the (thrifty) apportionment of funds and equipment—for the businesslike university management habitually harbors a larger number of departments than its disposable means will adequately provide for. So also each department competes with its fellow departments, as well as with similar departments in rival universities, for a clientele in the way of student registrations. These two lines of competition are closely interdependent. An adverse statistical showing in the number of students, or in the range, variety and volume of courses of instruction offered by any given department, is rated by the businesslike general directorate as a shortcoming, and it is therefore likely to bring a reduction of allowances. At the same time, of course, such an adverse showing reflects discredit on the chief of bureau, while it also wounds his self-respect. The final test of competency in such a chief, under business principles, is the statistical test; in part because numerical tests have a seductive air of businesslike accountancy, and also because statistical exhibits have a ready use as advertising material to be employed in appeals to the potential donors and the unlearned patrons of the university, as well as to the public at large.

So the chief of bureau, with the aid and concurrence of his loyal staff, will aim to offer as extensive and varied a range of instruction as the field assigned his

---

f. At least one such businesslike chief of bureau has seriously endeavored so to standardize and control the work of his staff as to have all courses of lectures professed in the department reduced to symmetrical and permanent shape under the form of certified syllabi, which could then be taken over by any member of the staff, at the discretion of the chief, and driven home in the lecture room with the accredited pedagogical circumstance and apparatus. The scheme has found its way into academic anecdote, on the lighter side, as being a project to supply standard erudition in uniform packages, "guaranteed under the pure food law, fully sterilized. and sealed without solder or acids"; to which it is only necessary to "add hot air and serve." [The "businesslike chief of bureau" alluded to here is unidentified. But the "scheme" in question almost certainly was one laid out in Morris L. Cooke's (1872–1960) *Academic and Industrial Efficiency* (1920), which aimed at developing conceptual tools for making "an estimate of the cost and the output both in teaching and research." –Ed.]

department will admit. Out of this competitive aggrandizement of departments there may even arise a diplomatic contention between heads of departments, as to the precise frontiers between their respective domains; each being ambitious to magnify his office and acquire merit by including much of the field and many of the students under his own dominion.[g] Such a conflict of jurisdiction is particularly apt to arise in case, as may happen, the number of scholastic departments exceeds the number of patently distinguishable provinces of knowledge; and competitive business principles constantly afford provocation to such a discrepancy, at the hands of an executive pushed by the need of a show of magnitude and large traffic. It follows, further, from these circumstances, that wherever contiguous academic departments are occupied with such closely related subject matter as would place them in a position to supplement one another's work, the negotiations involved in jealously guarding their respective frontiers may even take on an acrimonious tone, and may involve more or less of diplomatic mischief-making; so that, under this rule of competitive management, opportunities for mutual comfort and aid will not infrequently become occasion for mutual distrust and hindrance.

The broader the province and the more exuberant the range of instruction appropriated to a given department and its corps of teachers, the more creditable will be the statistical showing, and the more meagre and threadbare are likely to be the scientific results. The corps of instructors will be the more consistently organized and controlled with a view to their dispensing accumulated knowledge, rather than to pursue further inquiry in the direction of their scholarly inclination or capacity; and frequently, indeed, to dispense a larger volume and a wider range of knowledge than they are in any intimate sense possessed of.

It is by no means that no regard is had to the special tastes, aptitudes, and attainments of the members of the staff, in so apportioning the work; these things are, commonly, given such consideration as the exigencies of academic competition will permit; but these exigencies decide that the criterion of special fitness becomes a secondary consideration. Wherever the businesslike demands of a

---

g. So, e. g., it is known to have, on occasion, became a difficult question of inter-bureaucratic comity, whether commercial geography belongs of right to the department of geology or to that of economics; whether given courses in Hebrew are equitably to be assigned to the department of Semitics or to that of Religions; whether Church History is in fairness to be classed with profane History or with Divinity, etc.—questions which, except in point of departmental rivalry, have none but a meretricious significance. [At the University of Chicago in Veblen's day, "difficult questions of inter-bureaucratic comity" reflected the remarkably atomistic form of the University's initial departmental organization, as well as the power of chairs (several of whom were former college or university presidents) who headed individual departments. At the outset, Chicago's academic departments were not organized into divisions; hence, no divisional deans existed to arbitrate disputes among department heads. –Ed.]

rounded and extensive schedule of courses traverse the lines of special aptitude and training, the requirements of the schedule must rule the case; whereas, of course, the interests of science and scholarship, and of the best efficiency in the instruction given, would decide that no demands of the schedule be allowed to interfere with each man's doing the work which he can do best, and nothing else.

A schedule of instruction drawn on such lines of efficiency would avoid duplication of course, and would curtail the number of courses offered by any given department to such a modicum as the special fitness of the members of the staff would allow them to carry to the best effect. It would also proceed on the obvious assumption that co-ordinate departments in the several universities should supplement one another's work—an assumption obvious to the meanest academic common sense. But amicable working arrangements of this kind between departments of different universities, or between the several universities as a whole, are of course virtually barred out under the current policy of competitive duplication. It is out of the question, in the same manner and degree as the like co-operation between rival department stores is out of the question. Yet so urgently right and good is such a policy of mutual supplement and support, except as a business proposition, that some exchange of academic civilities paraded under its cloak is constantly offered to view in the maneuvers of the competing captains of erudition. The well-published and nugatory[h] periodic conferences of presidents commonly have such an ostensible purpose.

Competitive enterprise, reinforced with a sentimental penchant for large figures, demands a full schedule of instruction. But to carry such a schedule and do the work well would require a larger staff of instructors in each department, and a larger allowance of funds and equipment, than business principles will countenance. There is always a dearth of funds, and there is always urgent use for more than can be had; for the enterprising directorate is always eager to expand and project the business of the concern into new provinces of school work, secondary, primary, elementary, normal, professional, technical, manual-training, art schools, schools of music, elocution, book-keeping, housekeeping, and a further variety that will more readily occur to those who have been occupied with devising

h. Nugatory, that is, for the ostensible purpose of reducing inter-academic rivalry and duplication. However, there are other matters of joint interest to the guild of university executives, as, e.g., the inter-academic, or inter-executive, blacklist, and similar recondite matters of presidential courtesy and prestige, necessary to be attended to though not necessary to be spread abroad. [A "blacklist" is a list of people or organizations that are viewed with suspicion and disapproval and are to be avoided or punished. There is no evidence that early twentieth-century American university presidents kept or consulted actual blacklists of controversial professors. But because university presidents at the time operated as the primary gatekeepers of the faculty, in many cases they did correspond about individual professors seeking appointments. –Ed.]

ways and means of extending the competitive traffic of the university. Into these diverse and sundry channels of sand the pressure of competitive expansion is continually pushing additional half-equipped, under-fed and over-worked ramifications of the academic body. And then, too, sane competitive business practice insists on economy of cost as well as a large output of goods. It is "bad business" to offer a better grade of goods than the market demands, particularly to customers who do not know the difference, or to turn out goods at a higher cost than other competing concerns. So business exigencies, those exigencies of economy to which the businesslike governing boards are very much alive, preclude any department confining itself to the work which it can do best, and at the same stroke they preclude the authorities from dealing with any department according to such a measure of liberality as would enable it to carry on the required volume of work in a competent manner.

In the businesslike view of the captains of erudition, taken from the standpoint of the counting-house, learning and university instruction are a species of skilled labor, to be hired at competitive wages and to turn out the largest merchantable output that can be obtained by shrewd bargaining with their employees; whereas, of course, in point of fact and of its place in the economic system, the pursuit of learning is a species of leisure, and the work of instruction is one of the modes of a life so spent in "the increase and diffusion of knowledge among men." It is to be classed as "leisure" only in such a sense of that term as may apply to other forms of activity that have no economic, and more particularly no pecuniary, end or equivalence. It is by no means hereby intended to imply that such pursuit of knowledge is an aimless or indolent manner of life; nothing like dissipation has a legitimate place in it, nor is it "idle" in any other sense than that it is extra-economic, not without derogation to be classed as a gainful pursuit. Its aim is not the increase or utilization of the material means of life; nor can its spirit and employment be bought with a price. Any salary, perquisites, or similar emoluments assigned the scholars and scientists in the service of civilization, within the university or without, are (should be) in the nature of a stipend, designed to further the free use of their talent in the prosecution of this work, the value of which is not of a pecuniary kind. But under the stress of businesslike management in the universities the drift of things sets toward letting the work of science and scholarship to the lowest bidder, on a roughly applicable piece-wage plan. The result is about such a degree of inefficiency, waste and stultification as might fairly be expected; whereof there are abundantly many examples, that humble the pride of the scholars and rejoice the heart of the captains of erudition.

The piece-wage plan[27] never goes into effect in set form, or has not hitherto done so—although there are schools of nominally university grade in which there is a recognized and avowed endeavor so to apportion the weekly hours of class-room exercises to the pay of the teachers as to bring the pay per class-hour per semester to a passably uniform level for the general body of the staff. That the piece-wage plan has so little avowed vogue in the academic wage scheme may at first sight seem strange; the body of academic employees are as defenseless and unorganized as any class of the wage-earning population,[28] and it is among the unorganized and helpless that the piece-wage plan is commonly applied with the best effect; at the same time the system of scholastic accountancy, worked out for other purposes and already applied both to instructors, to courses of instruction, and to divisions of the school year, has already reduced all the relevant items to such standard units and thorough equivalence as should make a system of piece-wages almost a matter of course. That it has not formally been put in practice appears to be due to tradition, and to that long-term common sense appreciation of the nature of learning that will always balk at rating this work as a frankly materialistic and pecuniary occupation. The academic personnel, e. g., are unable to rid themselves of a fastidious—perhaps squeamish—persuasion that they are engaged in this work not wholly for pecuniary returns; and the community at large are obscurely, but irretrievably and irresponsibly, in the same suspicious frame of mind on that head. The same unadvised and unformulated persuasion that academic salaries are after all not honestly to be rated as wages, is doubtless accountable for certain other features of academic management touching the pay-roll; notably the failure of the employees to organize anything like a trades-union, or to fall into line on any workable basis of solidarity on such an issue as a wage-bargain, as also the equivocal footing on which the matter of appointments and removals is still allowed to stand; hence also the unsettled ethics of the trade in this respect.

For diverse reasons, but mainly reasons of competitive statistics, which resolve themselves, again, in the main into reasons of expedient publicity, it is desired

27. In a "piece wage" plan, compensation is based on the number of units of work produced by an individual or a team. In theory, such a plan is designed to provide greater incentives for higher productivity.

28. In 1918, "academic employees" were not quite as "defenseless and unorganized" as Veblen suggests here. The formation of the American Association of University Professors (AAUP) in 1915, and its subsequent issue of a *Declaration of Principles of Academic Freedom and Tenure*, made it clear that the first and foremost task of the new national association was to alter the prevailing view of university professors as employees serving at the sufferance of their employers. Now remembered as a landmark in the history of American higher education, the founding of the AAUP goes unmentioned in *The Higher Learning in America*.

that the enrolment should be very large and should always and unremittingly increase—due regard being always had, of course, to the eminent desirability of drawing into the enrolment many students from the higher levels of gentility and pecuniary merit. To this end it is well, as has already been remarked above, to announce a very full schedule of instruction and a free range of elective alternatives, and also to promote a complete and varied line of scholastic accessories, in the way of athletics, clubs, fraternities, "student activities," and similar devices of politely blameless dissipation.

These accessories of college life have been strongly on the increase since the business régime has come in. They are held to be indispensable, or unavoidable; not for scholarly work, of course, but chiefly to encourage the attendance of that decorative contingent who take more kindly to sports, invidious intrigue and social amenities than to scholarly pursuits. Notoriously, this contingent is, on the whole, a serious drawback to the cause of learning, but it adds appreciably, and adds a highly valued contribution, to the number enrolled; and it gives also a certain, highly appreciated, loud tone ("college spirit") to the student body; and so it is felt to benefit the corporation of learning by drawing public attention. Corporate means expended in provision for these academic accessories—"side shows," as certain ill-disposed critics have sometimes called them—are commonly felt to be well spent. Persons who are not intimately familiar with American college life have little appreciation of the grave solicitude given to these matters.

During some considerable number of years past, while the undergraduate enrolment at the universities has been increasing rapidly, the attitude of the authorities has progressively been undergoing a notable change touching these matters of extra-scholastic amenity. It is in great measure a continuation of changes that have visibly been going forward in the older universities of the country for a longer period, and it is organically bound up with the general shifting of ground that marks the incursion of business principles.

While the authorities have turned their attention primarily to the undergraduate division and its numerical increase, they have at the same time, and largely with the same end in view, endeavored to give it more of the character of a "gentleman's college," that is to say, an establishment for the cultivation of the graces of gentility and a suitable place of residence for young men of spendthrift habits. The improvement sought in these endeavors is not so much the increase and acceleration of scholarly pursuits, as a furthering of "social" proficiency. A "gentleman's college" is an establishment in which scholarship is advisedly made subordinate to genteel dissipation, to a grounding in those methods of conspicuous consumption[29] that should engage the thought and energies of a well-to-do man of the world. Such an ideal, more or less overtly, appears to be gaining ground among the larger universities; and, needless to say, it is therefore also gaining, by force of precedent and imitation, among the younger schools engaged in more of a struggle to achieve a secure footing of respectability.

Its bearing on the higher learning is, of course, sufficiently plain; and its intimate connection with business principles at large should be equally plain. The scheme of reputability in the pecuniary culture comprises not only the imperative duty of acquiring something more than an equitable share of the community's wealth, but also the dutiful privilege of spending this acquired wealth, and the leisure that goes with it, in a reputably conspicuous way, according to the ritual of decorum in force for the time being. So that proficiency in the decorously conspicuous waste of time and means is no less essential in the end than proficiency in the gainful conduct of business. The ways and means of reputably consuming time and substance, therefore, is by prescriptive necessity to be included in the training offered at any well-appointed undergraduate establishment that aims in any comprehensive sense to do its whole duty by the well-to-do young men under its tutelage.[i] It is, further and by compulsion of the same ideals, incumbent on such an establishment to afford these young men a precinct dedicate to cultured leisure, and conventionally sheltered from the importunities of the municipal police, where an adequate but guarded indulgence may be had for those extravagances of adolescence that count for so much in shaping the canons of genteel intercourse.

There is, of course, no intention here to find fault with this gentlemanly ideal of undergraduate indoctrination, or with the solicitude shown in this behalf by the captains of erudition, in endeavoring to afford time, place and circumstance for its due inculcation among college men. It is by no means here assumed that learning is substantially more to be desired than proficiency in genteel dissipation. It is only that the higher learning and the life of fashion and affairs are two widely distinct and divergent lines, both lying within the current scheme of civi-

---

i. The English pattern of boys' schools and gentlemanly university residence has doubtless afforded notable guidance to the "Educators" who have labored for the greater gentility of American college life; at the same time that the grave authenticity of these English customs has at many a difficult passage sewed opportunely to take the edge off the gentlemen-educators' sense of shame. [A more sympathetic way of putting this would be to say that, as the years passed and undergraduate enrollment steadily increased, American university presidents and boards became more interested in forging American undergraduate education in the model of the Oxford collegiate system. –Ed.]

29. Ostentatious display of accumulate or wasteful wealth. "Conspicuous consumption" is another phrase Veblen made current by the success of his earlier book *The Theory of the Leisure Class.*

lization; and that it is the university's particular office in this scheme to conserve and extend the domain of knowledge. There need be no question that it is a work of great social merit and consequence to train adepts in the ritual of decorum, and it is doubtless a creditable work for any school adapted to that purpose to equip men for a decorative place in polite society, and imbue them with a discriminating taste in the reputable waste of time and means. And all that may perhaps fall, not only legitimately, but meritoriously, within the province of the undergraduate school; at least it is not here intended to argue the contrary. At the same time a secure reputation for efficiency and adequate facilities along this line of aspirations on the part of any such school will serve a good business purpose in duly attracting students—or residents—from the better classes of society, and from those classes that aspire to be "better."

But this is essentially not university work. In the nature of the case it devolves on the college, the undergraduate school; and it cannot be carried through with due singleness of purpose in an establishment bound by tradition to make much of that higher learning that is substantially alien to the spirit of this thing. If, then, as indications run, the large undergraduate schools are in due course to develop somewhat unreservedly into gentlemen's colleges, that is an additional reason why, in the interest of both parties, the divorce of the university from the collegiate division should be made absolute. Neither does the worldly spirit that pervades the gentlemen's college further the university's interest in scholarship, nor do the university's scholarly interests further the college work in gentility.

Well to the front among these undergraduate appurtenances of gentleman-ship are the factional clubs known as Greek-letter fraternities. These touch the province of learning in the universities only incidentally and superficially, as they do not in practice enter the graduate division except by way of a thin aftermath of factional animus, which may occasionally infect such of the staff as are gifted with a particularly puerile temperament. They are, in effect, competitive organizations for the elaboration of the puerile irregularities of adolescence, and as such they find little scope among the graduate students or among the adult personnel at large. But as part of the apparatus of the undergraduate division they require a strict surveillance to keep them within the (somewhat wide) limits of tolerance; and so their presence affects the necessary discipline of the school at large, entailing a more elaborate and rigorous surveillance and more meddling with personal habits than would otherwise be required, and entailing also some slight corporate expense.

Much the same is true for the other social clubs, not of an advisedly factional character, that are latterly being installed by authority under university patronage

Figure 4. William Rainey Harper (*in bowler hat, right of drum*) and the University of Chicago Band, ca. 1900. University of Chicago Archives

and guaranteed by the university funds; as, also, and in a more pronounced degree, for college athletics, except that the item of expense in connection with these things is much more serious and the resulting diversion of interest from all matters of learning is proportionally greater. Among these means of dissipating energy and attention, college athletics is perhaps still the most effective; and it is also the one most earnestly pushed by the businesslike authorities,[30] at the same time that it is the most widely out of touch with all learning, whether it be the pursuit of knowledge or the perfunctory task work of the collegiate division. So notorious, indeed, is the discrepancy between college athletics and scholarly work that few college authorities latterly venture to avow as cordial a support of this training in sportsmanship as they actually give. Yet so efficient a means of attracting a certain class of young men is this academic enterprise in sports that, in practical effect, few schools fail to give it all the support that the limits of deco-

30. In Veblen's time, this was especially the case at the University of Chicago, where president William Rainey Harper was a leading booster of intercollegiate football. Harper considered Chicago's football team a traveling advertisement for the university and exploited its early success to cultivate wider civic and alumni support (see Figure 4). During Harper's years in office, no other program or department at the University received as much local and national newspaper comment. Chicago's football team became nationally known for what turned out to be its precedent-setting interregional games and travel.

rum will admit. There is probably no point at which specious practices and habitual prevarication[31] are carried so far as here. Little need be said of the threadbare subterfuges by which (ostensibly surreptitious) pecuniary inducements are extended to students and prospective students who promise well as college athletes;[j] or of the equally threadbare expedients by which these members of the guild of sportsmen are enabled to meet the formal requirements of scholarship imposed by shamefaced intercollegiate bargaining.[k]

But apart from such petty expedients, however abundant and commonplace, there is the more significant practice of retaining trainers and helpers at the university's expense and with academic countenance. There is the corps of workmen and assistants to take care of the grounds, buildings and apparatus, and there is the corps of trainers and coaches, masseurs and surgeons, masquerading under the caption of "physical culture,"[32] whose chief duty is to put the teams in form for the various contests. One may find a football or baseball coach retained officially as a member of the faculty and carried on the academic payroll, in a university that practices a penurious economy in the equipment and current supply of

j. Illustrative instances have little value as anecdotes and not much more as circumstantial evidence; their abundance and *outrance* are such as to have depreciated their value in both respects. Yet to any who may not know of this traffic by familiar contact one or two commonplace instances may perhaps not seem too much. So, a few years ago, in one of the greater of the new universities, a valued member of one of the athletic teams was retained at an allowance of $40 a month as bookkeeper to the janitor of one of the boys' dormitories on the campus. At the same university and about the same time two other athletes were carried on university pay as assistants to the editor of the weekly bulletin announcing the program of academic events for the week; though in this case, to the relief of the editor in question, only one of the two assistants reported at his office, and that only once, during the year of their incumbency. These, as already remarked, are commonplace occurrences. The more spectacular instances of shrewd management in these premises cannot well be dealt with otherwise than by a canny silence; that being also the course approved by current practice. [Nothing more is known of this episode than what Veblen relates in this footnote. During his time at the University of Chicago, other instances of "shrewd management" included creating a special diet at a designated "training table" for athletes and putting a portion of a luxurious new University residence hall at their disposal. –Ed.]

k. A single instance may tolerantly be admitted here. Among the formal requirements that would admit students to a free pursuit of sportsmanship, at the same university as above mentioned, without imputation of professionalism, was specified the ability to read at sight such a passage in a given foreign language as would satisfy the instructor in charge that the candidate was competent in the language in question. The instructor responsible in this case, a man of high academic rank and gifted with a sympathetic good-will toward the "boys," submitted in fulfilment of the test a copy of the Lord's Prayer in this foreign tongue, and passed the (several) candidates on finding them able passably to repeat the same in English. It would scarcely be fair to distinguish this episode by giving names and places, since equally ingenious expedients have been in use elsewhere. [Nothing more is known about this episode than what Veblen relates in this footnote. We do know, however, that in his time, as in our own, the specter of academic ineligibility was constant for university athletes, especially football players. Remedies, then as now, included additional academic support and steering athletes to courses taught by sympathetic faculty. See Robin Lester, *Stagg's University: The Rise, Decline, and Fall of Big-Time Football at Chicago* (Urbana: University of Illinois Press, 1995. –Ed.]

31. Deviation from the truth; lying.

32. In Britain and America, the phrase "physical culture" had been in use since the 1830s to describe and idealize the quest for individual health and fitness. In Veblen's day, the term was closely identified with school and college athletics and exercise programs.

materials and services necessary to the work of its scientific laboratories, and whose library is in a shameful state of neglect for want of adequate provision for current purchases and attendance. The qualifications of such a "professor" are those of a coach, while in point of scholarly capacity and attainments it would be a stretch of charity to say that he is of quite a neutral composition. Still, under the pressure of intercollegiate competition for the services of such expert *lanistae*,[33] he may have to be vested with the highest academic rank and conceded the highest scholastic honors, with commensurate salary. Expediency may so decide, partly to cloak the shamefulness of the transaction, partly to meet the exacting demands of a coach whose professional services have a high commercial rating in the sporting community, and who is presumed to be indispensable to the university's due success in intercollegiate athletics.[34]

The manifest aim, and indeed the avowed purpose, of these many expedients of management and concessions to fashion and frailty is the continued numerical growth of the undergraduate school—the increase of the enrolment and the obtaining of funds by use of which to achieve a further increase. To bring this assiduous endeavor into its proper light, it is to be added that most of these undergraduate departments are already too large for the best work of their kind. Since these undergraduate schools have grown large enough to afford a secure contrast as against the smaller colleges that are engaged in the same general field, it is coming to be plain to university men who have to do with the advanced instruction that, for the advanced work in science and scholarship, the training given by a college of moderate size commonly affords a better preparation than is had in the very large undergraduate schools of the great universities. This holds true, in a general way, in spite of the fact that the smaller schools are handicapped by an inadequate equipment, are working against the side-draft of a religious bias, with a corps of under-paid and over-worked teachers in great part selected on denominational grounds, and are under-rated by all concerned. The proposition, however, taken in a general way and allowing for exceptions, is too manifestly true to admit of much question; particularly in respect of preparation for the sciences proper, as contrasted with the professions.

The causes of this relative inefficiency that seems to attach unavoidably to the excessively large undergraduate establishments cannot be gone into here; in part they are obvious, in part quite obscure. But in any case the matter cannot be gone

33. Latin: owners and trainers of gladiators.
34. The paragraph alludes to president William Rainey Harper's 1891 appointment of Amos Alonzo Stagg (1862–1965) as associate professor and director of the Department of Physical Culture and Athletics at Chicago. Harper made Stagg the first tenured professor of "physical culture" and thus the first tenured football coach anywhere.

into here, except so far as it has an immediate bearing on the advanced work of the university, through the inclusion of these collegiate schools in the university corporation and under the same government. As has already been remarked, by force of the competitive need of a large statistical showing and a wide sweep of popular prestige and notoriety, and by reason of other incentives of a nature more intimate to the person of the executive, it is in effect a matter of course that the undergraduate school and its growth becomes the chief object of solicitude and management with a businesslike executive; and that so its shaping of the foundations of the establishment as a whole acts irresistibly to fashion the rest of the university administration and instruction in the image of the undergraduate policy. Under the same compulsion it follows also that whatever elements in the advanced work of the university will not lend themselves to the scheme of accountancy, statistics, standardization and coercive control enforced in and through the undergraduate division, will tend to be lost by disuse and neglect, as being selectively unfit to survive under that system.

The advanced work falls under the same stress of competition in magnitude and visible success; and the same scheme of enforced statistical credits will gradually insinuate itself into the work for the advanced degrees; so that these as well as the lower degrees will come to be conferred on the piece-work plan. Throughout the American universities there is apparent such a movement in the direction of a closer and more mechanical specification of the terms on which the higher degrees are to be conferred—a specification in terms of stipulated courses of classroom work and aggregate quantity of standard credits and length of residence. So that his need of conformity to the standard credit requirements will therefore constrain the candidate for an advanced degree to make the substantial pursuit of knowledge subordinate to the present pursuit of credits, to be attended to, if at all, in the scant interstitial intervals allowed by a strictly drawn accountancy. The effect of it all on their animus, and on the effective prosecution of the higher learnings by the instructors, should be sufficiently plain; but in case of doubt any curious person may easily assure himself of it by looking over the current state of things as they run in any one of the universities that grant degrees.

Nothing but continued workday familiarity with this system of academic grading and credit, as it takes effect in the conduct and control of instruction, and as its further elaboration continues to employ the talents and deliberation of college men, can enable any observer to appreciate the extraordinary lengths to which this matter is carried in practice, and the pervasive way in which it resistlessly bends more and more of current instruction to its mechanical tests and progressively sterilizes all personal initiative and ambition that comes within its sweep.

And nothing but the same continued contact with the relevant facts could persuade any outsider that all this skilfully devised death of the spirit is brought about by well-advised efforts of improvement on the part of men who are intimately conversant with the facts, and who are moved by a disinterested solicitude for the best academic good of the students under their charge. Yet such, unmistakably, are the facts of the case.

While the initial move in this sterilization of the academic intellect is necessarily taken by the statistically-minded superior officers of the corporation of learning, the detail of schedules and administrative routine involved is largely left in the discretion of the faculty. Indeed, it is work of this character that occupies nearly the whole of the attention of the faculty as a deliberative body, as well as of its many and various committees. In these matters of administrative routine and punctilio the faculty, collectively and severally, can exercise a degree of initiative and discretion. And these duties are taken as seriously as well may be, and the matters that so come within the faculty's discretion are handled in the most unambiguous spirit of responsible deliberation. Each added move of elaboration is taken only after the deliberative body has assured itself that it embodies a needed enhancement of the efficiency of the system of control. But each improvement and amplification also unavoidably brings the need of further specification and apparatus, desired to take care of further refinements of doubt and detail that arise out of the last previous extensions of the mechanism. The remedy sought in all such conjunctures is to bring in further specifications and definitions, with the effect of continually making two specifications grow where one grew before, each of which in its turn will necessarily have to be hedged about on both sides by like specifications, with like effect;[1] with the consequence that the grading and credit system is subject to a ceaseless proliferation of ever more meticulous detail. The underlying difficulty appears to be not that the collective wisdom of the faculty is bent on its own stultification, as an unsympathetic outsider might hastily conclude, but that there is in all the deliberations of such a body a total disregard of common sense. It is, presumably, not that the constituent members are quite devoid of that quality, but rather that no point in their elaboration of apparatus can feasibly be reached, beyond which a working majority can be brought conscientiously to agree that dependence may safely be placed on common sense rather than on further and more meticulous and rigorous specification.

1. "And then there came another locust and carried off another grain of wheat, and then there came another locust," etc., etc. [Variant quote from folktale "The English Tale," in Sidney Oldhall Addy, *Household Tales and Other Traditional Remains* (1855). –Ed.]

It is at this point that the American system of fellowships falls into the scheme of university policy; and here again the effect of business principles and undergraduate machinery is to be seen at work. At its inception the purpose of these fellowships was to encourage the best talent among the students to pursue disinterested advanced study farther and with greater singleness of purpose and it is quite plain that at that stage of its growth the system was conceived to have no bearing on intercollegiate competition or the statistics of registration. This was something over thirty years ago. A fellowship was an honorable distinction; at the same time it was designed to afford such a stipend as would enable the incumbent to devote his undivided energies to scholastic work of a kind that would yield no pecuniary return. Ostensibly, such is still the sole purpose of the fellowships; the traditional decencies require (voluble and reiterated) professions to that effect. But in point of practical effect, and progressively, concomitant with the incursion of business principles into university policy, the exigencies of competitive academic enterprise have turned the fellowships to account in their own employ. So that, in effect, today the rival universities use the fellowships to bid against one another for fellows to come into residence, to swell the statistics of graduate registration and increase the number of candidates for advanced degrees. And the eligible students have learned so to regard the matter, and are quite callously exploiting the system in that sense.

Not that the fellowships have altogether lost that character of a scholarly stipendiary with which they started out; but they have, under businesslike management, acquired a use not originally intended; and the new, competitive use of them is unequivocally their main use today. It would be hazardous to guess just how far the directorates of the rival universities consciously turn the fellowships to account in this enterprising way, or how far, on the other hand, they are able to let self-deception cover the policy of competitive bargaining in which they are engaged; but it would be difficult to believe that their right hand is altogether ignorant of what their left hand is doing. It would doubtless also be found that both the practice and the animus back of it differ appreciably from one school to another. But there is no element of hazard in the generalization that, by and large, such competitive use of the fellowships is today their chief use; and that such is the fact is quite openly avowed among the academic staff of some universities at least.

As a sequel and symptom of this use of the fellowship stipends in bargaining for an enlarged enrolment of advanced students, it has become a moot question in academic policy whether a larger number of fellowships with smaller stipends will give a more advantageous net statistical result than a smaller number of more adequate stipends. An administration that looks chiefly to the short-term returns—as is commonly the practice in latter-day business enterprise—will sensibly incline to make the stipends small and numerous; while the converse will be true where regard is had primarily to the enrolment of carefully selected men who may reflect credit on the institution in the long run. Up-to-date business policy will apparently commend the former rather than the latter course; for business practice, in its later phases, is eminently guided by consideration of short-term gains. It is also true that the average stipend attached to the fellowships offered today is very appreciably lower than was the practice some two or three decades ago; at the same time that the cost of living—which these stipends were originally designed to cover—has increased by something like one hundred per cent. As final evidence of the decay of scholarly purpose in the matter of fellowships,[35] and as a climax of stultification, it is to be added that stipends originally established as an encouragement to disinterested scholarship are latterly being used to induce enrolment in the professional schools attached to the universities.[m]

One further point of contact and contamination is necessary to be brought into this account of the undergraduate administration and its bearing on advanced work. The scholastic accessories spoken of above—clubs, fraternities, devotional organizations, class organizations, spectacles and social functions, athletics, and "student activities" generally—do not in any appreciable degree bear directly on the advanced work, in as much as they find no ready lodgment among the university students proper. But they count, indirectly and effectually, toward lowering the scholarly ideals and keeping down the number of advanced students, chiefly by diverting the interest and energies of the undergraduate men from scholarly pursuits and throwing them into various lines of business and sportsmanship.

The subsidized clubs work, in these premises, to much the same effect as the fraternities; both are, in effect, designed to cultivate expensive habits of life. The

m. More than one instance might be cited where a student whose privately avowed and known aim was the study and practice of Law has deliberately been induced by the offer of a fellowship stipend to register, for the time being, as an academic graduate student and as candidate for the academic doctor's degree. In the instances that come to mind the students in question have since completed their law studies and entered practice, without further troubling about the academic degree for which they once were ostensible candidates. [When the University of Chicago Law School was organized, prospective law students in the undergraduate student body were allowed to count the first year of their professional legal training as the last year of their undergraduate study. Chicago also created a "pre-legal" program for the first year of professional education. –Ed.]

35. Veblen is correct in saying that the original purpose of American university "fellowships" was to provide graduate students with the means to devote themselves exclusively to their studies. But "the decay" of their original exclusively scholarly purpose was driven by a second purpose he does not mention: utilization of graduate students as teachers, which eventually became an integral practice of American research universities.

same is true in a higher degree of athletic sports. The full round of sportsmanlike events, as well as the round schedule of social amenities for which the polite side of undergraduate life (partly subsidized) is designed to give a taste and training, are beyond the compass of men devoted to scholarship. In effect these things come in as alternatives to the pursuit of knowledge. These things call for a large expenditure of time and means, neither of which can be adequately met by the scientist or scholar. So that men who have been trained to the round of things that so go to make up the conventional scheme of undergraduate interests cannot well look to a career in the higher learning as a possible outcome of their residence in college. On the other hand, young men habitually, and no doubt rightly, expect a business career to yield an income somewhat above the average of incomes in the community, and more particularly in excess of the commonplace incomes of academic men; such an income, indeed, as may afford the means to cover the conventional routine of such polite expenditures. So that, in the absence of an independent income, some sort of a business career that promises well in the pecuniary respect becomes the necessary recourse of the men to whom these amenities of expenditure have become habitual through their undergraduate training. With like effect the mental discipline exercised by these sports and polite events greatly favors the growth of tactful equivocation and a guarded habit of mind, such as makes for worldly wisdom and success in business, but which is worse than useless in the scholar or scientist. And further and perhaps more decisively, an undergraduate who does his whole duty in the way of sports, fraternities, clubs, and reputable dissipation at large, commonly comes through his undergraduate course with a scanty and superficial preparation for scholarly or scientific pursuits, if any. So that even in case he should still chance to harbor a penchant for the pursuit of learning he will be unfit by lack of training.

CHAPTER IV

Academic Prestige and the Material Equipment

In the course of the preceding chapter it has appeared that the introduction of business principles into university policy has had the immediate and ubiquitous effect of greatly heightening the directorate's solicitude for a due and creditable publicity, a convincing visible success, a tactful and effectual showing of efficiency reflected in an uninterrupted growth in size and other tangible quantitative features. This is good policy as seen from the point of view of competitive business enterprise. In competitive business it is of the gravest importance to keep up the concern's prestige,[1] or "good will." A business concern so placed must be possessed of such prestige as will draw and hold a profitable traffic; otherwise the enterprise is in a precarious case. For the objective end and aim of business enterprise is profitable sales, or the equivalent of such sales if the concern is not occupied with what would strictly be called sales. The end sought is a net gain over costs; in effect, to buy cheap and sell dear. The qualities that count as of prime consequence in business enterprise, therefore, particularly in such business enterprise as has to do with many impressionable customers, are the salesman-like virtues of effrontery[2] and tact. These are high qualities in all business, because their due exercise is believed to bring a net return above the cost of the goods to the seller, and, indeed, above their value to the buyer. Unless the man in competitive business is able, by force of these businesslike aptitudes, to get something more than he gives, it is felt that he has fallen short of the highest efficiency. So the efficient salesman, and similarly the efficiently managed business concern, are enabled to add to their marketable goods an immaterial increment of "prestige value," as some of the economists are calling it. A margin of prepossessions or illusions as to their superior, but intangible and inexpensive, utility attaches to a given line of goods because of the advertiser's or salesman's work—work spent not so much on the goods as on the customer's sensibilities.

---

1. Admiration or respect that someone or something gets for being important or successful.
2. A very confident way of behaving that is rude or shocking.

In case these illusions of superior worth are of an enduring character, they will add an increment of such intangible utility also to goods or other marketable items subsequently to be offered by the same concern; and they can be added up as a presumptive aggregate and capitalized as intangible assets of the business concern in question. Such a body of accumulated and marketable illusions constitute what is known as "good-will," in the stricter sense of the term. The illusions in question need, of course, not be delusions; they may be well or ill founded; for the purpose in hand that is an idle question.

The most familiar and convincing illustrations of such good will are probably those afforded by the sales of patent medicines, and similar proprietary articles of household consumption; but intangible values of a similar nature are involved in nearly all competitive business. They are the product of salesmanship, not of workmanship; and they are useful to the seller, not to the buyer. They are useful for purposes of competitive gain to the businessman, not for serviceability to the community at large, and their value to their possessor lies in the differential advantage which they give to one seller as against another. They have, on the whole, no aggregate value or utility. From the point of view of the common good, work and expenditure so incurred for these competitive purposes are bootless waste.

Under compulsion of such precedents, drawn from the conduct of competitive business, publicity and "goodwill" have come to take a foremost place in the solicitude of the academic directorate.[3] Not that this notoriety and prestige, or the efforts that go to their cultivation, conduce in any appreciable degree to any ostensible purpose avowed, or avowable, by any university. These things, that is to say, rather hinder than help the cause of learning, in that they divert attention and effort from scholarly workmanship to statistics and salesmanship. All that is beyond cavil. The gain which so accrues to any university from such an accession of popular illusions is a differential gain in competition with rival seats of learning, not a gain to the republic of learning or to the academic community at large; and it is a gain in marketable illusions, not in serviceability for the ends of learning or for any other avowed or avowable end sought by the universities. But as competitors for the good-will of the unlettered patrons of learning[4] the university directorates are constrained to keep this need of a reputable notoriety[5] constantly in mind, however little it may all appeal to their own scholarly tastes.

3. A group of managers that controls a company or organization; a board of directors.
4. Doubtless an example of what Veblen has in mind here were the University of Chicago's elaborate quarterly convocation exercises, which were often held in downtown Chicago during his years on the faculty
5. State of being famous or well known for some bad deed or quality.

It is in very large part, if not chiefly, as touches the acquirement of prestige, that the academic work and equipment are amenable to business principles—not overlooking the pervasive system of standardization and accountancy that affects both the work and the equipment, and that serves other purposes as well as those of publicity; so that "business principles" in academic policy comes to mean, chiefly, the principles of reputable publicity. It means this more frequently and more consistently than anything else, so far as regards the academic administration, as distinguished from the fiscal management of the corporation.

Of course, the standards, ideals, principles and procedure of business traffic enter into the scheme of university policy in other relations also, as has already appeared and as will be shown more at large presently; but after all due qualification is had, it remains true that this business of publicity necessarily, or at least commonly, accounts for a disproportionately large share of the business to be taken care of in conducting a university, as contrasted with such an enterprise, e. g., as a bank, a steel works, or a railway company, on a capital of about the same volume. This follows from the nature of the case. The common run of business concerns are occupied with industrial enterprise of some kind, and with transactions in credit—with a running sequence of bargains from which the gains of the concern are to accrue—and it is upon these gains that attention and effort center, and to which the management of the concern constantly looks. Such concerns have to meet their competitors in buying, selling, and effecting contracts of all kinds, from which their gains are to come. A university, on the other hand, can look to no such gains in the work which is its sole ostensible interest and occupation; and the pecuniary transactions and arrangements which it enters into on the basis of its accumulated prestige are a relatively very trivial matter. There is, in short, no appreciable pecuniary gain to be looked for from any traffic resting on the acquired prestige, and therefore there is no relation of equivalence or discrepancy between any outlay incurred in this behalf and the volume of gainful business to be transacted on the strength of it; with the result that the academic directorate applies itself to this pursuit without *arrière pensée*.[6] So far as the acquired prestige is designed to serve a pecuniary end it can only be useful in the way of impressing potential donors, a highly speculative line of enterprise, offering a suggestive parallel to the drawings of a lottery.

Outlay for the purpose of publicity is not confined to the employment of field-agents and the circulation of creditable gossip and reassuring printed matter. The greater share of it comes in as incidental to the installation of plant and equip-

6. French: mental reservation.

ment and the routine of academic life and ceremony. As regards the material equipment, the demands of a creditable appearance are pervading and rigorous; and their consequences in the way of elaborate and premeditated incidentals are, perhaps, here seen at their best. To the laity a "university" has come to mean, in the first place and indispensably, an aggregation of buildings and other improved real-estate.[7] This material equipment strikes the lay attention directly and convincingly; while the pursuit of learning is a relatively obscure matter, the motions of which cannot well be followed by the unlettered, even with the help of the newspapers and the circular literature that issues from the university's publicity bureau. The academic work is, after all, unseen, and it stays in the background. Current expenditure for the prosecution of this work, therefore, offers the enterprise in advertisement a less advantageous field for the convincing use of funds than the material equipment, especially the larger items—laboratory and library buildings, assembly halls, curious museum exhibits, grounds for athletic contests, and the like. There is consequently a steady drift of provocation towards expenditure on conspicuous extensions of the "plant," and a correlative constant temptation to parsimony in the more obscure matter of necessary supplies and service, and similar running expenses without which the plant cannot effectually be turned to account for its ostensible use; with the result, not infrequently, that the usefulness of an imposing plant is seriously impaired for want of what may be called "working capital."[a]

7. Veblen is not exaggerating here. The new visibility of the emerging American university system, as John Thelin has pointed out, was literally most evident in its architecture. With their elaborate landscapes and magnificent buildings, the largest and wealthiest American universities captured popular interest as both new tourist destinations and new sources of national cultural pride. See John R. Thelin, *A History of American Higher Education* (Baltimore: Johns Hopkins University Press, 2004), 115–116.

a. A single illustrative instance may serve to show how the land lies in this respect, even though it may seem to the uninitiated to be an extreme if not an exaggerated case; while it may perhaps strike those familiar with these matters as a tedious commonplace. A few years ago, in one of the larger, younger and more enterprising universities, a commodious laboratory, well-appointed and adequately decorated, was dedicated to one of the branches of biological science. To meet the needs of scientific work such a laboratory requires the services of a corps of experienced and intelligent assistants and caretakers, particularly where the establishment is equipped with modern appliances for heating, ventilation and the like, as was the case in this instance. In this laboratory the necessary warmth was supplied by what is sometimes called the method of indirect steam heat; that is to say, the provision for heat and for ventilation were combined in one set of appliances, by bringing the needed air from the open through an outdoor "intake," passing it over steam-heated coils (in the basement of the building), and so distributing the air necessary for ventilation, at the proper temperature, throughout the building by means of a suitable arrangement of air-shafts. Such was the design. But intelligent service comes high, and ignorant janitors are willing to undertake what may be asked of them. And sufficient warmth can be had in an inclement climate and through a long winter season only at an appreciable expense. So, with a view to economy, and without the knowledge of the scientific staff who made use of the laboratory, the expedient was hit upon by the academic executive, in consultation with a suitable janitor, that the outdoor intake be boarded up tightly. so that the air which passed over the heating coils and through the air-shafts to the laboratory rooms was thenceforth drawn not from the extremely cold atmosphere

Indeed, instances might be cited where funds that were much needed to help out in meeting running expenses have been turned to use for conspicuous extensions of the plant in the way of buildings, in excess not only of what was needed for their alleged purpose but in excess of what could conveniently be made use of. More particularly is there a marked proclivity to extend the plant and the school organization into new fields of scholastic enterprise, often irrelevant or quite foreign to the province of the university as a seminary of learning; and to push these alien ramifications, to the neglect of the urgent needs of the academic work already in hand, in the way of equipment, maintenance, supplies, service and instruction.[8]

The running-expenses are always the most urgent items of the budget, as seen from the standpoint of the academic work; and they are ordinarily the item that is most parsimoniously provided for. A scanty provision at this point unequivocally means a disproportionate curtailment of the usefulness of the equipment as well as of the personnel—as, e.g., the extremely common and extremely unfortunate practice of keeping the allowance for maintenance and service in the university libraries so low as seriously to impair their serviceability. But the exigencies of prestige will easily make it seem more to the point, in the eyes of a businesslike executive, to project a new extension of the plant; which will then be half-employed, on a scanty allowance, in work which lies on the outer fringe or beyond the university's legitimate province.[b]

---

of outdoors but from the more temperate supply that filled the basement and had already had the benefit of circulating over the steam coils and through the ventilating shafts. By this means an obvious saving in fuel would be effected, corresponding to the heat differential between the outdoor air, at some 0° to −20° and that already confined in the building, at some 60°. How long this fuel-saving expedient was in force cannot well be ascertained, but it is known to have lasted at least for more than one season.

The members of the scientific staff meantime mysteriously but persistently fell sick after a few weeks of work in the laboratory, recurrently after each return from enforced vacations. Until, in the end, moved by persistent suspicions of sewer-gas—which, by the way, had in the meantime cost some futile inconvenience and expense occasioned by unnecessary overhauling of the plumbing—one of the staff pried into the janitor's domain in the basement; where he found near the chamber of the steam coils a loosely closed man-hole leading into the sewers, from which apparently such air was drawn as would necessarily go to offset the current leakage from this closed system of ventilation. [Nothing more is known about this episode than what Veblen relates in this note. –Ed.]

b. This is a nearly universal infirmity of American university policy, but it is doubtless not to be set down solely to the account of the penchant for a large publicity on the part of the several academic executives. It is in all likelihood due as much to the equally ubiquitous inability of the governing boards to appreciate or to perceive what the current needs of the academic work are, or even what they are like. Men trained in the conduct of business enterprise, as the governing boards are, will have great difficulty in persuading themselves that expenditures which yield neither increased dividends nor such a durable physical product as can be invoiced and added to the capitalization, can be other than a frivolous waste of good money; so that what is withheld from current academic expenditure is felt to be saved, while that expenditure which leaves a tangible residue of (perhaps useless) real estate is, by force of ingrained habit, rated as new investment.

8. Veblen here describes an ongoing phenomenon in American universities that critics speak of as "mission creep."

In so discriminating against the working capacity of the university, and in favour of its real-estate, this pursuit of reputable publicity further decides that the exterior of the buildings and the grounds should have the first and largest attention. It is true, the initial purpose of this material equipment, it is ostensibly believed, is to serve as housing and appliances for the work of inquiry and instruction. Such, of course, continues to be avowed its main purpose, in a perfunctorily ostensible way. This means a provision of libraries, laboratories, and lecture rooms. The last of these is the least exacting, and it is the one most commonly well supplied. It is also, on the whole, the more conspicuous in proportion to the outlay. But all these are matters chiefly of interior arrangement, appliances and materials, and they are all of a relatively inconspicuous character. Except as detailed in printed statistics they do not ordinarily lend themselves with appreciable effect to the art of advertising. In meeting all these material requirements of the work in hand a very large expenditure of funds might advantageously be made—advantageously to the academic use which they are to serve—without much visible effect as seen in perspective from the outside. And so far as bears on this academic use, the exterior of the buildings is a matter of altogether minor consequence, as are also the decorative appointments of the interior.[9]

In practice, under compulsion of the business principles of publicity, it will be found, however, that the exterior and the decorative appointments are the chief object of the designer's attention; the interior arrangement and working appointments will not infrequently become a matter of rude approximation to the requirements of the work, care being first taken that these arrangements shall not interfere with the decorative or spectacular intent of the outside. But even with the best-advised management of its publicity value, it is always appreciably more difficult to secure appropriations for the material equipment of a laboratory or library than for the shell of the edifice, and still more so for the maintenance of an adequate corps of caretakers and attendants.

As will be found true of other lines of this university enterprise in publicity, so also as to this presentation of a reputable exterior; it is designed to impress not the academic personnel, or the scholarly element at large, but the laity. The academic folk and scholars are commonly less susceptible to the appeal of curious

9. The first buildings of Johns Hopkins University that Veblen encountered as a graduate student in 1881 were separate structures in Baltimore with nothing in their overall plan that gave the university a distinct architectural identity. The same was true of Clark University, which opened in 1887 in one large and utilitarian structure built to house most of its faculty and classrooms. By contrast, both the University of Chicago and Stanford came to life as costly, carefully planned, and self-enclosed campuses, with buildings whose neo-historicist architectural styles—neo-Gothic at Chicago, Mission Revival at Stanford—were thought to represent the proper expression of a great American university. See Paul Venable Turner, *Campus: An American Planning Tradition* (Cambridge, MA: MIT Press, 1984), 163–214.

facades and perplexing feats of architecture; and then, such an appeal would have no particular motive in their case; it is not necessary to impress them. It is in the eyes of the unlettered, particularly the business community, that it is desirable for the university to present an imposing front; that being the feature of academic installation which they will readily appreciate. To carry instant conviction of a high academic worth to this large element of the populace, the university buildings should bulk large in the landscape, should be wastefully expensive, and should conform to the architectural mannerisms in present vogue. In a few years the style of architectural affectations will change, of course, as fashions necessarily change in any community whose tastes are governed by pecuniary standards; and any particular architectural contrivance will therefore presently lose much of its prestige value; but by the time it so is overtaken by obsolescence, the structures which embody the particular affectation in question will have made the appeal for which they were designed, and so will have served their purpose of publicity. And then, too, edifices created with a thrifty view to a large spectacular effect at a low cost are also liable to so rapid a physical decay as to be ready for removal and replacement before they have greatly outlived their usefulness in this respect.

In recent scholastic edifices one is not surprised to find lecture rooms acoustically ill designed, and with an annoying distribution of light, due to the requirements of exterior symmetry and the decorative distribution of windows; and the like holds true even in a higher degree for libraries and laboratories, since for these uses the demands in these respects are even more exacting. Nor is it unusual to find waste of space and weakness of structure, due, e. g., to a fictitious winding stair, thrown into the design to permit such a facade as will simulate the defensive details of a medieval keep, to be surmounted with embrasured battlements and a (make-believe) loop-holed turret. So, again, space will, on the same ground, be wasted in heavy-ceiled, ill-lighted lobbies; which might once have served as a mustering place for a body of unruly men-at-arms, but which mean nothing more to the point today, and in these premises, than so many inconvenient flagstones to be crossed in coming and going.

These principles of spectacular publicity demand a nice adjustment of the conspicuous features of the plant to the current vagaries in decorative art and magnificence, that is to say, conformity to the sophistications current on that level of culture on which these unlettered men of substance live and move and have their being. As touches the case of the seats of learning, these current lay sophistications draw on several more or less diverse, and not altogether congruous, lines of conventionally approved manifestation of the ability to pay. Out of the past comes the conventional preconception that these scholastic edifices should show something of the revered traits of ecclesiastical and monastic real estate; while out of the present comes an ingrained predilection for the more sprightly and exuberant effects of decoration and magnificence to which the modern concert-hall, the more expensive cafes and clubrooms, and the Pullman coaches have given a degree of authentication. Any one given to curious inquiry might find congenial employment in tracing out the manner and proportion in which these, and the like, strains of aesthetic indoctrination are blended in the edifices and grounds of a well-advised modern university.

It is not necessary here to offer many speculations on the enduring artistic merit of these costly stage properties of the seats of learning, since their permanent value in that respect is scarcely to be rated as a substantial motive in their construction. But there is, e. g., no obvious reason why, with the next change in the tide of mannerism, the disjointed grotesqueries of an eclectic and modified Gothic should not presently pass into the same category of apologetic neglect, with the architectural evils wrought by the mid-Victorian generation. But there is another side to this architecture of notoriety, that merits some slight further remark. It is consistently and unavoidably meretricious.[10] Just at present the enjoined vogue is some form of bastard antique.[11] The archaic forms which it ostensibly preserves are structurally out of date, ill adapted to the modern materials and the modern builder's use of materials. Modern building, on a large scale and designed for durable results, is framework building. The modern requirements of light, heating, ventilation and access require it to be such; and the materials used lend themselves to that manner of construction. The strains involved in modern structures are framework strains; whereas the forms which these edifices are required to simulate are masonry forms. The outward conformation and ostensible structure of the buildings, therefore, are commonly meaningless, except as an architectural prevarication. They have to be adapted, simulated, deranged, because in modern use they are impracticable in the shape, proportion and combination that of right belonged to them under the circumstances of materials and uses under which they were once worked out. So there results a meaningless juxtaposition of details, that prove nothing in detail and contradict one another in assemblage. All of which may suggest reflections on the fitness of housing the quest of truth in an edifice of false pretenses.[12]

10. Attracting attention in a vulgar manner.

11. "Bastard antique" probably means neo-Gothic, which was the architectural style that pervaded the nineteen buildings constructed at the University of Chicago during its first decades.

12. In short, as with several other defining features of the new American university system, Veblen believed that its borrowed and ostentatious architectural styles undermined its commitment to "higher learning."

These architectural vagaries serve no useful end in academic life. As an object lesson they conduce, in their measure, to inculcate in the students a spirit of disingenuousness. But they spread abroad the prestige of the university as an ornate and spendthrift establishment; which is believed to bring increased enrolment of students and, what is even more to the point, to conciliate the good-will of the opulent patrons of learning. That these edifices are good for this purpose, and that this policy of architectural *mise en scene*[13] is wise, appears from the greater readiness with which funds are procured for such ornate constructions than for any other academic use. It appears that the successful men of affairs to whom the appeal for funds is directed, find these wasteful, ornate and meretricious edifices a competent expression of their cultural hopes and ambitions.

13. French: stage setting; arrangements of action and machinery for a theatrical production.

CHAPTER V

The Academic Personnel

As regards the personnel[1] of the academic staff the control enforced by the principles of competitive business is more subtle, complex and far-reaching, and should merit more particular attention. The staff is the university—or it should so be if the university is to deserve the place assigned it in the scheme of civilization. Therefore the central and gravest question touching current academic policy is the question of its bearing on the personnel and the work which there is for them to do. In the apprehension of many critics the whole question of university control is comprised in the dealings of the executive with the staff.

Whether the power of appointment vests formally in one man or in a board, in American practice it commonly vests, in effect, in the academic executive. In practice, the power of removal, as well as that of advancement, rests in the same hands. The businesslike requirements of the case bring it to this outcome *de facto*, whatever formalities of procedure may intervene *de jure*.[2]

It lies in the nature of the case that this appointing power will tend to create a faculty after its own kind. It will be quick to recognize efficiency within the lines of its own interests, and slower to see fitness in those lines that lie outside of its horizon, where it must necessarily act on outside solicitation and hearsay evidence.

The selective effect of such a bias, guided as one might say, by a "consciousness of kind,"[3] may be seen in those establishments that have remained under clerical tutelage; where, notoriously, the first qualification looked to in an applicant for work as a teacher is his religious bias. But the bias of these governing boards and executives that are under clerical control has after all been able to effect only a partial, though far-reaching, conformity to clerical ideals of fitness in

---

1. People employed in an organization or engaged in an organized undertaking. Within American colleges and universities during the first decades of the twentieth century, "academic personnel" was routinely used as a synonym for the faculty.

2. Latin: *de facto*: in fact, in deed, actually; *de jure*: based on or according to law.

3. A pleasurable state of mind prompted by innate collective feelings of belonging or similarity. A concept associated with the American sociologist Franklin H. Giddings (1855–1931), which he derived from Adam Smith's (1733–1790) concept of "sympathy" in *Theory of Moral Sentiments* (1759).

the faculties so selected; more especially in the larger and modernized schools of this class. In practice it is found necessary somewhat to wink at devotional short-comings among their teachers; clerical, or pronouncedly devout, scientists that are passably competent in their science, are of very rare occurrence; and yet something presentable in the way of modern science is conventionally required by these schools, in order to live, and so to effect any part of their purpose. Half a loaf is better than no bread. None but the precarious class of schools made up of the lower grade and smaller of these colleges, such as are content to save their souls alive without exerting any effect on the current of civilization, are able to get along with faculties made up exclusively of God-fearing men.

Something of the same kind, and in somewhat the same degree, is true for the schools under the tutelage of businessmen. While the businesslike ideal may be a faculty wholly made up of men highly gifted with business sense, it is not prac-ticable to assemble such a faculty which shall at the same time be plausibly competent in science and scholarship. Scientists and scholars given over to the pursuit of knowledge are conventionally indispensable to a university, and such are commonly not largely gifted with business sense, either by habit or by native gift. The two lines of interest—business and science—do not pull together; a com-petent scientist or scholar well-endowed with business sense is as rare as a de-vout scientist—almost as rare as a white blackbird. Yet the inclusion of men of scientific gifts and attainments among its faculty is indispensable to the univer-sity, if it is to avoid instant and palpable stultification.

So that the most that can practically be accomplished by a businesslike selec-tion and surveillance of the academic personnel will be a compromise; whereby a goodly number of the faculty will be selected on grounds of businesslike fitness, more or less pronounced, while a working minority must continue to be made up of men without much business proficiency and without pronounced loyalty to commercial principles.

This fluctuating margin of limitation has apparently not yet been reached, perhaps not even in the most enterprising of our universities. Such should be the meaning of the fact that a continued commercialization of the academic staff appears still to be in progress, in the sense that businesslike fitness counts pro-gressively for more in appointments and promotions. These businesslike quali-fications do not comprise merely facility in the conduct of pecuniary affairs, even if such facility be conceived to include the special aptitudes and proficiency that go to the making of a successful advertiser. In academic circles as elsewhere busi-nesslike fitness includes solvency as well as commercial genius. Both of these qualifications are useful in the competitive maneuvers in which the academic body is engaged. But while the two are apparently given increasing weight in the selection and grading of the academic personnel, the precedents and specifications for a standard rating of merit in this bearing have hitherto not been worked out to such a nicety as to allow much more than a more or less close approach to a consistent application of the principle in the average case. And there lies always the infirmity in the background of the system that if the staff were selected consistently with an eye single to business capacity and business animus the university would presently be *functa officio*,[4] and the captain of erudition would find his occupation gone.

A university is an endowed institution of culture; whether the endowment take the form of assigned income, as in the state establishments, or of funded wealth, as with most other universities. Such fraction of the income as is assigned to the salary roll, and which therefore comes in question here, is apportioned among the staff for work which has no determinate market value. It is not a matter of *quid pro quo*;[5] since one member of the exchange, the stipend or salary, is measurable in pecuniary terms and the other is not. This work has no business value, in so far as it is work properly included among the duties of the academic men. Indeed, it is a fairly safe test; work that has a commercial value does not belong in the university. Such services of the academic staff as have a business value are those portions of their work that serve other ends than the higher learning; as, e. g., the prestige and pecuniary gain of the institution at large, the pecuniary advantage of a given clique or faction within the university, or the profit and renown of the directive head. Gains that accrue for services of this general character are not, properly speaking, salary or stipend payable toward "the increase and diffusion of knowledge among men," even if they are currently so designated, in the absence of suitable distinctions. Instances of such a diversion of corporate funds to private ends have in the past occurred in certain monastic and priestly orders, as well as in some modern political organizations. Organized malversation[6] of this character has latterly been called "graft." The long-term common sense of the community would presently disavow any corporation of learning overtly pursuing such a course, as being faithless to its trust, and the conservation of learning would so pass into other hands. Indeed, there are facts current which broadly suggest that the keeping of the higher learning is beginning to pass into other, and presumptively more disinterested, hands.

The permeation of academic policy by business principles is a matter of more

---

4. Latin: of no further legal efficacy or official authority.
5. Latin: this for that.
6. Misbehavior; especially corruption in an office, trust, or commission.

or less, not of absolute, dominance. It appears to be a question of how wide a deviation from scholarly singleness of purpose the long-term common sense of the community will tolerate. The cult of the idle curiosity sticks too deep in the instinctive endowment of the race,[7] and it has in modern civilization been too thoroughly ground into the shape of a quest of matter-of-fact knowledge, to allow this pursuit to be definitively set aside or to fall into abeyance. It is by too much an integral constituent of the habits of thought induced by the discipline of work-day life. The faith in and aspiration after matter-of-fact knowledge is too profoundly ingrained in the modern community, and too consonant with its work-day habit of mind, to admit of its supersession by any objective end alien to it—at least for the present and until some stronger force than the technological discipline of modern life shall take over the primacy among the factors of civilization, and so give us a culture of a different character from that which has brought on this modern science and placed it at the center of things human.[8]

The popular approval of business principles and businesslike thrift is profound, disinterested, alert and insistent; but it does not, at least not yet, go the length of unreservedly placing a businesslike exploitation of office above a faithful discharge of trust. The current popular animus may not, in this matter, approach that which animates the business community, specifically so-called, but it is sufficiently "practical" to approve practical sagacity and gainful traffic wherever it is found; yet the furtherance of knowledge is after all an ideal which engages the modern community's affections in a still more profound way, and, in the long run, with a still more unqualified insistence. For good or ill, in the apprehension of the civilized peoples, matter-of-fact knowledge is an end to be sought; while gainful enterprise is, after all, a means to an end. There is, therefore, always this massive hedge of slow but indefeasible popular sentiment that stands in the way of making the seats of learning over into something definitively foreign to the purpose which they are popularly believed to serve.[a]

---

a. It was a very wise and adroit politician who found out that "You cannot fool all the people all the time." [Quotation is part of a famous remark attributed to Abraham Lincoln (1809–65): "You can fool some of the people all of the time, and all of the people some of the time, but you cannot fool all of the people all of the time."]

7. Cf. chapter I, "Introductory," note b.

8. Science was never more revered in the United States than it was in Veblen lifetime, when the findings of "modern science" were for the most part intellectually accessible to the educated lay public. In the late nineteenth and early twentieth century, "science" also was understood more as a method and spirit, than a specific body of knowledge, and so was thought to be easily transferable from physical and biological to other human sciences. Science was not associated with specific disciplines, then, so much as an intellectual process thought to be transmitted by all legitimate academic disciplines. To Veblen's dismay, William Rainey Harper and other university presidents of his day were committed to using "science" to improve society, not just to generate new knowledge and expertise.

Perhaps the most naive way in which a predilection for men of substantial business value expresses itself in university policy is the unobtrusive, and in part
unformulated, preference shown for teachers with sound pecuniary connections,
whether by inheritance or by marriage. With no such uniformity as to give evidence of an advised rule of precedence or a standarized schedule of correlation,
but with sufficient consistency to merit, and indeed to claim, the thoughtful attention of the members of the craft, a scholar who is in a position to plead personal
wealth or a wealthy connection has a perceptibly better chance of appointment
on the academic staff, and on a more advantageous scale of remuneration, than
men without pecuniary antecedents.[9] Due preferment also appears to follow more
as a matter of course where the candidate has or acquires a tangible standing of
this nature.

This preference for well-to-do scholars need by no means be an altogether
blind or impulsive predilection for commercial solvency on the part of the appointing power; though such a predilection is no doubt ordinarily present and
operative in a degree. But there is substantial ground for a wise discrimination
in this respect. As a measure of expediency, particularly the expediency of publicity, it is desirable that the incumbents of the higher stations on the staff should
be able to live on such a scale of conspicuous expensiveness as to make a favorable impression on those men of pecuniary refinement and expensive tastes with
whom they are designed to come in contact. The university should be worthily
represented in its personnel, particularly in such of its personnel as occupy a
conspicuous place in the academic hierarchy; that is to say, it should be represented with becoming expensiveness in all its social contact with those classes
from whose munificence large donations may flow into the corporate funds.
Large gifts of this kind are creditable both to him that gives and him that takes,
and it is the part of wise foresight so to arrange that those to whom it falls to
represent the university, as potential beneficiary, at this juncture should do so
with propitiously creditable circumstance. To meet and convince the opulent patrons of learning, as well as the parents and guardians of possible opulent students, it is, by and large, necessary to meet them on their own ground, and to
bring into view such evidence of culture and intelligence as will readily be appreciated by them. To this end a large and well-appointed domestic establishment is

9. A quantitative study of the socioeconomic background of American university professors in
Veblen's time found that the largest number had businessmen for fathers, although ministers, farm-
ers, and other established professions were also well represented. In 1915, a study of 885 leading
American scientists (not all of whom were professors) showed that the fathers of 381 were professional
men; 188 fathers were farmers; and 316 were businessmen. See Laurence Veysey, *The Emergence of the
American University* (Chicago: University of Chicago Press, 1965), 300–301, n. 134.

more fortunate than a smaller one; abundant, well-chosen and well-served viands, beverages and narcotics will also felicitously touch the sensibilities of these men who are fortunate enough to have learned their virtue; the better, that is to say, on the whole, the more costly, achievements in dress and equipage will "carry farther" in these premises than a penurious economy. In short, it is well that those who may be called to stand spokesmen for the seat of learning in its contact with men and women of substantial means, should be accustomed to, and should be pecuniarily competent for, a scale of living somewhat above that which the ordinary remuneration for academic work will support. An independent income, therefore, is a meritorious quality in an official scholar.[10]

The introduction of these delegates from the well-to-do among the academic personnel has a further, secondary effect that is worth noting. Their ability freely to meet any required pecuniary strain, coupled with that degree of social ambition that commonly comes with the ability to pay, will have a salutary effect in raising the standard of living among the rest of the staff—salutary as seen from the point of view of the bureau of publicity. In the absence of outside resources, the livelihood of academic men is somewhat scant and precarious. This places them under an insidious temptation to a more parsimonious manner of life than the best (prestige) interests of the seat of learning would dictate. By undue saving out of their current wages they may easily give the academic establishment an untoward[11] air of indigence, such as would be likely to depreciate its prestige in those well-to-do circles where such prestige might come to have a commercial value, in the way of donations, and it might at the same time deter possible customers of the same desirable class from sending their young men to the university as students.

The American university is not an eleemosynary institution; it does not plead indigence, except in that Pickwickian[12] sense in which indigence may without shame be avowed in polite circles; nor does it put its trust in donations of that sparseness and modesty which the gifts of charity commonly have. Its recourse necessarily is that substantial and dignified class of gifts that are not given thriftily on compunction of charity, but out of the fullness of the purse. These dignified

10. "Well-to-do scholars" had other advantages Veblen does not mention. At a time when university funds for research were relatively scarce, they could pay for research expenses not supported by extramural resources. Some also were not shy about approaching Board members to support their work, although this typically was through the mediation of the President's Office. The early twentieth-century American professoriate was closed in other ways Veblen does not mention either: almost all were white, male, Protestant, and East Coast Americans.

11. Not proper or appropriate.

12. Resembling the character of Samuel Pickwick in Charles Dickens's (1812–1870) *The Pickwick Papers* (1836), especially in being naively kind or benevolent.

gifts commonly aim to promote the most reputable interests of humanity, rather than the sordid needs of creature comfort, at the same time that they serve to fortify the donor' s good name in good company. Donations to university funds have something of the character of an investment in good fame; they are made by gentlemen and gentlewomen, to gentlemen, and the transactions begin and end within the circle of pecuniary respectability. An impeccable respectability, authentic in the pecuniary respect, therefore, affords the only ground on which such a seminary of learning can reasonably claim the sympathetic attention of the only class whose attentions are seriously worth engaging in these premises; and respectability is inseparable from an expensive scale of living, in any community whose scheme of life is conventionally regulated by pecuniary standards.

It is accordingly expedient, for its collective good repute, that the members of the academic staff should conspicuously consume all their current income in current expenses of living. Hence also the moral obligation incumbent on all members of the staff—and their households—to take hands and help in an end-less chain of conspicuously expensive social amenities, where their social profi-ciency and their ostensible ability to pay may effectually be placed on view. An effectual furtherance to this desirable end is the active presence among the staff of an appreciable number who are ready to take the lead at a pace slightly above the competency of the common run of university men. Their presence insures that the general body will live up to their limit; for in this, as in other games of emulation, the pace maker is invaluable.

Besides the incentive so given to polite expenditure by the presence of a highly solvent minority among the academic personnel, it has also been found expedient that the directorate take thought and institute something in the way of an authen-tic curriculum of academic festivities and exhibitions of social proficiency. A de-gree of expensive gentility is in this way propagated by authority, to be paid for in part out of the salaries of the faculty.

Something in this way of ceremonial functions and public pageants has long been included in the ordinary routine of the academic year among the higher American schools. It dates back to the time when they were boys' schools under the tutelage of the clergy, and it appears to have had a ritualistic origin, such as would comport with what is found expedient in the service of the church. By re-moter derivation it should probably be found to rest on a very ancient and archaic faith in the sacramental or magical efficacy of ceremonial observances. But the present state of the case can by no means be set down to the account of aimless survival alone. Instead of being allowed in any degree to fall into abeyance by neglect, the range and magnitude of such observances have progressively grown appreciably greater since the principles of competitive business have come to rule the counsels of the universities. The growth, in the number of such observances, in their pecuniary magnitude, in their ritualistic circumstance, and in the importance attached to them, is greater in the immediate present than at any period in the past; and it is, significantly, greater in those larger new establishments that have started out with few restraints of tradition. But the move so made by these younger, freer, more enterprising seats of learning falls closely in with that spirit of competitive enterprise that animates all alike though unequally.[b]

That it does so, that this efflorescence of ritual and pageantry[13] intimately belongs in the current trend of things academic, is shown by the visible proclivity of the older institutions to follow the lead given in this matter by the younger ones, so far as the younger ones have taken the lead. In the mere number of authorized events, as contrasted with the average of some twenty-five or thirty years back, the present average appears, on a somewhat deliberate review of the available data, to compare as three or four to one. For certain of the younger and more exuberant seats of learning today, as compared with what may be most nearly comparable in the academic situation of the eighties, the proportion is perhaps twice as large as the larger figure named above. Broadly speaking, no requirement of the academic routine should be allowed to stand in the way of an available occasion for a scholastic pageant.

These genteel solemnities, of course, have a cultural significance, probably of a high order, both as occasions of rehearsal in all matters of polite conformity and as a stimulus to greater refinement and proficiency in expenditure on seemly dress and equipage. They may also be believed to have some remote, but presumably salutary, bearing on the higher learning. This latter is an obscure point, on which it would be impossible at present to offer anything better than abstruse speculative considerations; since the relation of these genteel exhibitions to scientific inquiry or instruction is of a peculiarly intangible nature. But it is none of these cultural bearings of any such round of polite solemnities and stately pageants

---

b. *La gloria di colui che tutto muove,*
  Per l'universo penétra e risplende
  In una parte più e meno altr'ove.

[Italian quoted from Dante's *The Paradiso,* canto I, lines 1–3: "The glory of Him who moves all things rays forth / through all the universe and is reflected / from each thing in proportion to its worth." English translation from *The Paradiso,* trans. John Ciardi (New York: The New American Library, 1961), 24. –Ed.]

13. William Rainey Harper was a well-known devotee of "ritual and pageantry." During his years as president of the University of Chicago, he frequently called administrators and faculty to don caps and gowns, partly because Chicago then granted degrees at quarterly convocations rather than at a single convocation at the end of the year. Ritual and pageantry were especially prominent in 1896 and 1901, when the university celebrated its fifth and tenth anniversaries.

that comes in question here. It is their expediency in point of businesslike enterprise, or perhaps rather their businesslike motive, on the one hand, and their effect upon the animus and efficiency of the academic personnel, on the other hand.

In so far as their motive should not (by unseemly imputation) be set down to mere boyish exuberance of make-believe, it must be sought among considerations germane to that business enterprise that rules academic policy. However attractive such a derivation might seem, this whole traffic in pageantry and ceremonial amenities cannot be traced back to ecclesiastical ground, except in point of remote pedigree; it has grown greater since the businessmen took over academic policy out of the hands of the clergy. Nor can it be placed to the account of courtly, diplomatic, or military antecedents or guidance; these fields of activity, while they are good breeding ground for pomp and circumstance, do not overlap, or even seriously touch, the frontiers of the republic of learning. On the other hand, in seeking grounds or motives for it all, it is also not easy to find any close analogy in the field of business enterprise of the larger sort, that has to do with the conduct of industry. There is little of this manner of expensive public ceremonial and solemn festivities to be seen, e. g., among business concerns occupied with railroading or banking, in cotton-spinning, or sugar-refining, or in farming, shipping, coal, steel, or oil. In this field phenomena of this general class are of rare occurrence, sporadic at the best; and when they occur they will commonly come in connection with competitive sales of products, services or securities, particularly the latter. Nearer business analogues will be found in retail merchandising, and in enterprises of popular amusement, such as concert halls, beer gardens, or itinerant shows. The street parades of the latter, e. g., show a seductive, though, it is believed, misleading analogy to the ceremonial pageants that round off the academic year.

Phenomena that come into view in the later and maturer growth of the retail trade, as seen, e. g., in the larger and more reputable department stores, are perhaps nearer the point. There are formal "openings" to inaugurate the special trade of each of the four seasons, desired to put the patrons of the house on a footing of good-humored familiarity with the plant and its resources, with the customs of the house, the personnel and the stock of wares in hand, and before all to arrest the attention and enlist the interest of those classes that may be induced to buy. There are also occasional gatherings of a more ceremonial character, by special invitation of select customers to a promised exhibition of peculiarly rare and curious articles of trade. This will then be illuminated with shrewdly conceived harangues setting forth the alleged history, adventures and merits, past and future, of the particular branch of the trade, and of the particular house at whose expense the event is achieved. In addition to these seasonal and occasional set pieces of mercantile ceremony, there will also run along in the day's work an unremitting display of meritorious acts of commission and omission. Like their analogues in academic life these ceremonials of trade are expensive, edifying, enticing, and surrounded with a solicitous regard for publicity; and it will be seen that they are, all and several, expedients of advertising.

To return to the academic personnel and their implication in these recurrent spectacles and amenities of university life. As was remarked above, apart from outside resources the livelihood that comes to a university man is, commonly, somewhat meagre. The tenure is uncertain and the salaries, at an average, are not large. Indeed, they are notably low in comparison with the high conventional standard of living which is by custom incumbent on university men. University men are conventionally required to live on a scale of expenditure comparable with that in vogue among the well-to-do businessmen, while their university incomes compare more nearly with the lower grades of clerks and salesmen. The rate of pay varies quite materially, as is well known. For the higher grades of the staff, whose scale of pay is likely to be publicly divulged, it is, perhaps, adequate to the average demands made on university incomes by polite usage; but the large majority of university men belong on the lower levels of grade and pay; and on these lower levels the pay is, perhaps, lower than any outsider appreciates.[c]

c. In a certain large and enterprising university, e. g., the pay of the lowest, and numerous, rank regularly employed to do full work as teachers, is proportioned to that of the highest—much less numerous—rank about as one to twelve at the most, perhaps even as low as one to twenty. And it may not be out of place to enter the caution that the nominal rank of a given member of the staff is no secure index of his income, even where the salary "normally" attached to the given academic rank is known. Not unusually a "normal" scale of salaries is formally adopted by the governing board and spread upon their records, and such a scale will then be surreptitiously made public. But departures from the scale habitually occur, whereby the salaries actually paid come to fall short of the "normal" perhaps as frequently as they conform to it.

There is no trades-union among university teachers, and no collective bargaining. There appears to be a feeling prevalent among them that their salaries are not of the nature of wages, and that there would be a species of moral obliquity implied in overtly so dealing with the matter. And in the individual bargaining by which the rate of pay is determined the directorate may easily be tempted to seek an economical way out, by offering a low rate of pay coupled with a higher academic rank. The plea is always ready to hand that the university is in want of the necessary funds and is constrained to economize where it can. So an advance in nominal rank is made to serve in place of an advance in salary, the former being the less costly commodity for the time being. Indeed, so frequent are such departures from the normal scale as to have given rise to the (no doubt ill-advised) suggestion that this may be one of the chief uses of the adopted schedule of normal salaries. So an employee of the university may not infrequently find himself constrained to accept, as part payment, an expensive increment of dignity attaching to a higher rank than his salary account would indicate. Such an outcome of individual bargaining is all the more likely in the academic community, since there is no settled code of professional ethics governing the conduct of business enterprise in academic management, as contrasted with the traffic of ordinary competitive business. [Veblen again paints too bleak a picture here, perhaps in part because it appears that he largely completed the manuscript of *The Higher Learning in America* before

With men circumstanced as the common run of university men are, the temptation to parsimony is ever present, while on the other hand, as has already been noted, the prestige of the university—and of the academic head—demands of all its members a conspicuously expensive manner of living. Both of these needs may, of course, be met in some poor measure by saving in the obscurer items of domestic expense, such as food, clothing, heating, lighting, floor-space, books, and the like; and making all available funds count toward the collective end of reputable publicity, by throwing the stress on such expenditures as come under the public eye, as dress and equipage, bric-a-brac, amusements, public entertainments, etc. It may seem that it should also be possible to cut down the proportion of obscure expenditures for creature comforts by limiting the number of births in the family, or by foregoing marriage. But, by and large, there is reason to believe that this expedient has been exhausted. As men have latterly been at pains to show, the current average of children in academic households is not high; whereas the percentage of celibates is. There appears, indeed, to be little room for additional economy on this head, or in the matter of household thrift, beyond what is embodied in the family budgets already in force in academic circles.

So also, the tenure of office is somewhat precarious; more so than the documents would seem to indicate. This applies with greater force to the lower grades than to the higher. Latterly, under the rule of business principles, since the prestige value of a conspicuous consumption has come to a greater currency in academic policy, a member of the staff may render his tenure more secure, and may perhaps assure his due preferment, by a sedulous attention to the academic social amenities, and to the more conspicuous items of his expense account; and he will then do well in the same connection also to turn his best attention in the day's work to administrative duties and schoolmasterly discipline, rather than to the increase of knowledge. Whereas he may make his chance of preferment less assured, and may even jeopardize his tenure, by a conspicuously parsimonious manner of life, or by too pronounced an addiction to scientific or scholarly pur-

---

the American Association of University Professors (AAUP) was founded in 1915 (Cf. chapter III, "The Academic Administration," note 28.) The AAUP was not an academic trade union. In the two years after its founding, however, more than thirty complaints of alleged infractions of academic freedom were brought to the attention of its new Committee A: the Committee on Academic Freedom and Tenure, which was the successor to the committee of university professors that had drafted the AAUP's founding 1915 *Declaration of Principles on Academic Freedom and Tenure*. In 1916 and 1917, Committee A's published reports outlined procedures that the AAUP set in place to investigate future alleged infractions. These procedures included factual inquiry, attempted conciliation, and—in especially difficult cases—investigation by an *ad hoc* committee. Since then, a steady stream of AAUP's Committee A reports has developed into a small library of scholarly commentary on the subjects of academic freedom and tenure. –Ed.]

suits, to the neglect of those polite exhibitions of decorum that conduce to the maintenance of the university's prestige in the eyes of the (pecuniarily) cultured laity.

A variety of other untoward circumstances, of a similarly extra-scholastic bearing, may affect the fortunes of academic men to a like effect; as, e. g., unearned newspaper notoriety that may be turned to account in ridicule; unconventional religious, or irreligious convictions—so far as they become known; an undesirable political affiliation; an impecunious marriage, or such domestic infelicities as might become subject of remark. None of these untoward circumstances need touch the serviceability of the incumbent for any of the avowed, or avowable, purposes of the seminary of learning; and where action has to be taken by the directorate on provocation of such circumstances it is commonly done with the (unofficial) admission that such action is taken not on the substantial merits of the case but on compulsion of appearances and the exigencies of advertising. That some such effect should be had follows from the nature of things, so far as business principles rule.

In the degree, then, in which these and the like motives of expediency are decisive, there results a husbanding of time, energy and means in the less conspicuous expenditures and duties, in order to a freer application to more conspicuous uses, and a meticulous cultivation of the bourgeois virtues. The workday duties of instruction, and more particularly of inquiry, are, in the nature of the case, less conspicuously in evidence than the duties of the drawing room, the ceremonial procession, the formal dinner, or the grandstand on some red-letter day of intercollegiate athletics.[d] For the purposes of a reputable notoriety the everyday work of the classroom and laboratory is also not so effective as lectures to popular audiences outside; especially, perhaps, addresses before an audience of devout and well-to-do women. Indeed, all this is well approved by experience.

d. So, e. g., the well-known president of a well and favorably known university was at pains a few years ago to distinguish one of his faculty as being his "ideal of a university man"; the grounds of this invidious distinction being a lifelike imitation of a country gentleman and a fair degree of attention to committee work in connection with the academic administration; the incumbent had no distinguishing marks either as a teacher or as a scholar, and neither science nor letters will be found in his debt. It is perhaps needless to add that for reasons of invidious distinction, no names can be mentioned in this connection. It should be added in illumination of the instance cited, that in the same university, by consistent selection and discipline of the personnel, it had come about that, in the apprehension of the staff as well as of the executive, the accepted test of efficiency was the work done on the administrative committees—rather than that of the class rooms or laboratories. [The "well-known president" Veblen alludes to here probably is Nicholas Murray Butler (1862–1947), president of Columbia University from 1901 to 1945, who once told the Columbia faculty that he expected them to observe one simple rule when it came to controversial issues: "behave like a gentleman." (On Butler, cf. chapter III, "The Academic Administration," note d.) –Ed.]

In many and devious ways, therefore, a university man may be able to serve the collective enterprise of his university to better effect than by an exclusive attention to the scholastic work on which alone he is ostensibly engaged.

Among the consequences that follow is a constant temptation for the members of the staff to take on work outside of that for which the salary is nominally paid. Such work takes the public eye; but a further incentive to go into this outside and non-academic work, as well as to take on supernumerary work within the academic schedule, lies in the fact that such outside or supernumerary work is specially paid, and so may help to eke out a sensibly scant livelihood. So far as touches the more scantily paid grades of university men, and so far as no alien considerations come in to trouble the working-out of business principles, the outcome may be schematized somewhat as follows. These men have, at the outset, gone into the university presumably from an inclination to scholarly or scientific pursuits; it is not probable that they have been led into this calling by the pecuniary inducements, which are slight as compared with the ruling rates of pay in the open market for other work that demands an equally arduous preparation and an equally close application. They have then been apportioned rather more work as instructors than they can take care of in the most efficient manner, at a rate of pay which is sensibly scant for the standard of (conspicuous) living conventionally imposed on them. They are, by authority, expected to expend time and means in such polite observances, spectacles and quasi-learned exhibitions as are presumed to enhance the prestige of the university. They are so induced to divert their time and energy to spreading abroad the university's good repute by creditable exhibitions of a quasi-scholarly character, which have no substantial bearing on a university man's legitimate interests; as well as in seeking supplementary work outside of their mandatory schedule, from which to derive an adequate livelihood and to fill up the complement of politely wasteful expenditures expected of them. The academic instruction necessarily suffers by this diversion of forces to extra-scholastic objects; and the work of inquiry, which may have primarily engaged their interest and which is indispensable to their continued efficiency as teachers, is, in the common run of cases, crowded to one side and presently drops out of mind. Like other workmen, under pressure of competition the members of the academic staff will endeavor to keep up their necessary income by cheapening their product and increasing their marketable output. And by consequence of this pressure of bread-winning and genteel expenditure, these university men are so barred out from the serious pursuit of those scientific and scholarly inquiries which alone can, academically speaking, justify their retention on the university faculty, and for the sake of which, in great part at least, they have chosen this vocation. No infirmity more commonly besets university men than this going to seed in routine work and extra-scholastic duties. They have entered on the academic career to find time, place, facilities and congenial environment for the pursuit of knowledge, and under pressure they presently settle down to a round of perfunctory labor by means of which to simulate the life of gentlemen.[e]

Before leaving the topic it should further be remarked that the dissipation incident to these polite amenities, that so are incumbent on the academic personnel, apparently also has something of a deteriorative effect on their working capacity, whether for scholarly or for worldly uses. *Prima facie* evidence to this effect might be adduced, but it is not easy to say how far the evidence would bear closer scrutiny. There is an appreciable amount of dissipation, in its several sorts, carried forward in university circles in an inconspicuous manner, and not designed for publicity. How far this is induced by a loss of interest in scholarly work, due to the habitual diversion of the scholars' energies to other and more exacting duties, would be hard to say; as also how far it may be due to the lead given by men-of-the-world retained on the faculties for other than scholarly reasons. At the same time there is the difficulty that many of those men who bear a large part in the ceremonial dissipation incident to the enterprise in publicity are retained, apparently, for their proficiency in this line as much as for their scholarly attainments, or at least so one might infer; and these men must be accepted with the defects of their qualities.

As bearing on this whole matter of pomp and circumstance, social amenities and ritual dissipation, quasi-learned demonstrations and meretricious publicity, in academic life, it is difficult beyond hope of a final answer to determine how much of it is due directly to the masterful initiative of the strong man who directs the enterprise, and how much is to be set down to an innate proclivity for all that sort of thing on the part of the academic personnel. A near view of these phenomena leaves the impression that there is, on the whole, less objection felt than expressed among the academic men with regard to this routine of demonstration;

---

e. Within the past few years an academic executive of great note has been heard repeatedly to express himself in facetious doubt of this penchant for scholarly inquiry on the part of university men, whether as "reseárch" or as "résearch"; and there is doubtless ground for scepticism as to its permeating the academic body with that sting of ubiquity that is implied in many expressions on this head. And it should also be said, perhaps in extenuation of the expression cited above, that the president was addressing delegations of his own faculty, and presumably directing his remarks to their special benefit; and that while he professed (no doubt ingenuously) a profound zeal for the cause of science at large, it had come about, selectively, through a long course of sedulous attention on his own part to all other qualifications than the main fact, that his faculty at the time of speaking was in the main an aggregation of slack-twisted schoolmasters and men about town. Such a characterization, however, does not carry any gravely invidious discrimination, nor will it presumably serve in any degree to identify the seat of learning to which it refers. [The "academic executive" alluded to here is unidentified. –Ed.]

that the reluctance with which they pass under the ceremonial yoke is not altogether ingenuous; all of which would perhaps hold true even more decidedly as applied to the faculty households.[f] But for all that, it also remains true that without the initiative and countenance of the executive head these boyish movements of sentimental spectacularity on the part of the personnel would come to little, by comparison with what actually takes place. It is after all a matter for executive discretion, and, from whatever motives, this diversion of effort to extra-scholastic ends has the executive sanction;[g] with the result that an intimate familiarity with current academic life is calculated to raise the question whether make-believe does not, after all, occupy a larger and more urgent place in the life of these thoughtful adult male citizens than in the life of their children.

f. The share and value of the "faculty wives" in all this routine of resolute conviviality is a large topic, an intelligent and veracious account of which could only be a work of naive brutality:

"But the grim, grim Ladies, Oh, my brothers!
    They are ladling bitterly.
They are ladling in the work-time of the others,
    In the country of the free."

(Mrs. Elizabret Harte Browning, in *The Cry of the Heathen Chinee*.)

[Veblen is having fun with his readers here. He has fashioned a fictitious poet and a fictitious poem bearing a name and a title that are hybrid echoes of two real poets and two real poems: Elizabeth Barrett Browning's (1806–61) "The Cry of the Children" (1843) and Bret Harte's (1836–1902) "The Heathen Chinee" (1870). Browning's once widely read poem condemned child labor in England and helped bring about child labor reforms; Harte's poem was a satire of anti-Chinese sentiment in Northern California. –Ed.]

g. What takes place without executive sanction need trouble no one.

CHAPTER VI

The Portion of the Scientist

The principles of business enterprise touch the life and work of the academic staff at diverse points and with various effect. Under their rule, and in so far as they rule, the remuneration shifts from the basis of a stipend designed to further the pursuit of knowledge, to that of a wage bargain, partaking of the nature of a piece-work scheme, designed to procure class-room instruction at the lowest practicable cost. A businesslike system of accountancy standardizes and measures this instruction by mechanically gauged units of duration and number, amplitude and frequency, and so discountenances work that rises above a staple grade of mediocrity. Usage and the urgent need of a reputable notoriety impose on university men an extraneous and excessively high standard of living expenses, which constrains them to take on supernumerary work in excess of what they can carry in an efficient manner. The need of university prestige enforces this high scale of expenses, and also pushes the members of the staff into a routine of polite dissipation, ceremonial display, exhibitions of quasi-scholarly proficiency and propagandist intrigue.

If these business principles were quite free to work out their logical consequences, untroubled by any disturbing factors of an un-businesslike nature, the outcome should be to put the pursuit of knowledge definitively in abeyance within the university, and to substitute for that objective something for which the language hitherto lacks a designation.

For diverse reasons of an un-businesslike kind, such a consummate ("sweat-shop"[1]) scheme has never fully been achieved, particularly not in establishments that are, properly speaking, of anything like university grade. This perfect scheme of low-cost perfunctory instruction, high-cost stage properties and press-agents, public song and dance, expensive banquets, speech-making and processions, is never fully rounded out. This amounts to admitting a partial defeat for the gild of businesslike "educators." While, as a matter of speculative predilection, they may

1. Place where people work long hours for low pay and in unhealthy conditions.

not aim to leave the higher learning out of the university, the rule of competitive business principles consistently pushes their administration toward that end; which they are continually prevented from attaining, by the necessary conditions under which their competitive enterprise is carried on.

For better or worse, there are always and necessarily present among the academic corps a certain number of men whose sense of the genteel properties is too vague and meagre, whose grasp of the principles of official preferment is too weak and inconsequential, whose addiction to the pursuit of knowledge is too ingrained, to permit their conforming wholly to the competitive exigencies of the case. By force of the exigencies of competitive prestige there is, of course, a limit of tolerance that sets decent bounds both to the number of such supererogatory[2] scholars harbored by the university, and the latitude allowed them in their intemperate pursuit of knowledge; but their presence in the academic body is, after all, neither an irrelevant accident nor a transient embarrassment. It is, in one sense of the expression, for the use of such men, and for the use which such men find for it, that the university exists at all; in some such sense, indeed, as a government, a political machine, a railway corporation or a toll-road, may be said to exist for the use of the community from which they get their living. It is true in the sense that this ostensible use cannot be left out of account in the long run. But even from day to day this scholarly purpose is never quite lost sight of. The habit of counting it in, as a matter of course, affects all concerned, in some degree; and complacent professions of faith to that effect cross one another from all quarters. It may frequently happen that the enterprising men in whom academic discretion centers will have no clear conception of what is implied in this scholarly purpose to which they give a perfunctory matter-of-course endorsement, and much of their professions on that head may be *ad captandum;*[3] but that it need be a matter of course argues that it must be counted with.

Still, in the degree in which business principles rule the case the outcome will be of much the same complexion as it might be in the absence of any such prepossession, intelligent or otherwise, in favor of the higher learning on the part of the directorate; for competition has the same effect here as elsewhere, in that it permits none of the competitors to forego any expedient that has been found advantageous by any one of them. So that, whatever course might be dictated by the sentiments of the directorate, the course enjoined by the principles of competitive business sets toward the suppression or elimination of all such scholarly or scien-

2. Superfluous, unnecessary.
3. Latin: designed to attract or please a crowd, often used to describe an argument designed to appeal chiefly to the emotions.

tific work from the university as does not contribute immediately to its prestige—except so far as the conditions alluded to make such a course impracticable.

It is not an easy or a graceful matter for a businesslike executive to get rid of any un-decorative or indecorous scientist, whose only fault is an unduly pertinacious pursuit of the work for which alone the university claims to exist, whose failure consists in living up to the professions of the executive instead of professing to live up to them. Academic tradition gives a broad, though perhaps uncertain, sanction to the scientific spirit that moves this obscure element in the academic body. And then, their more happily gifted, more worldly-wise colleagues have also a degree of respect for such a single-minded pursuit of knowledge, even while they may view these naive children of impulse with something of an amused compassion; for the general body of the academic staff is still made up largely of men who have started out with scholarly ideals, even though these ideals may have somewhat fallen away from them under the rub of expediency. At least in a genial, speculative sense of the phrase, scholarship still outranks official preferment in the esteem of the generality of academic men, particularly so long as the question does not become personal and touch their own preferment. In great part the academic corps still understands and appreciates the scholarly animus, and looks, on the whole, kindly and sympathetically—indeed, with a touch of envy—on those among them who are so driven to follow their own scientific bent, to the neglect of expedient gentility and publicity.

The like can, of course, not be so freely said of that body of businessmen in whom is vested the final control; yet this sentiment of genial approval that pervades the academic body finds some vague response even among these; and in any event it is always to be reckoned with and is not to be outraged, unless for a good and valuable consideration. It cannot altogether be set aside, although, it is true, the conduct of certain executive heads, grown old in autocratic rule and self-complacency, may at times appear to argue the contrary. So that, by and large, there results an unstable compromise between the requirements of scholarly fitness and those of competitive enterprise, with a doubtful and shifting issue. Just at present, under the firm hand of an enterprising and autocratic executive, the principles of competitive business are apparently gaining ground in the greater universities, where the volume of traffic helps to cloud the details of suppression, and the cult of learning is gradually falling into a more precarious position.

In a curious way, too, the full swing of business principles in academic life is hindered by the necessary ways and means through which these principles are worked out; so much so, indeed, as to throw a serious doubt on their ultimately achieving an undivided dominion. Taken as a business concern, the university is

in a very singular position. The reason for its being, at all, is the educational aspiration that besets modern mankind. Its only ostensible reason for being, and so
for its being governed and managed, competitively or otherwise, is the advancement of learning. And this advancement of learning is in no degree a business
proposition; and yet it must, for the present at least, remain the sole ostensible
purpose of the businesslike university. In the main, therefore, all the competitive
endeavors and maneuvers of the captains of erudition in charge must be made
under cover of an ostensible endeavor to further this non-competitive advancement of learning, at all costs. Since learning is not a competitive matter; since,
indeed, competition in any guise or bearing in this field is detrimental to learning;[4] the competitive maneuvers of the academic executive must be carried on
surreptitiously, in a sense, cloaked as a non-competitive campaign for the increase
of knowledge without fear or favor.

All this places the executive in a very delicate position. On the one hand the
principles of competitive business, embodied in a plenary board of control and in
a critical scrutiny from the side of the business community at large, demand that
all appointments, promotions, dismissals, ceremonials, pronouncements and expenditures, must be made with a constant view to their highest advertising effect;
whereas the notions current as to what is fitting in a seminary of the higher
learning, on the other hand, somewhat incongruously demand that all these
deeds of commission and omission be done with an eye single to the increase of
knowledge, regardless of appearances. And this double responsibility falls, of necessity, on the executive head of the university, under the present régime of centralized autocratic rule. Any ethical code that shall permit the executive head to
accomplish what is expected of him in the way of a competitive enterprise under
these circumstances, will necessarily be vague and shifty, not to say tenuous and
shadowy; and man who have tried to do their whole duty in these premises are
ready to admit that they have been called on to face many distasteful situations,
where honesty would not approve itself as the best policy.[a]

Whatever expedients of decorative real-estate, spectacular pageantry, bureaucratic
magnificence, elusive statistics, vocational training, genteel solemnities and sweat-
shop instruction, may be imposed by the exigencies of a competitive business
policy, the university is after all a seat of learning, devoted to the cult of the idle

a. Cf. John Jay Chapman (1862–1933), "Professional Ethics," in *University Control*, 453–61, for an
estimate of the inefficiency of academic opinion as a corrective of the executive power on his head.
[Chapman graduated from Harvard in 1884, studied at Harvard Law School, and then practiced law
before pursuing a career as a reforming American editor and writer –Ed.]
4. Cf. chapter II, "The Academic Administration," note 14.

curiosity—otherwise called the scientific spirit. And stultification, broad and final, waits on any university directorate that shall dare to avow any other end as its objective. So the appearance of an unwavering devotion to the pursuit of knowledge must be kept up. Hence the presence of scholars and scientists of accepted standing is indispensable to the university, as a means of keeping up its prestige. The need of them may be a need of their countenance rather than of their work, but they are indispensable, and they bring with them the defects of their qualities. When a man achieves such notoriety for scientific attainments as to give him a high value as an article of parade, the chances are that he is endowed with some share of the scientific animus, and he is likely to have fallen into the habit of rating the triumphs of science above those of the market place. Such a person will almost unavoidably affect the spirit of any academic corps into which he is intruded. He will also, in a measure, bend the forces of the establishment to a long-term efficiency in the pursuit of knowledge, rather than to the pursuit of a reputable notoriety from day to day. To the enterprising captain of erudition he is likely to prove costly and inconvenient, but he is unavoidable.

This will hold true in a general way, and with due exceptions, for men prominent in those material sciences that have to do with data of such a tangible character, and give their results in such terms of mechanical fact, as to permit a passably close appreciation of their worth by the laity. It applies only more loosely, with larger exceptions and a wider margin of error, in the humanities and the so-called moral and social sciences. In this latter field a clamorous conformity to current prepossessions, particularly the conventional prepossessions of respectability, or an edifying and incisive rehearsal of commonplaces, will commonly pass in popular esteem for scholarly and scientific merit. A truculent quietism is often accepted as a mark of scientific maturity. The reason for this will appear presently. But so far as popular esteem is a truthful index of scientific achievement. the proposition holds, that scientists who have done great things have a business value to the captain of erudition as a means of advancing the university's prestige; and so far the indicated consequences follow. In some measure the scientific men so intruded into the academic body are in a position to give a direction to affairs within their field and within the framework of the general policy. They are able to claim rank and discretion, and their choice, or at least their assent, must be consulted in the selection of their subalterns, and in a degree also in the organization of the department's work. It is true, men whose talent, interest and experience run chiefly within the lines of scientific inquiry, are commonly neither skilled nor shrewd managers in that give and take of subtleties and ambiguities by which the internal machinery of the university is kept in line and running under a businesslike administration; but even so, their aims and prepossessions will in a measure affect the animus and shape the work of the academic body. All this applies particularly on the higher levels of research, as contrasted with the commonplace (undergraduate) work of instruction. But at this point, therefore, the principles of competitive publicity carry with them a partial neutralization of their own tendency.

This necessity of employing scientists of a commanding force and rank raises a point of some delicacy in the administration of the competitive university. It is necessary to assign these men a relatively high rank in the academic hierarchy; both because they will accept no subordinate place and because the advertising value of their prestige will be curtailed by reducing them to an inconspicuous position. And with high rank is necessarily associated a relatively large discretion and a wide influence in academic affairs, at least on the face of things. Such men, so placed, are apt to be exacting in matters which they conceive to bear on the work in their own sciences, and their exactions may not be guided chiefly by the conspicuousness of the equipment which they require or of the results at which they aim. They are also not commonly adroit men of affairs, in the business sense of the term; not given to conciliatory compromises and an exhibition of complaisant statistics. The framing of shrewd lines of competitive strategy, and the bureaucratic punctilios of university administration, do not commonly engage their best interest, even if it does not stir them to an indecorous impatience.[b]

Should such a man become unduly insistent in his advocacy of scholarship, so as seriously to traverse the statistical aspirations of the executive, or in any way to endanger the immediate popular prestige of the university, then it may become an open question whether his personal prestige has not been bought at too high a cost. As a business proposition, it may even become expedient to retire him. But his retirement may not be an easy matter to arrange. The businesslike grounds of it cannot well be avowed, since it is involved in the scheme of academic decorum, as well as in the scheme of publicity, that motives of notoriety must not be avowed. Colorable grounds of another kind must be found, such as will divert the popular imagination from the point at issue. By a judicious course of vexation and equivocations, an obnoxious scientist may be maneuvered into such a position that his pride will force a "voluntary" resignation.[5] Failing this, it may become

---

b. "The lambs play always, they know no better, / They are only one times one." [Quoted from "Seven Times One. – Exultation," in *Songs of Seven*, by Jean Ingelow (1820–77), English poet, novelist, and children's author. –Ed.]

5. Probable allusion to Veblen's departures from Chicago and Stanford, both of which were "voluntary resignations" shaped largely by his unhappy and unconsummated first marriage to Ellen Rolfe. As Veblen and his first wife grew increasingly estranged, she undertook letter-writing campaigns and

necessary, however distasteful, delicately to defame his domestic life, or his racial, religious or political status. In America such an appeal to the baser sentiments will commonly cloud the issue sufficiently for the purpose in hand, even though it all has nothing to do with the man's fitness for university work. Such a step, however, is not to be taken unless the case is urgent; if there is danger of estranging the affections of potential donors, or if it involves anything like overt disloyalty to the executive head.

This is one of the points at which it is necessary to recall the fact that no settled code of business ethics has yet been worked out for the guidance of competitive university management; nor is it easy to see how such a code can be worked out, so long as the university remains ostensibly a seat of learning, unable to avow any other ground of action than a single-minded pursuit of knowledge. It has been alleged—indeed it is fast becoming a tradition—that the executives of the great competitive universities habitually allow some peculiar latitude as touches the canons of truth and fair dealing. If this describes the facts, it should not be counted against these discreet men who so have to tax their ingenuity, but against the situation in which they are placed, which makes it impracticable to observe a nice discrimination in matters of veracity. Statements of fact, under such conditions, will in great part be controlled by the end to be accomplished, rather than by antecedent circumstances; such statements are necessarily of a teleological order. As in other competitive business, facts have in this connection only a strategic value; but the exigencies of strategy here are peculiarly exacting, and often rigorous.

Academic tradition and current common sense unite in imposing on the universities the employment of prominent scholars and scientists, in that men of note in this class have a high prestige value for purposes of publicity; and it was suggested above that a reservation of some breadth must be made on this head. Common notoriety is the due test of eminence which the competitive university must apply in the selection of its notables. But in the sciences that deal with the less tangible and measureable data, the so-called moral or social sciences, common notoriety is not even an approximately accurate index of scientific capacity or attainments; and still it is, of course, the standing of the incumbents in point of

visits with the presidents of Chicago and Stanford to inform them of what she took to be Veblen's neglect and misbehavior. In 1905, William Rainey Harper forwarded her allegations to Chicago newspapers, which refused to print them. Despite the often repeated claim that Harper fired Veblen, Veblen in fact had successfully negotiated a contract for a new and better appointment at Stanford before he tendered his resignation in May 1906, some four months after Harper had died. In October, 1909, after sharing Veblen's wife's second round of letters with his Stanford faculty advisory board, David Starr Jordan met with Veblen. He refused to discuss his personal affairs and resigned the same day.

common notoriety that must chiefly be had in view in any strict valuation of them for purposes of academic prestige. They are needed for the advertising value which they bring, and for this purpose they are valuable somewhat in proportion to the rank awarded them by common report among that unlearned element, whose good opinion the competitive university must conciliate. But in the nature of the case, within the range of sciences named, the estimate of the unlearned is necessarily in the wrong.

With the exception of archaeological inquiries and the study of law, as commonly pursued, these moral or social sciences are occupied with inquiry into the nature of the conventions under which men live, the institutions of society—customs, usages, traditions, conventions, canons of conduct, standards of life, of taste, of morality and religion, law and order. No faithful inquiry into these matters can avoid an air of skepticism as to the stability or finality of someone or other among the received articles of institutional furniture. An inquiry into the nature and causes, the working and the outcome, of this institutional apparatus, will disturb the habitual convictions and preconceptions on which they rest, even if the outcome of the inquiry should bear no color of iconoclasm; unless, indeed, the inquirer were so fortunate as to start with an inalienable presumption that the received convictions on these matters need no inquiry and are eternally right and good; in which case he does best to rest content at his point of departure. Skepticism is the beginning of science. Herein lies the difference between homiletical[6] exposition and scientific inquiry.

Now, on these matters of habit and convention, morality and religion, law and order—matters which intimately touch the community's accepted scheme of life—all men have convictions; sentimental convictions to which they adhere with an instinctive tenacity, and any disturbance of which they resent as a violation of fundamental truth. These institutions of society are made up of the habits of thought of the people who live under them. The consensus of the unlearned, or unscientific, as regards the scientific validity of inquiries which touch these matters means little else than the collective expressions of a jealous orthodoxy with respect to the articles of the current social creed. One who purports to be a scientist in this field can gain popular approval of his scientific capacity, particularly the businessmen's approval, only by accepting and confirming current convictions regarding those elements of the accepted scheme of life with which his science is occupied. Any inquiry which does not lead to corroboration of the opinions in vogue among the unlearned is condemned as being spurious and

6. Resembling the art of preaching.

dangerously wrong-headed; whereas an unbiased inquiry into these things, of course, neither confirms nor disputes the scheme of things into which it inquires. And so, at the best, it falls into the same class with the fabled Alexandrine books[7] that either agreed with the Koran or disagreed with it, and were therefore either idle or sacrilegious.

Within this field, vulgar sentiment will tolerate a skeptical or non-committal attitude toward vulgar convictions only as regards the decorative furnishings, not as regards the substance of the views arrived at. Some slight play of hazardous phrases about the fringe of the institutional fabric may be tolerated by the popular taste, as an element of spice, and as indicating a generous and unbiased mind; but in such cases the conclusive test of scientific competency and leadership, in the popular apprehension, is a serene and magniloquent return to the orthodox commonplaces, after all such playful excursions. In fact, substantially nothing but homiletics[8] and woolgathering[9] will pass popular muster as science in this connection.

So it comes about that the men who are by common notoriety held to be the leaders in this field of learning, and who therefore are likely to be thrown up by official preferment, are such as enlarge on the commonplace and aphoristic wisdom of the laity. Not that the official sanction falls unfailingly on the paragons of mediocrity; there are many and illustrious exceptions, a fair proportion of whom would be illustrious even without the official sanction; and in this connection it is in place to recall that business principles have not hitherto held undivided and sovereign dominion in this province, and that there is even reason to believe that they are not yet coming fully into their own.

These putative leaders of science referred to are, in the common run of cases, not men with whom the science will have to count; but by virtue of their eligibility as academic spokesmen of the science, they are men with whom their contemporaries in the science will have to count. As is shown by the experience of the past, they are likely to be well forgotten by the generation that follows them, but they are, perforce, equally well remembered by their contemporaries. It is not the long-term serviceability of these official scientists that counts toward their availability for academic leadership, but their popular prestige. They may not be such

7. "Fabled Alexandrine books" were books held in the great library of Alexandria, the ancient world's single most important archive of knowledge, which was destroyed after the conquest of the city by the army of Caliph 'Umar in 641 AD. According to a story that first circulated in late seventeenth-century Western scholarship, the commander of the Arab army was inclined to spare the library. But the Caliph decreed otherwise. If the library's books agreed with the Koran, he declared, they were useless and need not be preserved; if they disagreed, they were pernicious and ought to be destroyed.

8. The art of preaching.

9. Indulgence in idle daydreaming.

leaders as the science needs, but they are such exponents of opinion as are believed to commend themselves to the tastes of the well-to-do laity. A citation of instances would seem invidious, nor, presumably, is it called for. The anecdotal history of contemporary events is particularly full at this juncture; while to outsiders who are not in a position to appreciate either the urgency or the subtlety of the motives of academic expediency in this bearing, a recital of illustrative instances might seem either libelous or farcical. The exigencies of competitive academic enterprise, especially in its relation to the maintenance and increase of endowment, place the executive in a very delicate position in this matter and leave little room for squeamish deliberation.

At the risk of tedium, it is necessary to push the analysis of businesslike motives and their bearing a step farther at this point. It is not simply the vulgar, commonplace convictions of the populace that must receive consideration in this field of the moral and social sciences—including such matters as religion, sociology, economics, and political science, so-called. What is especially to be conciliated by the official scientists is the current range of convictions on all these heads among those well-to-do classes from whom the institution hopes to draw contributions to its endowment, on the one hand, and the more reputable part of its undergraduate clientèle, on the other hand. Which comes, broadly, to saying that a jealous eye must be had to the views and prepossessions prevalent among the respectable, conservative middle class; with a particular regard to that more select body of substantial citizens who have the disposal of accumulated wealth. This select and substantial element are on the whole more conservative, more old-fashioned in their views of what is right, good and true, and hold their views on more archaic grounds of conviction, than the generality of the vulgar. And within this conservative body, again, it is the elderly representatives of the old order that are chiefly to be considered—since it is the honorable custom among men of large means not to give largely to institutions of learning until late in life.

It is to be accounted one of the meritorious customs of the greater businessmen that, one with another, they eventually convert a share of their takings to the installation of schools and similar establishments designed to serve and to conserve the amenities of civilized life. Usually it is in later life, or as an act of leave-taking, that this munificence is exercised. Usually, too, the great men who put forth this large munificence do not hamper their bounty with many restrictions on the character of the enlightenment which it is to serve. Indeed, there is in this respect a certain large modesty and continence customarily associated with the large donations. But like other men of force and thoughtfulness, the large and elderly businessmen have well-assured convictions and preferences; and as is the

case with other men of the passing generation, so with the superannuated businessmen, their convictions and preferences fall out on the side of the old order
rather than contrariwise. A wise academic policy, conducted by an executive looking to the fiscal interests of the university, will aim not to alienate the affections
of the large businessmen of a ripe age, by harboring specialists whose enquires
are likely to traverse these old-settled convictions in the social, economic, political, or religious domain. It is bad business policy to create unnecessary annoy-
ance. So it comes about that the habitual munificence of the captains of industry
who have reached their term will have grave consequences for that range of academic science that is occupied with matters on which they hold convictions.[c]

There results a genial endeavor to keep step with the moribund captains of
industry and the relics of the wealthy dead. Remotely by force of a worldly-wise
appointing power, proximately by force of the good taste and sober sense of well-
chosen incumbents, something of filial piety comes to pervade the academic handling of those institutional phenomena that touch the sentiments of the passing
generation. Hence it comes that current academic work in the province of the
social, political, and economic sciences, as well as in the sciences that touch the
religious interest, has a larger reputation for assurance and dignity than for an
incisive canvassing of the available material.

Critics of the latter-day university policies have from time to time called attention to an apparent reluctance on the part of these academic scientists to encoun-
ter present-day facts hand-to-hand, or to trace out the causes to which current conditions are due. Distempered critics have even alleged that the academic leaders in
the social sciences are held under some constraint, as being, in some sort, in the
pay of the well-to-do conservative element; that they are thereby incapacitated
from following up any inquiry to its logical conclusion, in case the conclusion
might appear to traverse the interest or the opinions of those on whom these
leaders are in this way pecuniarily dependent.

Now, it may be conceded without violence to notorious facts, that these official
leaders of science do commonly reach conclusions innocuous to the existing law
and order, particularly with respect to religion, ownership, and the distribution

c. "He was a trusted and efficient employee of an institution made possible and maintained by
men of great wealth, men who not only live on the interest of their money, but who expend millions
in the endowment of colleges and universities in which enthusiastic young educators. . . find lucrative
and honorable employment."—Editorial on the dismissal of Dr. Nearing, in the *Minneapolis Journal,*
August 11, 1915. ["Dr. Nearing" was Scott Nearing (1883–1983). In June 1915, the board of trustees at
the Wharton School of the University of Pennsylvania ignored the recommendation of its faculty and
refused to renew Nearing's appointment as assistant professor. The case attracted national attention,
partly because Nearing was then a well-known figure immersed in various progressive causes in Phil-
adelphia and whose views ran afoul those of the Wharton trustees. –Ed.]

of wealth. But this need imply no constraint, nor even any peculiar degree of tact, much less a moral obliquity. It may confidently be asserted, without fear of contradiction from their side, that the official leaders in this province of academic research and indoctrination are, commonly, in no way hindered from pushing their researches with full freedom and to the limit of their capacity; and that they are likewise free to give the fullest expression to any conclusions or convictions to which their inquiries may carry them. That they are able to do so is a fortunate circumstance, due to the fact that their intellectual horizon is bounded by the same limits of commonplace insight and preconceptions as are the prevailing opinions of the conservative middle class. That is to say, a large and aggressive mediocrity is the prime qualification for a leader of science in these lines, if his leadership is to gain academic authentication.[10]

All this may seem too much like loose generality. With a view to such precision as the case admits, it may be remarked that this province of academic science as habitually pursued, is commonly occupied with questions of what ought to be done, rather than with theories of the genesis and causation of the present-day state of things, or with questions as to what the present-day drift of things may be, as determined by the causes at work. As it does in popular speculation, so also in this academic quasi-science, the interest centers on what ought to be done to improve conditions and to conserve those usages and conventions that have by habit been imbedded in the received scheme of use and wont, and so have come to be found good and right. It is of the essence of popular speculations on this range of topics that they are focused on questions of use; that they are of a teleological order; that they look to the expediency of the observed facts and to their exploitation, rather than to a scientific explanation of them. This attitude, of course, is the attitude of expediency and homiletics, not of scientific inquiry.

A single illustrative instance of the prevalence of this animus in the academic social sciences may be in place. It is usual among economists, e.g., to make much of the proposition that economics is an "art"—the art of expedient management of the material means of life; and further that the justification of economic theory

---

10. Veblen exaggerates the extent to which the views of early twentieth-century American social scientists mirrored the "prevailing opinions of the conservative middle class." It is true that, within Veblen's own generation of university-trained social scientists, there were scholars whose attitudes toward science and reform resembled those of the previous, largely conservative generation. But there were also numerous then prominent social scientists—e.g., Richard T. Ely, Franz Boas, E. A. Ross, John R. Commons, and Albion Small—with a different outlook and openly reformist ideals. The defining feature of this more reform-minded group was a shared conception of modern social science as a product of close empirical investigation. They also shared a desire to use their knowledge to solve social problems. See Dorothy Ross, "The Development of the Social Sciences," in *Discipline and History: Political Science in the United States* (Ann Arbor: University of Michigan Press, 1993), 88–91.

lies in its serviceability in this respect. Such a quasi-science necessarily takes the current situation for granted as a permanent state of things; to be corrected and brought back into its normal routine in case of aberration, and to be safeguarded with apologetic defense at points where it is not working to the satisfaction of all parties. It is a "science" of complaisant interpretations, apologies, and projected remedies.[11]

The academic leaders in such a quasi-science should be gifted with the aspirations and limitations that so show up in its pursuit. Their fitness in respect of this conformity to the known middle-class animus and apprehension of truth may, as it expediently should, be considered when their selection for academic office and rank is under advisement; but, provided the choice be a wise one, there need be no shadow of constraint during their incumbency. The incumbent should be endowed with a large capacity for work, particularly for "administrative" work, with a lively and enduring interest in the "practical" questions that fall within his academic jurisdiction, and with a shrewd sense of the fundamental rightness of the existing order of things, social, economic, political, and religious. So, by and large, it will be found that these accredited leaders of scientific inquiry are fortunate enough not narrowly to scrutinize, or to seek particular explanation of, those institutional facts which the conservative common sense of the elderly businessman accepts as good and final; and since their field of inquiry is precisely this range of institutional facts, the consequence is that their leadership in the science conduces more to the stability of opinions than to the advancement of knowledge.

The result is by no means that nothing is accomplished in this field of science under this leadership of forceful mediocrity, but only that, in so far as this leadership decides, the work done lies on this level of mediocrity. Indeed, the volume of work done is large and of substantial value, but it runs chiefly on compilation of details and on the scrutiny and interpretation of these details with a view to their conformity with the approved generalizations of the day before yesterday— generalizations that had time to grow into aphoristic commonplaces at a date before the passing generation of businessmen attained their majority.

11. Veblen believed that economics would become a "science" only when it embraced an evolutionary framework of explanation along Darwinian lines. The neoclassical economics taught in American universities in his day was a "complaisant" science, he believed, because it naively assumed that all humans were motivated by hedonistic or rational principles and that economic growth as such constituted social progress. By contrast, in *The Theory of the Leisure Class*, Veblen argued that the accumulation of wealth and the political and social power that came with wealth carried over into modern life practices of hierarchy and coercion that had their origins in earlier "barbaric" or feudal societies. See Howard Brick, *Transcending Capitalism: Visions of a New Society in Modern American Thought* (Ithaca, NY: Cornell University Press, 2006), 47–50.

What has just been said of this academic leadership in the social sciences, of course, applies only with due qualification. It applies only in so far as the principles of competitive enterprise control the selection of the personnel, and even then only with exceptions. There is no intention to depreciate the work of those many eminent scholars, of scientific animus and intellectual grasp, whose endeavors are given to this range of inquiry. Its application, indeed, is intended to reach no farther than may serve to cover the somewhat tactful and quietistic attitude of the moral sciences in the universities. As they are cultivated in the great seminaries of learning, these sciences are commonly of a somewhat more archaic complexion than the contemporary material sciences; they are less iconoclastic, have a greater regard for prescriptive authority and authenticity, are more given to rest their inquiry on grounds of expediency, as contrasted with grounds of cause and effect. They are content to conclude that such and such events are expedient or inexpedient, quite as often and as easily as that such are the causes or the genetic sequence of the phenomena under discussion. In short, under this official leadership these sciences will have an attitude toward their subject of inquiry resembling that taken by the material sciences something like a century ago.

To the credit of this academic leadership in the social sciences, then, it should be said that both the leaders and their disciples apply themselves with admirable spirit to these inquiries into the proper, expedient, and normal course of events; and that the conclusions arrived at also shed much salutary light on what is proper, expedient, and normal in these premises. Inquiries carried on in this spirit in the field of human institutions belong, of course, in the category of worldly wisdom rather than of science. "Practical" questions occupy these scientists in great part, and practical, or utilitarian, considerations guide the course of the inquiry and shape the system of generalizations in these sciences, to a much greater extent than in the material sciences with which they are here contrasted. An alert sense of the practical value of their inquiries and their teaching is one of the chief requisites for official recognition in the scientists who occupy themselves with these matters, and it is one of the chief characteristics of their work. So that, in so far as it all conforms to the principles of competitive business, the line of demarcation between worldly wisdom and theoretical validity becomes peculiarly indistinct in this province of science. And, it may be remarked by the way, the influence of this academic science, both in its discipline and in its tenets, appears to be wholly salutary; it conduces, on the whole, to a safe and sane, if not an enthusiastic, acceptance of things as they are, without undue curiosity as to why they are such.

What has here been said of the place and use of the scientist under the current régime of competitive enterprise describes what should follow from the unrestrained dominion of business principles in academic policy, rather than what has actually been accomplished in any concrete case; it presents an ideal situation rather than a relation of events, though without losing touch with current facts at any point. The run of the facts is, in effect, a compromise between the scholar's ideals and those of business, in such a way that the ideals of scholarship are yielding ground, in an uncertain and varying degree, before the pressure of businesslike exigencies.

CHAPTER VII

Vocational Training

In this latter-day academic enterprise, that looks so shrewdly to practical expediency, "vocational training" has, quite as a matter of course, become a conspicuous feature. The adjective is a new one, installed expressly to designate this line of endeavor, in the jargon of the educators; and it carries a note of euphemism. "Vocational training"[1] is training for proficiency in some gainful occupation, and it has no connection with the higher learning, beyond that juxtaposition given it by the inclusion of vocational schools in the same corporation with the university; and its spokesmen in the university establishments accordingly take an apologetically aggressive attitude in advocating its claims. Educational enterprise of this kind has, somewhat incontinently, extended the scope of the corporation of learning by creating, "annexing," or "affiliating" many establishments that properly lie outside the academic field and deal with matters foreign to the academic interest—fitting schools, high-schools, technological, manual and other training schools for mechanical, engineering and other industrial pursuits, professional schools of diverse kinds, music schools, art schools, summer schools, schools of "domestic science," "domestic economy," "home economics" (in short, housekeeping), schools for the special training of secondary-school teachers, and even schools that are avowedly of primary grade; while a variety of "university extension" bureau have also been installed, to comfort and edify the unlearned with lyceum lectures, to dispense erudition by mail-order, and to maintain some putative contact with amateur scholars and dilettanti beyond the pale.[2]

On its face, this enterprise in assorted education simulates the precedents given by the larger modern business coalitions, which frequently bring under one gen-

---

1. Vocational training became a conspicuous feature of the American university system because of the steady expansion of the number of occupations for which formal study was possible and demanded. Veblen's complaint here is that the development of the American university system blurred an important long-standing distinction between the connotation of "profession" and that of "vocation."

2. Allusion to William Rainey Harper's master plan for the University of Chicago, whose capacious goals were to encompass all sectors of American society, including adult students and nontraditional learners. Cf. chapter I, "Introductory," note 5.

eral business management a considerable number and variety of industrial plants. Doubtless a boyish imitation of such business enterprise has had its share in the propagation of these educational excursions. It all has an histrionic[3] air, such as would suggest that its use, at least in good part, might be to serve as an outlet for the ambition and energies of an executive gifted with a penchant for large and difficult undertakings, and with scant insight into the needs and opportunities of a corporation of the higher learning, and who might therefore be carried off his scholastic footing by the glamour of the exploits of the trust-makers. No doubt, the histrionic proclivities of the executive, backed by a similar sensibility to dramatic effect on the part of their staff and of the governing boards, must be held accountable for much of this headlong propensity to do many other things halfway rather than do the work well that is already in hand. But this visible histrionic sensibility, and the glamour of great deeds, will by no means wholly account for current university enterprise along this line; not even when there is added the urgent competitive need of a show of magnitude, such as besets all the universities; nor do these several lines of motivation account for the particular direction so taken by these excursions *in partes infidelium*.[4] At the same time, reasons of scholarship or science plainly have no part in the movement.

Apart from such executive weakness for spectacular magnitude, and the competitive need of formidable statistics, the prime mover in the case is presumably the current unreflecting propensity to make much of all things that bear the signature of the "practical." These various projections of university enterprise uniformly make some plausible claim of that nature. Any extension of the corporation's activity can be more readily effected, is accepted more as an expedient matter of course, if it promises to have such a "practical" value. "Practical" in this connection means useful for private gain; it need imply nothing in the way of serviceability to the common good.

The same spirit shows itself also in a ceaseless revision of the schedule of instruction offered by the collegiate or undergraduate division as such, where it leads to a multiplication of courses desired to give or to lead up to vocational training. So that practical instruction, in the sense indicated, is continually thrown more into the foreground in the courses offered, as well as in the solicitude of the various administrative boards, bureau and committees that have to do with the organization and management of the academic machinery.

As has already been remarked, these directive boards, committees, and chiefs

---

3. Deliberately affected; theatrical.
4. Latin: in the land of the infidels; originally refers to non-Christians.

of bureau are chosen, in great part, for their businesslike efficiency, because they are good office-men, with "executive ability"; and the animus of these academic businessmen, by so much, becomes the guiding spirit of the corporation of learning, and through their control it acts intimately and pervasively to order the scope and method of academic instruction. This permeation of the university's everyday activity by the principles of competitive business is less visible to outsiders than the various lines of extraneous enterprise already spoken of, but it touches the work within the university proper even more radically and insistently; although, it is true, it affects the collegiate (undergraduate) instruction more immediately than what is fairly to be classed as university work. The consequences are plain. Business proficiency is put in the place of learning. It is said by advocates of this move that learning is hereby given a more practical bent; which is substantially a contradiction in terms. It is a case not of assimilation, but of displacement and substitution, garnished with circumlocution of a more or less ingenuous kind.

Historically, in point of derivation and early growth, this movement for vocational training is closely related to the American system of "electives" in college instruction, if it may not rather be said to be a direct outgrowth of that pedagogical expedient.[a] It dates back approximately to the same period for its beginnings, and much of the arguments adduced in its favor are substantially the same as have been found convincing for the system of electives. Under the elective system a

a. "Our professors in the Harvard of the '50s were a set of rather eminent scholars and highly respectable men. They attended to their studies with commendable assiduity and drudged along in a dreary, humdrum sort of way in a stereotyped method of classroom instruction. . . .

"And that was the Harvard system. It remains in essence the system still—the old, outgrown, pedagogic relation of the large class-recitation room. The only variation has been through Eliot's effort to replace it by the yet more pernicious system of premature specialization. This is a confusion of the college and university functions and constitutes a distinct menace to all true higher education. The function of the college is an all-around development, as a basis for university specializations. Eliot never grasped that fundamental fact, and so he undertook to turn Harvard College into a German university—specializing the student at 18. He instituted a system of one-sided contact in place of a system based on no contact at all. It is devoutly to be hoped that, some day, a glimmer of true light will effect an entrance into the professional educator's head. It certainly hadn't done so up to 1906."— Charles Francis Adams II (1835–1915), An Autobiography (1916). [Adams was the grandson and great-grandson of past American presidents, and brother of Henry Adams (1838–1918). After graduating from Harvard in 1856, he served as a colonel in the Union Army during the Civil War and then pursued a mixed career as businessman, civic leader, and man of letters. The "Harvard system" Adams speaks of was the "free elective" undergraduate curriculum implemented by Charles W. Eliot (1834–1926) shortly after he became president in 1869. Eliot eventually became the national spokesman and symbol of the system, arguing that a true university "must try to teach every subject . . . for which there is any demand; and to teach it thoroughly enough to carry the individual student to the confines of present knowledge and to make him capable of original research." The problem Veblen spots with this line of argument is that advocates of the "free elective" system had little sense of the logical extremes of a system that still shapes deliberations about curriculum reform now usually bent on encouraging institutional differentiation and hence a steady proliferation of subjects for academic study. –Ed.]

considerable and increasing freedom has been allowed the student in the choice of what he will include in his curriculum; so that the colleges have in this way come to refer the choice of topics in good part to the guidance of the student's own interest. To meet the resulting range and diversity of demands, an increasing variety of courses has been offered, at the same time that a narrower specialization has also taken effect in much of the instruction offered. Among the other leadings of interest among students, and affecting their choice of electives, has also been the laudable practical interest that these young men take in their own prospective material success.[b] So that this—academically speaking, extraneous—interest has come to mingle and take rank with the scholarly interests proper in shaping the schedule of instruction. A decisive voice in the ordering of the affairs of the higher learning has so been given to the novices, or rather to the untutored probationers of the undergraduate schools, whose entrance on a career of scholarship is yet a matter of speculative probability at the best.

Those who have spoken for an extensive range of electives have in a very appreciable measure made use of that expedient as a means of displacing what they have regarded as obsolete or dispensable items in the traditional college curriculum. In so advocating a wider range and freedom of choice, they have spoken for the new courses of instruction as being equally competent with the old in point of discipline and cultural value; and they have commonly not omitted to claim—somewhat in the way of an *obiter dictum*,[5] perhaps—that these newer and more vital topics, whose claims they advocate, have also the peculiar merit of conducing in a special degree to good citizenship and the material welfare of the community. Such a line of argument has found immediate response among those pragmatic spirits within whose horizon "value" is synonymous with "pecuniary value," and to whom good citizenship means proficiency in competitive business. So it has come about that, while the initial purpose of the elective system appears to have been the sharpening of the students' scholarly interests and the cultivation of a more liberal scholarship, it has by force of circumstances served to propagate a movement at cross purposes with all scholarly aspiration.[6]

All this advocacy of the practical in education has fallen in with the aspirations of such young men as are eager to find gratuitous help toward a gainful career, as well as with the desires of parents who are anxious to see their sons equipped

b. The college student's interest in his studies has shifted from the footing of an avocation to that of a vocation. [An avocation is a diversion or distraction; a vocation is a regular occupation, for which one is particularly suited or qualified. –Ed.]

5. Latin: an incidental or collateral opinion that is uttered by a judge but not binding; comment made in passing.

6. Cf. note a, *supra*.

for material success; and not least has it appealed to the sensibilities of those substantial citizens who are already established in business and feel the need of a free supply of trained subordinates at reasonable wages. The last mentioned is the more substantial of these incentives to gratuitous vocational training, coming in, as it does, with the endorsement of the community's most respected and most influential men. Whether it is training in any of the various lines of engineering, in commerce, in journalism, or in the mechanic and manual trades, the output of trained men from these vocational schools goes, in the main, to supply trained employees for concerns already profitably established in such lines of business as find use for this class of men; and through the gratuitous, or half gratuitous, opportunities offered by these schools, this needed supply of trained employees comes to the business concerns in question at a rate of wages lower than what they would have to pay in the absence of such gratuitous instruction.

Not that these substantial citizens, whose word counts for so much in commendation of practical education, need be greatly moved by selfish consideration of this increased ease in procuring skilled labor for use in their own pursuit of gain; but the increased and cheaper supply of such skilled workmen is "good for business," and, in the common sense estimation of these conservative businessmen, what is good for business is good, without reservation. What is good for business is felt to be serviceable for the common good; and no closer scrutiny is commonly given to that matter. While any closer scrutiny would doubtless throw serious doubt on this general proposition, such scrutiny cannot but be distasteful to the successful businessmen; since it would unavoidably also throw a shadow of doubt on the meritoriousness of that business traffic in which they have achieved their success and to which they owe their preferential standing in the community.

In this high rating of things practical the captains of industry are also substantially at one with the current common-sense award of the vulgar, so that their advocacy of practical education carries the weight of a self-evident principle. It is true, in the long run and on sober reflection the award of civilized common sense runs to the effect that knowledge is more to be desired than things of price; but at the same time the superficial and transient workday sense of daily needs—the "snap judgment" of the vulgar—driven by the hard usage of competitive breadwinning, says that a gainful occupation is the first requisite of human life; and accepting it without much question as the first requisite, the vulgar allow it uncritically to stand as the chief or sole and that is worth an effort. And in so doing they are not so far out of their bearings; for to the common man, under the com-

petitive system, there is but a scant margin of energy or interest left over and disposable for other ends after the instant needs of bread-winning have been met.

Proficiency and single-mindedness in the pursuit of private gain is something
that can readily be appreciated by all men who have had the usual training given
by the modern system of competitive gain and competitive spending. Nothing is
so instantly recognized as being of great urgency, always and everywhere, under
this modern, pecuniary scheme of things. So that, without reflection and as a
matter of course, the first and gravest question of any general bearing in any
connection has come to be that classic of worldly wisdom: What profiteth it a
man?[7] and the answer is, just as uncritically, sought in terms of pecuniary gain.
And the men to whom has been entrusted the custody of that cultural heritage
of mankind that cannot be bought with a price, make haste to play up to this
snap judgment of the vulgar, and so keep them from calling to mind, on second
thought, what it is that they, after all, value more highly than the means of competitive spending.

Concomitant with this growing insistence on vocational training in the schools,
and with this restless endeavor of the academic authorities to gratify the demand,
there has also come an increasing habitual inclination of the same uncritical
character among academic men to value all academic work in terms of livelihood
or of earning capacity.[c] The question has been asked, more and more urgently
and openly, What is the use of all this knowledge?[d] Pushed by this popular prejudice, and themselves also drifting under compulsion of the same prevalent bias,

c. So, e. g., in the later eighties, at the time when the confusion of sentiments in this matter of
electives and practical academic instruction was reaching its height, one of the most largely endowed
of the late-founded universities set out avowedly to bend its forces singly to such instruction as would
make for the material success of its students; and, moreover, to accomplish this end by an untram-
meled system of electives, limited only by the general qualification that all instruction offered was to
be of this pragmatic character. The establishment in question, it may be added, has in the course of
years run a somewhat inglorious career, regard being had to its unexampled opportunities, and has in
the event come to much the same footing of compromise between learning and vocational training,
routine and electives, as its contemporaries that have approached their present ambiguous position
from the contrary direction; except that, possibly, scholarship as such is still held in slightly lower esteem among the men of this faculty—selected on grounds of their practical bias—than among the
generality of academic men. [Possible allusion to developments at Harvard where president Charles
Eliot had steadily expanded the domain of "free election" during the 1880s. By 1885, all subject requirements for sophomores, juniors, and seniors were abolished; by 1897, the entire prescribed course of
undergraduate study at Harvard had been reduced to a year of freshman rhetoric. –Ed.]

d. "And why the sea is boiling hot,
And whether pigs have wings."

[Quotation from Lewis Carroll (1832–98), "The Walrus and the Carpenter," in *Through the Looking
Glass, and What Alice Found There* (1871). –Ed.]

7. Allusion to Mark 8:36: "For what shall it profit a man, if he shall gain the whole world, and lose
his soul?"

even the seasoned scholars and scientists—Matthew Arnold's "Remnant"[8]—have taken to heart this question of the use of the higher learning in the pursuit of gain. Of course it has no such use, and the many shrewdly devised solutions of the conundrum have necessarily run out in a string of sophistical dialectics. The place of disinterested knowledge in modern civilization is neither that of a means to private gain, nor that of an intermediate step in "the roundabout process of the production of goods."

As a motto for the scholars' craft, *Scientia pecuniae ancillans*[9] is nowise more seemly than the Schoolmen's *Philosophia theologiae ancillans*.[10,e] Yet such inroads have pecuniary habits of valuation made even within the precincts of the corporation of learning, that university men—and even the scholarly ones among them—are no more than half ashamed of such a parcel of fatuity. And relatively few among university executives have not, within the past few years, taken occasion to plead the merits of academic training as a business proposition. The man of the world—that is to say, of the business world puts the question, What is the use of this learning? and the men who speak for learning, and even the scholars occupied with the "humanities," are at pains to find some colorable answer that shall satisfy the worldly-wise that this learning for which they speak is in some way useful for pecuniary gain.[f]

If he were not himself infected with the pragmatism of the market-place, the scholar's answer would have to be. Get thee behind me!

Benjamin Franklin—high-bred pragmatist that he was—once put away such a question with the rejoinder: What is the use of a baby?[11] To civilized men—with the equivocal exception of the warlike politicians—this latter question seems foolish, criminally foolish. But there once was a time, in the high days of barbarism,

e. Cf. Adam Smith (1723–90) on the "idle curiosity," in *Theory of Moral Sentiments* (1759), 351, esp. 355. [There is no mention of "idle curiosity" in these pages, where Smith's topic is actually "public virtue." –Ed.]

f. So, a man eminent as a scholar and in the social sciences has said, not so long ago: "The first question I would ask is, has not this learning a large part to play in supplementing those practical powers, instincts and sympathies which can be developed only in action, only through experience? . . . That broader training is just what is needed by the higher and more responsible ranks of business, both private and public. . . . Success in large trading has always needed breadth of view." [Quotation is unidentified. –Ed.]

8. Veblen read in Matthew Arnold (1822–88), "Spinoza and the Bible," in *Essays in Criticism, Second Series* (1865) that after "the ruin of their state . . . the only election Jews now have is that of the *pious*, the *remnant*, which has always taken place, in every other state."

9. Latin: science is the servant of money.

10. Latin: philosophy is the servant of theology.

11. In 1783, Benjamin Franklin (1706–90) was among the witnesses in Paris of the world's first-known hot-air balloon flight. Asked what possible use the invention could be, Franklin allegedly replied, "What good is a newborn baby?"

when thoughtful men were ready to canvass that question with as naive a gravity as this other question, of the use of learning, is canvassed by the substantial citizens of the present day. At the period covered by that chapter in ancient history, a child was, in a way, an article of equipment for the upkeep of the family and its prestige, and more remotely for the support of the sovereign and his prestige. So that a male child would be rated as indubitably worthwhile if he gave promise of growing into a robust and contentious man. If the infant were a girl, or if he gave no promise of becoming an effective disturber of the peace, the use or expediency of rearing the child would become a matter for deliberation; and not infrequently the finding of those old-time utilitarians was adverse, and the investment was cancelled. The habit of so deliberating on the pragmatic advisability of child-life has been lost, latterly; or at any rate such of the latter-day utilitarians as may still entertain a question of this kind in any concrete case are ashamed to have it spoken of nakedly. Witness the lame but irrepressible sentimental protest against the Malthusian doctrine of population.[12]

It is true, in out-of-the-way corners and on the lower levels—and on the higher levels of imperial politics—where men have not learned to shrink from shameful devices, the question of children and of the birth-rate is still sometimes debated as a question of the presumptive use of offspring for some ulterior end. And there may still be found those who are touched by the reflection that a child born may become a valuable asset as a support for the parents' old age. Such a pecuniary rating of the parental relation, which values children as a speculative means of gain, may still be met with. But wherever modern civilization has made its way at all effectually, such a provident rating of offspring is not met with in good company. Latter-day common sense does not countenance it.

Not that a question of expediency is no longer entertained, touching this matter of children, but it is no longer the patriarchal-barbarian question as to eventual gains that may be expected to accrue to the parent or the family. Except in the view of those statesmen of the barbarian line who see the matter of birth-rate from the higher ground of dynastic politics, a child born is not rated as a means, but as an end. At least conventionally, it is no longer a question of pecuniary gain for the parent but of expediency for the child. No mother asks herself if her child will pay.

Civilized men shrink from anything like rating children as a contrivance for use in the "round-about process of the production of goods."[13] And in much the

12. Allusion to Thomas Robert Malthus (1766–1837), *An Essay on the Principle of Population* (1798), which argued that unchecked populations increase at geometric ratios, while food supplies increase only at arithmetic ratios. Malthus's grim prospect is of a world with too many people and not enough food to feed them.

13. Concept that describes a process in which capital goods are produced first, and then with the

same spirit, and in the last analysis on much the same grounds, although in a less secure and more loosely speculative fashion, men also look to the higher learning as the ripe fulfilment of material competency, rather than as a means to material success. In their thoughtful intervals, the most businesslike pragmatists will avow such an ideal. But in workday detail, when the question turns concretely on the advisability of the higher education, the workday habit of pecuniary traffic asserts itself, and the matter is then likely to be argued in pecuniary terms. The barbarian animus,[14] habitual to the quest of gain, reverts, and the deliberation turns on the gainfulness of this education, which has in all sobriety been acknowledged the due end of culture and endeavor. So that, in working out the details, this end of living is made a means, and the means is made an end.

No doubt, what chiefly urges men to the pursuit of knowledge is their native bent of curiosity—an impulsive proclivity to master the logic of facts; just as the chief incentive to the achievement of children has, no doubt, always been the parental bent. But very much as the boorish element in the present and recent generations will let the pecuniary use of children come in as a large subsidiary ground of decision, and as they have even avowed this to be their chief concern in the matter; so, in a like spirit, men trained to the business system of competitive gain and competitive spending will not be content to find that they can afford the quest of that knowledge which their human propensity incites them to cultivate, but they must back this propensity with a shamefaced apology for education on the plea of its gainfulness.

What is here said of the businesslike spirit of the latter-day "educators" is not to be taken as reflecting disparagingly on them or their endeavors. They respond to the call of the times as best they can. That they do so, and that the call of the times is of this character, is a fact of the current drift of things; which one may commend or deprecate according as one has the fortune to fall in with one or the other side of the case; that is to say according to one's habitual bent; but in any event it is to be taken as a fact of the latter-day situation, and a factor of some force and permanence in the drift of things academic, for the present and the calculable future. It means a more or less effectual further diversion of interest and support from science and scholarship to the competitive acquisition of wealth, and therefore also to its competitive consumption. Through such a diversion of energy and attention in the schools, the pecuniary animus at large, and pecuniary

---

new goods produced, desired consumer goods are produced. The concept was developed by Austrian economist Eugen von Böhm-Bawerk (1851–1914) in arguing that consumer demand, not the supply of savings, is the primary determinant of capital investment in any industry.

14. Cf. chapter I, "Introductory," note 11.

standards of worth and value, stand to gain, more or less, at the cost of those other virtues that are, by the accepted tradition of modern Christendom, held to be of graver and more enduring import. It means an endeavor to substitute the pursuit of gain and expenditure in place of the pursuit of knowledge, as the focus of interest and the objective end in the modern intellectual life.

This incursion of pecuniary ideals in academic policy is seen at its broadest and baldest in the Schools of Commerce—"Commerce and Politics," "Business Training," "Commerce and Administration," "Commerce and Finance," or whatever may be the phrase selected to designate the supersession of learning by worldly wisdom.[15] Facility in competitive business is to take the place of scholarship, as the goal of university training, because, it is alleged, the former is the more useful. The ruling interest of Christendom, in this view, is pecuniary gain. And training for commercial management stands to this ruling interest of the modern community in a relation analogous to that in which theology and homiletics stood to the ruling interest in those earlier times when the salvation of men's souls was the prime object of solicitude. Such a seminary of business has something of a sacerdotal dignity. It is the appointed keeper of the higher business animus.[g]

Such a school, with its corps of instructors and its equipment, stands in the university on a tenure similar to that of the divinity school. Both schools are equally extraneous to that "intellectual enterprise" in behalf of which, ostensibly, the university is maintained. But while the divinity school belongs to the old order and is losing its preferential hold on the corporation of learning, the school of commerce belongs to the new order and is gaining ground. The primacy among pragmatic interests has passed from religion to business, and the school of commerce is the exponent and expositor of this primacy. It is the perfect flower of the secularization of the universities. And as has already been remarked above, there is also a wide-sweeping movement afoot to bend the ordinary curriculum of the

g. Cf. *Report of a Conference on Commercial Education and Business Progress*, in connection with the dedication of the Commerce Building, at the University of Illinois, 1913. The somewhat raucous note of self-complacency that pervades this characteristic document should not be allowed to lessen its value as evidence of the spirit for which it speaks. Indeed, whatever it may show, of effrontery and disingenuousness, is rather to be taken as of the essence of the case. It might prove difficult to find an equally unabashed pronouncement of the like volume and consistency put forth under the like academic auspices; but it does by no means stand alone, and its perfections should not be counted against it. [The School of Commerce at the University of Illinois was founded in 1902. –Ed.]

15. Strictly speaking, "commerce" means activities related to the buying and selling of goods and services. In Veblen's time, the word was routinely used as a synonym for business. When Veblen arrived at the University of Chicago in 1893, the Wharton School of Finance, founded in 1881, was the only freestanding institution dedicated exclusively to providing professional business education for undergraduates. Opened in 1908, the Harvard Business School was the first university-based professional school with full-time faculty to offer master's degrees in business administration.

higher schools to the service of this cult of business principles, and so to make the ordinary instruction converge to the advancement of business enterprise, very much as it was once dutifully arranged that the higher instruction should be subservient to religious teaching and consonant with the demands of devout observances and creeds.

It is not that the College of Commerce stands alone as the exponent of worldly wisdom in the modern universities; nor is its position in this respect singular, except in the degree of its remoteness from all properly academic interests. Other training schools, as in engineering and in the other professions, belong under the same general category of practical aims, as contrasted with the aims of the higher learning. But the College of Commerce stands out preeminent among these various training schools in two respects: (a) While the great proportion of training for the other professions draws largely on the results of modern science for ways and means, and therefore includes or presumes a degree of familiarity with the work, aims and methods of the sciences, so that these schools have so much of a bond of community with the higher learning, the school of commerce on the other hand need scarcely take cognizance of the achievements of science, nor need it presume any degree of acquaintance on the part of its students or adepts with the matter or logic of the sciences;[h] (b) in varying degrees, the proficiency given by training in the other professional schools, and required for the efficient pursuit of the other professions, may be serviceable to the community at large; whereas the business proficiency inculcated by the schools of commerce has no such serviceability, being directed singly to a facile command of the ways and means of private gain.[i] The training that leads up to the several other profes-

h. This characterization applies without abatement to the schools of commerce as commonly designed at their foundation and set forth in their public announcements, and to their work in so far as they live up to their professions. At the same time it is to be noted that few of these schools successfully keep their work clear of all entanglement with theoretical discussions that have only a scientific bearing. And it is also quite feasible to organize a "school of commerce" on lines of scientific inquiry with the avowed purpose of dealing with business enterprise in its various ramifications as subject matter of theoretical investigation; but such is not the avowed aim of the established schools of this class, and such is not the actual character of the work carried on in these schools, except by inadvertence. [Veblen was not alone in doubting that business education would ever prove to be a legitimate academic subject. Twelve years after *The Higher Learning in America* first appeared, Abraham Flexner (1866–1939), then one of the most influential figures in American higher education, echoed Veblen's sentiments in his widely circulated *Universities: American, British, and German* (1930). Flexner was secretary of the General Education Board from 1913 to 1928, and the first director of the Institute for Advanced Study in Princeton, New Jersey, from 1930 to 1938. –Ed.]

i. It is doubtless within the mark to say that the training given by the American schools of commerce is detrimental to the community's material interests. In America, even in a more pronounced degree than elsewhere, business management centers on financiering and salesmanship; and American commercial schools, even in a more pronounced degree than those of other countries, center their attention on proficiency in these matters, because these are the matters which the common sense of the American business community knows how to value, and on which it insists as indispensable qual-

sions, of course, varies greatly in respect of its draught on scientific information, as well as in the degree of its serviceability to the community; some of the professions, as, e. g., Law, approach very close to the character of business training, both in the unscientific and unscholarly nature of the required training and in their uselessness to the community; while others, as, e. g., Medicine and the various lines of engineering, differ widely from commercial training in both of these respects. With the main exception of Law (and, some would add, of Divinity?) the professional schools train men for work that is of some substantial use to the community at large. This is particularly true of the technological schools. But while the technological schools may be occupied with work that is of substantial use, and while they may draw more or less extensively on the sciences for their materials and even for their methods, they cannot, for all that, claim standing in the university on the ground of that disinterested intellectual enterprise which is the university's peculiar domain.[16]

---

ifications in its young men. The besetting infirmity of the American business community, as witness the many and circumstantial disclosures of the "efficiency engineers," and of others who have had occasion to speak of the matter, is a notable indifference to the economical and mechanically efficient use, exploitation and conservation of equipment and resources, coupled with an equally notable want of insight into the technological needs and possibilities of the industries which they control. The typical American businessman watches the industrial process from ambush, with a view to the seizure of any item of value that may be left at loose ends. Business strategy is a strategy of "watchful waiting," at the center of a web; very alert and adroit, but remarkably incompetent in the way of anything that can properly be called "industrial enterprise." [The most prominent "efficiency engineer" of Veblen's day was Frederick Winslow Taylor (1856–1915), who spent his career searching for scientific law in the industrial workplace. –Ed.]

The concatenation of circumstances that has brought American business enterprise to this inglorious posture, and has virtually engrossed the direction of business affairs in the hands of men endowed with the spiritual and intellectual traits suitable to such prehensile enterprise, cannot be gone into here. The fact, however, is patent. It should suffice to call to mind the large fact, as notorious as it is discreditable, that the American business community has, with unexampled freedom, had at its disposal the largest and best body of resources that has yet become available to modern industry, in men, materials and geographical situation, and that with these means they have achieved something doubtfully second-rate, as compared with the industrial achievements of other countries less fortunately placed in all material respects.

What the schools of commerce now offer is further specialization along the same line of proficiency, to give increased facility in financiering and salesmanship. This specialization on commerce is like other specialization in that it draws off attention and interest from other lines than those in which the specialization falls; thereby widening the candidate's field of ignorance while it intensifies his effectiveness within his specialty. The effect, as touches the community's interest in the matter, should be an enhancement of the candidate's proficiency in all the futile ways and means of salesmanship and "conspiracy in restraint of trade." together with a heightened incapacity and ignorance bearing on such work as is of material use. ["Conspiracy in restraint of trade" is a phrase usually associated with the Sherman Anti-Trust Act (1890), which in Section 1 prohibited any and all business agreements—such as bid-rigging and price-fixing—that would restrain trade. –Ed.]

16. Early twentieth-century American "technological schools" developed from various sources. Some were survivors of antebellum mechanics' institutes; others arose in response to local demand for particular kinds of technicians; others were the creations of philanthropic self-made men such as Peter Cooper (1791–1883) and Enoch Pratt (1808–96), who preferred to endow schools and libraries for workmen rather than colleges or universities for the wealthy.

The professional knowledge and skill of physicians, surgeons, dentists, pharmacists, agriculturists, engineers of all kinds, perhaps even of journalists, is of some use to the community at large, at the same time that it may be profitable to the bearers of it. The community has a substantial interest in the adequate training of these men, although it is not that intellectual interest that attaches to science and scholarship. But such is not the case with the training designed to give proficiency in business. No gain comes to the community at large from increasing the business proficiency of any number of its young men. There are already much too many of these businessmen, much too astute and proficient in their calling, for the common good. A higher average business efficiency simply raises activity and avidity in business to a higher average pitch of skill and fervor, with very little other material result than a redistribution of ownership; since business is occupied with the competitive wealth, not with its production. It is only by a euphemistic metaphor that we are accustomed to speak of the businessmen as producers of goods. Gains due to such efficiency are differential gains only. They are a differential as against other businessmen on the one hand, and as against the rest of the community on the other hand. The work of the College of Commerce, accordingly, is a peculiarly futile line of endeavor for any public institution, in that it serves neither the intellectual advancement nor the material welfare of the community.

The greater the number and the higher the proficiency of the community's businessmen, other things equal, the worse must the rest of the community come off in that game of skilled bargaining and shrewd management by which the businessmen get their gains. Gratuitous or partly gratuitous training for business will presumably increase the number of highly proficient businessmen. As the old-fashioned economists would express it, it will increase the number of "middlemen," of men who "live by their wits."[17] At the same time it should presumably increase the average efficiency of this increased number. The outcome should be that the resulting body of businessmen will be able, between them, to secure a larger proportion of the aggregate wealth of the community; leaving the rest of the community poorer by that much, except for that (extremely doubtful) amount by which shrewd business management is likely to increase the material wealth-producing capacity of the community. Any such presumed increase of wealth-producing capacity is an incidental concomitant of business traffic, and in the nature of the case it cannot equal the aggregate increased gain that goes to the businessmen. At the best the question as to the effect which such an aggre-

17. People who "live by their wits" do not have regular employment, but survive by manipulating people and situations.

gate increased business efficiency will have on the community's material welfare is a question of how large the net loss will be; that it will entail a net loss on the community at large is in fact not an open question.

A college of commerce is designed to serve an emulative purpose only—individual gain regardless of, or at the cost of, the community at large—and it is, therefore, peculiarly incompatible with the collective cultural purpose of the university. It belongs in the corporation of learning no more than a department of athletics.[j] Both alike give training that is of no use to the community, except, perhaps, as a sentimental excitement. Neither business proficiency nor proficiency in athletic contests need be decried, of course. They have their value, to the businessmen and to the athletes, respectively, chiefly as a means of livelihood at the cost of the rest of the community, and it is to be presumed that they are worthwhile to those who go in for that sort of thing. Both alike are related to the legitimate ends of the university as a drain on its resources and an impairment of its scholarly animus. As related to the ostensible purposes of a university, therefore, the support and conduct of such schools at the expense of the universities is to be construed as a breach of trust.

What has just been said of the schools of commerce is, of course, true also of the other training schools comprised in this latter-day university policy, in the degree in which these others aim at the like emulative and unscholarly results. It holds true of the law schools, e. g., typically and more largely than of the generality of professional and technical schools. Both in point of the purely competitive value of their training and of the unscientific character of their work, the law schools are in very much the same case as the schools of commerce; and, no doubt, the accepted inclusion of law schools in the university corporation has made the intrusion of the schools of commerce much easier than it otherwise

j. Latterly, it appears, the training given by the athletic establishments attached to the universities is also coming to have a value as vocational training; in that the men so trained and vouched for by these establishments are finding lucrative employment as instructors, coaches, masseurs, etc., engaged in similar athletic traffic in various schools, public or private. So also, and for the same reason, they are found eligible as "muscular Christian" secretaries in charge of chapters of the YMCA and the like quasi-devout clubs and guilds. Indeed in all but the name, the athletic establishments are taking on the character of "schools" or "divisions" included under the collective academic administration, very much after the fashion of a "School of Education" or a "School of Journalism"; and they are in effect "graduating" students in Athletics, with due, though hitherto unofficial, certification of proficiency. So also, latterly, one meets with proposals, made in good faith, among official academic men to allow due "academic credit" for training in athletics and let it count toward graduation. By indirection and subreption, of course, much of the training given in athletics already does so count. [The Young Men's Christian Association (YMCA) was founded in 1844 in London to put Christian principles into practice by developing a healthy "mind, body, and spirit." In Veblen's time, the YMCA had local chapters at many American colleges and universities. "Muscular Christianity," first promoted by the YMCA, enjoyed its heyday in Britain and America in the late nineteenth century, stressing the need for a committed evangelicalism combined with the zealous pursuit of physical health and "manliness." –Ed.]

would have been. The law school's inclusion in the university corporation has the countenance of ancient tradition, it comes down as an authentic usage from the medieval era of European education, and from the pre-history of the American universities. But in point of substantial merit the law school belongs in the modern university no more than a school of fencing or dancing. This is particularly true of the American law schools, in which the Austinian conception of law[18] is followed, and it is more particularly true the more consistently the "case method"[19] is adhered to. These schools devote themselves with great singleness to the training of practitioners, as distinct from jurists; and their teachers stand in a relation to their students analogous to that in which the "coaches" stand to the athletes. What is had in view is the exigencies, expedients and strategy of successful practice; and not so much a grasp of even those quasi-scientific articles of metaphysics that lie at the root of the legal system. What is required and inculcated in the way of a knowledge of these elements of law is a familiarity with their strategic use.

The profession of the Law is, of course, an honorable profession, and it is doubtless believed by its apologists to be a useful profession, on the whole; but a body of lawyers somewhat less numerous, and with a lower average proficiency in legal subtleties and expedients, would unquestionably be quite as serviceable to the community at large as a larger number of such men with a higher efficiency; at the same time they would be less costly, both as to initial cost and as to the expenses of maintenance that come of that excessive volume and retardation of litigation due to an extreme facility in legal technique on the part of the members of the bar.

It will also be found true that both the schools of law and those of commerce, and in a less degree the other vocational schools, serve the advantage of one class as against another. In the measure in which these schools accomplish what they aim at, they increase the advantage of such men as already have some advantage over the common run. The instruction is half-way gratuitous; that is the purpose of placing these schools on a foundation or maintaining them at the public expense. It is presumed to be worth more than its cost to the students. The fees and other incidental expenses do not nearly cover the cost of the schools; otherwise

18. The "Austinian conception of law" was fashioned by John Austin (1790–1859), commonly known as the father of modern English jurisprudence. Austin argued for the separation of law and morality. His work broke a long-standing tradition of historical jurisprudence, which studied the development and evolution of law, as well as the tradition of Western natural law thinking, and insisted that to be valid and binding law must conform to moral standards.

19. The "case method" entails close study of decision-making in actual legal cases and was viewed by its first proponents as "scientific" preparation for the practice of law. It was pioneered in the United States in the 1870s by Harvard Law School Dean Christopher Langdell (1826–1906).

no foundation or support from the public funds would be required, and the universities would have no colorable excuse for going into this field. But even if the instruction and facilities offered by these schools are virtually gratuitous, yet the fees and incidental expenses, together with the expenditure of time and the cost of living required for a residence at the schools, make up so considerable an item of expense as effectually to exclude the majority of those young men who might otherwise be inclined to avail themselves of these advantages. In effect, none can afford the time and expense of this business training, whether in Commerce, Law, or the other professions, except those who are already possessed of something more than the average wealth or average income; and none, presumably, take kindly to this training, in commerce or law, e. g., except those who already have something more than the average taste and aptitude for business traffic, or who have a promising "opening" of this character in sight. So that this training that is desired to serve the private advantage of commercial students is, for the greater part, extended to a select body of young men; only such applicants being eligible, in effect, as do not on any showing need this gratuity.

In proportion to the work which it undertakes, the College of Commerce is—or it would be if it lived up to its professions—the most expensive branch of the university corporation. In this connection the case of the law school offers a significant object lesson of what to expect in the further growth of the schools of commerce. The law school is of older standing and maturer growth, at the same time that its aims and circumstances are of much the same general character as those that condition the schools of commerce; and it is therefore to be taken as indicating something of what must be looked for in the college of commerce if it is to do the work for which it is established. The indications, then, are (a) that the instruction in the field of commercial training may be expected gradually to fall into a more rigidly drawn curriculum, which will discard all irrelevant theoretical excursions and will diverge more and more widely from the ways of scientific inquiry, in proportion as experience and tactful organization bring the school to a maturer insight into its purposes and a more consistent adherence to its chief purpose of training expert men for the higher business practice; and (b) that the personnel of its staff must increasingly be drawn from among the successful businessmen, rather than from men of academic training.

Among the immediate consequences of this latter feature, as shown in the example of the law schools, is a relatively high cost. The schedule of salaries in the law schools attached to the universities, e. g., runs appreciably higher than in the university proper. the reason being, of course, that men suitable efficiently to serve as instructors and directive officials in a school of law are almost necessarily men whose services in the practice of the law would command a high rate of pay. What is needed in the law school (as in the school of commerce) is men who are practically conversant with the ways and means of earning large fees—that being the point of it all. Indeed, the scale of pay which their services will command in the open market is the chief and ordinary test of their fitness for the work of instruction. The salaries paid these men of affairs, who have so been diverted to the service of the schools, is commonly some multiple of the salary assigned to men of a comparable ability and attainments in the academic work proper. The academic rank assigned them is also necessarily, and for the like reason, commensurate with their higher scale of pay; all of which throws an undue preponderance of discretion and authority into the hands of these men of affairs, and so introduces a disproportionate bias in favor of unscientific and unscholarly aims and ideals in the university at large.

Judged by the example of the law schools, then, the college of commerce, if it is to live and thrive, may be counted on to divert a much larger body of funds from legitimate university uses, and to create more of a bias hostile to scholarly and scientific work in the academic body, than the mere numerical showing of its staff would suggest. It is fairly to be expected that capable men of affairs, drawn from the traffic of successful business for this service, will require even a higher rate of pay, at the same time that they will be even more cordially out of sympathy with the ideals of scholarship, than the personnel of the law schools. Such will necessarily be the outcome, if these schools are at all effectually to serve the purpose for which they are created.

But for the present, as matters stand now, near the inception of this enterprise in training masters of gain, such an outcome has not been reached. Neither have the schools of commerce yet been placed on such a footing of expensiveness and authoritative discretion as the high sanction of the quest of gain would seem properly to assign them; nor are they, as at present organized and equipped, at all eminently fit to carry out the work entrusted to their care. Commonly, it is to be admitted, the men selected for the staff are men of some academic training, rather than men of affairs who have shown evidence of fitness to give counsel and instruction, by eminently gainful success in business. They are, indeed, commonly men of moderate rating in the academic community, and are vested with a moderate rank and authority; and the emoluments of these offices are also such as attach to positions of a middling grade in academic work, instead of being comparable with the gains that come to capable men engaged in the large business outside. Yet it is from among these higher grades of expert businessmen outside that the schools of commerce must draw their staff of instructors and their administrative officers if they are to accomplish the task proposed to them. A movement in this direction is already visibly setting in.

It is reasonably to be expected that one or the other result should follow: either the college of commerce must remain, somewhat as in practice it now is, something in the way of an academic division, with an academic routine and standards, and with an unfulfilled ambition to serve the higher needs of business training; with a poorly paid staff of nondescript academic men, not peculiarly fitted to lead their students into the straight and narrow way of business success, nor yet eminently equipped for a theoretical inquiry into the phenomena of business traffic and their underlying causes so that the school will continue to stand, in effect, as a more or less pedantic and equivocal adjunct of a department of economics; or the schools must be endowed and organized with a larger and stricter regard to the needs of the higher business traffic; with a personnel composed of men of the highest business talent and attainments, tempted from such successful business traffic by the offer of salaries comparable with those paid the responsible officials of large corporations engaged in banking, railroading, and industrial enterprises—and they must also be fitted out with an equipment of a corresponding magnitude and liberality.

Apart from a large and costly material equipment, such a college would also, under current conditions, have to be provided with a virtually unlimited fund for travelling expenses, to carry its staff and its students to the several typical seats and centers of business traffic and maintain them there for that requisite personal contact with affairs that alone can contribute to a practical comprehension of business strategy. In short, the schools would have to meet those requirements of training and information which men who today aim to prepare themselves for the larger business will commonly spend expensive years of apprenticeship to acquire. It is eminently true in business training, very much as it is in military strategy, that nothing will take the place of first-hand observation and personal contact with the processes and procedure involved; and such first-hand contact is to be had only at the cost of a more or less protracted stay where the various lines of business are carried on.

The creation and maintenance of such a College of Commerce, on such a scale as will make it anything more than a dubious make-believe, would manifestly appear to be beyond the powers of any existing university. So that the best that can be compassed in this way, or that has been achieved, by the means at the

Figure 5. Thorstein Veblen (*front row, second from left*), Herbert J. Davenport (*front row, center*), Walter W. Stewart (*to right*), and University of Missouri School of Commerce students, ca. 1914. University of Missouri–Columbia Archives

disposal of any university hitherto, is a cross between a secondary school for bank-clerks and travelling salesmen and a subsidiary department of economics.[20]

All this applies with gradually lessened force to the other vocational schools, occupied with training for occupations that are of more substantial use to the community and less widely out of touch with the higher learning. In the light of their professions on the one side and the degree of their fulfilment on the other, it would be hazardous to guess how far the university directorate in any given case is animated with a spontaneous zeal for the furtherance of these "practical" aims which the universities so pursue, and how far on the other hand it may be a matter of politic management, to bring content to those commercially-minded laymen whose goodwill is rated as a valuable asset. These men of substance have

20. Veblen's animus against schools and colleges of "commerce," grounded in the assumption that business could never prove to be a profession that required or benefited from formal academic training, is curious in ways that will not be apparent to readers unfamiliar with his career. At the University of Chicago, the College of Commerce and Administration was partly the creation of J. Laurence Laughlin (1850–1933), who earlier had helped Veblen land his first appointment and remained his protector during his time at Chicago. After accepting a position as lecturer in the Economics Department at the University of Missouri in 1911, Veblen later served on the faculty of its School of Commerce, which became the new home of the department when the school opened in 1914 (see Figure 5).

a high appreciation of business efficiency—a species of self-respect, and therefore held as a point of honor—and are consequently inclined to rate all education in terms of earning-capacity. Failure to meet the presumed wishes of the businessmen in this matter, it is apprehended, would mean a loss of support in endowment and enrolment. And since endowment and enrolment, being the chief elements of visible success, are the two main ends of current academic policy, it is incumbent on the directorate to shape their policy accordingly.

So the academic authorities face the choice between scholarly efficiency and vocational training, and hitherto the result has been equivocal. The directorate should presumably be in a position to appreciate the drift of their own action, in so diverting the university's work to ends at variance with its legitimate purpose; and the effect of such a policy should presumably be repugnant to their scholarly tastes, as well as to their sense of right and honest living. But the circumstances of their office and tenure leave them somewhat helpless, for all their presumed insight and their aversion to this malpractice; and these conditions of office require them, as it is commonly apprehended, to take active measures for the defeat of learning—hitherto with an equivocal outcome. The schools of commerce, even more than the other vocational schools, have been managed somewhat parsimoniously, and the effectual results have habitually fallen far short of the clever promises held out in the prospectus.[21] The professed purpose of these schools is the training of young men to a high proficiency in the larger and more responsible affairs of business, but for the present this purpose must apparently remain a speculative, and very temperately ingenuous, aspiration, rather than a practicable working program.

21. Possible allusion to the unimpressive early results of Chicago's College of Commerce and Administration, which opened in 1898. In 1901–2, only 7 of 311 baccalaureate graduates completed their work in the new college.

CHAPTER VIII

Summary and Trial Balance[1]

As in earlier passages, so here in speaking of profit and loss, the point of view taken is neither that of material advantage, whether of the individuals concerned or of the community at large, nor that of expediency for the common good in respect of prosperity or of morals; nor is the appraisal here ventured upon to be taken as an expression of praise or dispraise at large, touching this incursion of business principles into the affairs of learning.

By and large, the intrusion of businesslike ideals, aims and methods into this field, with all the consequences that follow, may be commendable or the reverse. All that is matter for attention and advisement at the hands of such as aim to alter, improve, amend or conserve the run of institutional phenomena that goes to make up the current situation. The present inquiry bears on the higher learning as it comes into this current situation, and on the effect of this recourse to business principles upon the pursuit of learning.

Not that this learning is therefore to be taken as necessarily of higher and more substantial value than that traffic in competitive gain and competitive spending upon which business principles converge, and in which they find their consummate expression—even though it is broadly to be recognized and taken account of that such is the deliberate appraisal awarded by the common sense of civilized mankind. The profit and loss here spoken for is not profit and loss, to mankind or to any given community, in respect of that inclusive complex of interests that makes up the balanced total of good and ill; it is profit and loss for the cause of learning, simply; and there is here no aspiration to pass on ulterior questions. As required by the exigencies of such an argument, it is therefore assumed, *pro forma*, that profit and loss for the pursuit of learning is profit and loss without reservation; very much as a corporation accountant will audit income and outlay within the affairs of the corporation, whereas, qua accountant, he will perforce have nothing to say as to the ulterior expediency of the corporation and its affairs in any other bearing.

1. A "trial balance" is a statement of all open debit and credit items in a double-entry ledger, prepared to test their equality.

I[2]

Business principles take effect in academic affairs most simply, obviously and avowably in the way of a businesslike administration of the scholastic routine; where they lead immediately to a bureaucratic organization and a system of scholastic accountancy. In one form or another, some such administrative machinery is a necessity in any large school that is to be managed on a centralized plan; as the American schools commonly are, and as, more particularly, they aim to be. This necessity is all the more urgent in a school that takes over the discipline of a large body of pupils that have not reached years of discretion, as is also commonly the case with those American schools that claim rank as universities; and the necessity is all the more evident to men whose ideal of efficiency is the centralized control exercised through a system of accountancy in the modern large business concerns. The larger American schools are primarily undergraduate establishments—with negligible exceptions; and under these current American conditions, of excessive numbers, such a centralized and bureaucratic administration appears to be indispensable for the adequate control of immature and reluctant students; at the same time, such an organization conduces to an excessive size. The immediate and visible effect of such a large and centralized administrative machinery is, on the whole, detrimental to scholarship, even in the undergraduate work; though it need not be so in all respects and unequivocally, so far as regards that routine training that is embodied in the undergraduate curriculum. But it is at least a necessary evil in any school that is of so considerable a size as to preclude substantially all close or cordial personal relations between the teachers and each of these immature pupils under their charge, as, again, is commonly the case with these American undergraduate establishments. Such a system of authoritative control, standardization, gradation, accountancy, classification, credits and penalties, will necessarily be drawn on stricter lines the more the school takes on the character of a house of correction or a penal settlement; in which the irresponsible inmates are to be held to a round of distasteful tasks and restrained from (conventionally) excessive irregularities of conduct. At the same time this recourse to such coercive control and standardization of tasks has unavoidably given the schools something of the character of a penal[3] settlement.

2. Section I is largely a summary of points Veblen makes in the first seven chapters.

3. Relating to or used for punishment. Veblen's choice of words here needs some explanation. In saying that the American university has "something of the character of a penal settlement," part of what he had in mind was the widespread adoption of a practice then unheard of in European universities: regular compulsory tests and exams that forced American university undergraduate students to attend to their academic assignments. Veblen observed other kinds of "penal" arrangements put into

As intimated above, the ideal of efficiency by force of which a large-scale centralized organization commends itself in these premises is that pattern of shrewd management whereby a large business concern makes money. The underlying business-like presumption accordingly appears to be that learning is a merchantable commodity, to be produced on a piece-rate plan, rated, bought and sold by standard units, measured, counted and reduced to staple equivalence by impersonal, mechanical tests. In all its bearings the work is hereby reduced to a mechanistic, statistical consistency, with numerical standards and units; which conduces to perfunctory and mediocre work throughout, and acts to deter both students and teachers from a free pursuit of knowledge, as contrasted with the pursuit of academic credits. So far as this mechanistic system goes freely into effect it leads to a substitution of salesman-like proficiency—a balancing of bargains in staple credits—in the place of scientific capacity and addiction to study.

The salesman-like abilities and the men of affairs that so are drawn into the academic personnel are, presumably, somewhat under grade in their kind; since the pecuniary inducement offered by the schools is rather low as compared with the remuneration for office work of a similar character in the common run of business occupations, and since businesslike employees of this kind may fairly be presumed to go unreservedly to the highest bidder. Yet these more unscholarly members of the staff will necessarily be assigned the more responsible and discretionary positions in the academic organization; since under such a scheme of standardization, accountancy and control, the school becomes primarily a bureaucratic organization, and the first and unremitting duties of the staff are those of official management and accountancy. The further qualifications requisite in the members of the academic staff will be such as make for vendibility,[4] volubility,[5] tactful effrontery,[6] conspicuous conformity to the popular taste in all matters of opinion, usage and conventions.

The need of such a businesslike organization asserts itself in somewhat the same degree in which the academic policy is guided by considerations of magnitude and statistical renown; and this in turn is somewhat closely correlated with the extent of discretionary power exercised by the captain of erudition placed in

---

place at the University of Chicago. President William Rainey Harper initially championed the ideal that Chicago undergraduates were responsible young adults who needed no administrative or faculty supervision. But over time he implemented stringent attendance requirements and brought student dormitories and student publications under close administrative scrutiny. Harper also instituted sexual segregation in the classrooms during the first two undergraduate years. Chicago was fully co-educational at its start.

4. Marketable; saleable.
5. Glibness; loquaciousness.
6. Shamelessness.

control. At the same time, by provocation of the facilities which it offers for making an impressive demonstration, such bureaucratic organization will lead the university management to bend its energies with somewhat more singleness to the parade of magnitude and statistical gains. It also, and in the same connection, provokes to a persistent and detailed surveillance and direction of the work and manner of life of the academic staff, and so it acts to shut off initiative of any kind in the work done.[a]

Intimately bound up with this bureaucratic officialism and accountancy, and working consistently to a similar outcome, is the predilection for "practical efficiency" that is to say, for pecuniary success—prevalent in the American community.[b] This predilection is a matter of settled habit, due, no doubt, to the fact that preoccupation with business interests characterizes this community in an exceptional degree, and that pecuniary habits of thought consequently rule popular thinking in a peculiarly uncritical and prescriptive fashion. This pecuniary animus

a. "He has stifled all manly independence and individuality wherever it has exhibited itself at college. All noble idealism, and all the graces of poetry and art have been shriveled by his brutal and triumphant power. He has made mechanical efficiency and administrative routine the goal of the university's endeavor. The nobler ends of academic life will never be served so long as this spokesman of materialism remains in power."

History will relate that one of the eminent captains, through an incumbency of more than a quarter of a century, in a university of eminent wealth and volume, has followed a settled policy of defeating any overt move looking to scientific or scholarly inquiry on the part of any member of his faculty. Should a man of scholarly proclivities by any chance sift through the censorship exercised in virtue of the executive's appointing power, as might happen, since the captain was himself not qualified to pass a grounded opinion on any man's qualifications in that respect; and should he then give evidence of continuing to spend time and thought on matters of that nature, his burden of administrative and classroom tasks would presently be increased sufficiently to subdue his wayward bent; or, in an incorrigible case, the offender against the rule of academic sterility would eventually be retired by severance of his connection with this seat of learning.

In some sinister sense the case reflects credit on the American academic community at large, in that, by the close of this quarter-century of preventive regimen, the resulting academic staff had become a byword of nugatory intrigue and vacant pedantry.

[A second allusion to Joel Spingarn's dismissal from the Columbia University faculty in 1911. (Cf. chapter 3, "The Academic Administration and Policy," note d.) The quotation is taken from a statement Spingarn made about Columbia president Nicholas Murray Butler after he was dismissed. It appeared in the *New York Times* (10 April 1911). –Ed.]

b. So far has this predilection made its way in the counsels of the "educators" that much of the current discussion of *desiderata* [Latin for things that are need or wanted. –Ed.] in academic policy reads like controversial argument on "efficiency engineering,"—an "efficiency engineer" is an accountant competent to advise business concerns how best to increase their saleable output per unit of cost. And there has, indeed, been at least one tour of inspection of American universities by such an "efficiency engineer," undertaken in the service of an establishment founded with a view to academic welfare and governed by a board of university presidents. The report submitted by the inquiry in question duly conforms to the customary lines of "scientific management." [Allusion to Morris L. Cooke (1872–1960), a mechanical engineer and then relatively well-known protégée of Frederick Winslow Taylor (Cf. chapter VII, "Vocational Training," note h.). The Carnegie Foundation for the Advancement of Teaching was the "establishment" that funded and published Cooke's *Academic and Industrial Efficiency* (1911), a book in which he developed a calculus for measuring the efficiency and productivity of educational institutions much like that Taylor earlier had developed for industrial factories. –Ed.]

falls in with and reinforces the movement for academic accountancy, and combines with it to further a so-called "practical" bias in all the work of the schools.

It appears, then, that the intrusion of business principles in the universities goes to weaken and retard the pursuit of learning, and therefore to defeat the ends for which a university is maintained. This result follows, primarily, from the substitution of impersonal, mechanical relations, standards and tests, in the place of personal conference, guidance and association between teachers and students; as also from the imposition of a mechanically standardized routine upon the members of the staff, whereby any disinterested preoccupation with scholarly or scientific inquiry is thrown into the background and falls into abeyance. Few if any who are competent to speak in these premises will question that such has been the outcome. To offset against this work of mutilation and retardation there are certain gains in expedition, and in the volume of traffic that can be carried by any given equipment and corps of employees. Particularly will there be a gain in the statistical showing, both as regards the volume of instruction offered, and probably also as regards the enrolment; since accountancy creates statistics and its absence does not.

Such increased enrolment as may be due to businesslike management and methods is an increase of undergraduate enrolment. The net effect as regards the graduate enrolment—apart from any vocational instruction that may euphemistically be scheduled as "graduate"—is in all probability rather a decrease than an increase.[7] Through indoctrination with utilitarian (pecuniary) ideals of earning and spending, as well as by engendering spendthrift and sportsmanlike habits, such a businesslike management diverts the undergraduate students from going in for the disinterested pursuit of knowledge, and so from entering on what is properly university work; as witness the relatively slight proportion of graduate students outside of the professional schools—who come up from the excessively large undergraduate departments of the more expansive universities, as contrasted with the number of those who come into university work from the smaller and less businesslike colleges.

The ulterior consequences that follow from such businesslike standardization and bureaucratic efficiency are evident in the current state of the public schools;

7. During Veblen's years at Chicago, the number of undergraduate students grew much more rapidly than that of their graduate counterparts. In fall 1893, the beginning of Veblen's second year on the faculty, the university had 232 graduate students and 357 undergraduates. By fall 1901, the number of graduate students had grown very modestly to 246, while the number of undergraduates had ballooned to 1,522.

especially as seen in the larger towns, where the principles of business management have had time and scope to work out in a fair degree of consistency. The
resulting abomination of desolation[8] is sufficiently notorious. And there appears
to be no reason why a similarly stale routine of futility should not overtake the
universities, and give similarly foolish results, as fast as the system of standardization, accountancy and piece-work goes consistently into effect—except only
for the continued enforced employment of a modicum of impracticable scholars
and scientists on the academic staff, whose un-businesslike scholarly proclivities and inability to keep the miner's-inch[9] of scholastic credit always in mind,
must in some measure always defeat the perfect working of standardization and
accountancy.

As might be expected, this régime of graduated sterility has already made fair
headway in the undergraduate work, especially in the larger undergraduate
schools; and this in spite of any efforts on the part of the administration to hedge
against such an outcome by recourse to an intricate system of electives and a
wide diversification of the standard units of erudition so offered.

In the graduate work the like effect is only less visible, because the measures
leading to it have come into bearing more recently, and hitherto less unreservedly.
But the like results should follow here also, just so fast and so far as the same
range of business principles come to be worked into the texture of the university
organization in the same efficacious manner as they have already taken effect in
the public schools. And, pushed on as it is by the progressive substitution of men
imbued with the tastes and habits of practical affairs, in the place of unpractical
scholarly ideals, the movement toward a perfunctory routine of mediocrity
should logically be expected to go forward at a progressively accelerated rate. The
visible drift of things in this respect in the academic pursuit of the social sciences,
so-called, is an argument as to what may be hoped for in the domain of academic
science at large. It is only that the executive is actuated by a sharper solicitude to
keep the academic establishment blameless of anything like innovation or iconoclasm at this point; which reinforces the drift toward a mechanistic routine and
a curtailment of inquiry in this field; it is not that these sciences that deal with
the phenomena of human life lend themselves more readily to mechanical description and enumeration than the material sciences do, nor is their subject
matter intrinsically more inert or less provocative of questions.

8. Biblical phrase in Book of Daniel 24:15 describing latter-day divine judgment of the wicked
wherever they may be; also: extreme sadness caused by loss or loneliness.

9. Cf. chapter III, "The Academic Administration," note 20.

II

Throughout the above summary review, as also through the foregoing inquiry, the argument continually returns to or turns about two main interests—notoriety and the academic executive. These two might be called the two foci about which swings the orbit of the university world. These conjugate foci lie on a reasonably short axis; indeed, they tend to coincide; so that the orbit comes near the perfection of a circle; having virtually but a single center which may perhaps indifferently be spoken of as the university's president or as its renown, according as one may incline to conceive these matters in terms of tangible fact or of intangible.

The system of standardization and accountancy has this renown or prestige as its chief ulterior purpose: the prestige of the university or of its president, which largely comes to the same net result. Particularly will this be true in so far as this organization is designed to serve competitive ends; which are, in academic affairs, chiefly the ends of notoriety, prestige, advertising in all its branches and bearings. It is through increased creditable notoriety that the universities seek their competitive ends, and it is on such increase of notoriety, accordingly, that the competitive endeavors of a businesslike management are chiefly spent. It is in and through such accession of renown, therefore, that the chief and most tangible gains due to the injection of competitive business principles in the academic policy should appear.

Of course, this renown, as such, has no substantial value to the corporation of learning; nor, indeed, to anyone but the university executive by whose management it is achieved. Taken simply in its first incidence, as prestige or notoriety, it conduces in no degree to the pursuit of knowledge; but in its ulterior consequences, it appears currently to be believed, at least ostensibly, that such notoriety must greatly enhance the powers of the corporation of learning. These ulterior consequences are (believed to be), a growth in the material resources and the volume of traffic.

Such good effects as may follow from a sedulous attention to creditable publicity, therefore, are the chief gains to be set off against the mischief incident to "scientific management"[10] in academic affairs. Hence any line of inquiry into the business management of the universities continually leads back to the cares of publicity, with what might to an outsider seem undue insistence. The reason is

10. System of management advocated and made famous by Frederick Winslow Taylor (cf. chapter VII, "Vocational Training," note i); also known as "Taylorism." In Taylor's view, the task of "scientific" management was to break down every task into its component parts, time each part to determine how quickly it can be done, and then recombine them all into a more efficient whole.

that the businesslike management and arrangements in question are habitually—and primarily required either to serve the ends of this competitive campaign of publicity or to conform to its schedule of expediency. The felt need of notoriety and prestige has a main share in shaping the work and bearing of the university at every point. Whatever will not serve this end of prestige has no secure footing in current university policy.[11] The margin of tolerance on this head is quite narrow; and it is apparently growing incontinently narrower.

So far as any university administration can, with the requisite dignity, permit itself to avow a pursuit of notoriety, the gain that is avowedly sought by its means is an increase of funds—more or less ingenuously spoken of as an increase of equipment. An increased enrolment of students will be no less eagerly sought after, but the received canons of academic decency require this object to be kept even more discreetly masked than the quest of funds.

The duties of publicity are large and arduous, and the expenditures incurred in this behalf are similarly considerable. So that it is not unusual to find a Publicity Bureau[12]—often apologetically masquerading under a less telltale name—incorporated in the university organization to further this enterprise in reputable notoriety. Not only must a creditable publicity be provided for, as one of the running cares of the administration, but every feature of academic life, and of the life of all members of the academic staff, must unremittingly (though of course unavowedly) be held under surveillance at every turn, with a view to furthering whatever may yield a reputable notoriety, and to correcting or eliminating whatever may be conceived to have a doubtful or untoward bearing in this respect.

This surveillance of appearances, and of the means of propagating appearances, is perhaps the most exacting detail of duty incumbent on an enterprising executive. Without such a painstaking cultivation of a reputable notoriety, it is believed, a due share of funds could not be procured by any university for the prosecution of its work as a seminary of the higher learning. Its more alert and unabashed rivals, it is presumed, would in that case be able to divert the flow of loose funds to their own use, and would so outstrip their dilatory competitor in the race for size and popular acclaim, and therefore, it is sought to be believed, in scientific and scholarly application.

In the absence of all reflection—not an uncommon frame of mind in this connection—one might be tempted to think that all this academic enterprise of notoriety and conciliation should add something appreciable to the aggregate of

11. Cf. chapter IV, "The Academic Administration," note 24.
12. Today often called University Relations, a department that also can encompass related endeavors such as Communications and Marketing, Development, and Government and Community Relations.

funds placed at the disposal of the universities; and that each of these competitive advertising concerns should so gain something appreciable, without thereby cutting into the supply of funds available for the rest. But such is probably not the outcome, to any appreciable extent; assuredly not apart from the case of the state universities that are dependent on the favor of local politicians, and perhaps apart from gifts for conspicuous buildings.

With whatever (slight) reservation may be due, publicity in university management is of substantially the same nature and effect as advertising in other competitive business; and with such reservation as may be called for in the case of other advertising, it is an engine of competition, and has no aggregate effect. As is true of competitive gains in business at large, so also these differential gains of the several university corporations cannot be added together to make an aggregate. They are differential gains in the main, of the same nature as the gains achieved in any other game of skill and effrontery. The gross aggregate funds contributed to university uses from all sources would in all probability be nearly as large in the absence of such competitive notoriety and conformity.[13] Indeed, it should seem likely that such donors as are gifted with sufficient sense of the value of science and scholarship to find it worthwhile to sink any part of their capital in that behalf would be somewhat deterred by the spectacle of competitive waste and futile clamor presented by this academic enterprise; so that the outcome might as well be a diminution of the gross aggregate of donations and allowances. But such an argument doubtless runs on very precarious grounds; it is by no means evident that these munificent patrons of learning habitually distinguish between scholarship and publicity. But in any case it is quite safe to presume that to the cause of learning at large, and therefore to the community in respect of its interest in the advancement of learning, no appreciable net gain accrues from this competitive publicity of the seats of learning.

In some slight, or doubtful, degree this competitive publicity, including academic pageants, genteel solemnities, and the like, may conceivably augment the gross aggregate means placed at the disposal of the universities, by persuasively keeping the well-meaning men of wealth constantly in mind of the university's need of additional funds, as well as of the fact that such gifts will not be allowed to escape due public notice. But the aggregate increase of funds due to these en-

13. Veblen's claim here is open to argument. University presidents believed that "publicity" efforts were crucial to an institution's success, and sometimes with good reason. In 1892, for example, when Columbia's president Seth Low announced plans to move the entire college to a new and more spacious location in New York City at 116th and Broadway, he also launched a well-publicized challenge to the trustees and other wealthy New Yorkers that ignited the largest outpouring of philanthropy in Columbia's history.

deavors is doubtless not large enough to offset the aggregate expenditure on notoriety. Taken as a whole, and counting in all the wide-ranging expenditure entailed by this enterprise in notoriety and the maintenance of academic prestige,
university publicity doubtless costs appreciably more than it brings. So far as it
succeeds in its purpose, its chief effect is to divert the flow of funds from one to
another of the rival establishments. In the aggregate this expedient for procuring means for the advancement of learning doubtless results in an appreciable
net loss.

The net loss, indeed, is always much more considerable than would be indicated by any statistical showing; for this academic enterprise involves an extensive and almost wholly wasteful duplication of equipment, personnel and output
of instruction, as between the rival seats of learning, at the same time that it also
involves an excessively parsimonious provision for actual scholastic work, as
contrasted with publicity; so also it involves the overloading of each rival corps of
instructors with a heterogeneous schedule of courses, beyond what would conduce to their best efficiency as teachers. This competitive parcelment, duplication
and surreptitious thrift, due to a businesslike rivalry between the several schools,
is perhaps the gravest drawback to the American university situation.[14]

It should be added that no aggregate gain for scholarship comes of diverting
any given student from one school to another duplicate establishment by specious offers of a differential advantage; particularly when, as frequently happens,
the differential inducement takes the form of the extra-scholastic amenities spoken of in an earlier chapter, or the greater alleged prestige of one school as against
another, or, as also happens, a surreptitiously greater facility for achieving a given
academic degree.

In all its multifarious ways and means, university advertising carried beyond
the modicum that would serve a due "publicity of accounts"[15] as regards the work
to be done, accomplishes no useful aggregate result. And, as is true of advertising in other competitive business, current university publicity is not an effective
means of spreading reliable information; nor is it designed for that end. Here as
elsewhere, to meet the requirements of competitive enterprise, advertising must
somewhat exceed the point of maximum veracity.

14. Veblen here repeats his earlier criticism of the new American system for its "extensive and
wasteful duplication of plant, organization, and personnel." His criticism of what became a distinctively American commitment to mass higher education is usually overlooked in discussion of his book.
15. Early twentieth-century legal term for one of several new regulations that progressive American
reformers sought to apply to corporations doing interstate business. As a condition for being granted
a license to do inter-state business, "publicity of accounts" would require a corporation to gain commission approval of all its affairs, from its capitalization to its business practices.

In no field of human endeavor is competitive notoriety and a painstaking conformity to extraneous standards of living and of conduct so gratuitous a burden, since learning is in no degree a competitive enterprise; and all mandatory observance of the conventions—pecuniary or other—is necessarily a drag on the pursuit of knowledge. In ordinary competitive business, as, e. g., merchandising, advertisement is a means of competitive selling, and is justified by the increased profits that come to the successful advertiser from the increased traffic; and on the like grounds a painstaking conformity to conventional usage, in appearances and expenditure, is there wisely cultivated with the same end in view. In the affairs of science and scholarship, simply as such and apart from the personal ambitions of the university's executive, there is nothing that corresponds to this increased traffic or these competitive profits,[c]—nor will the discretionary officials avow that such increased traffic is the purpose of academic publicity. Indeed, an increased enrollment of students yields no increased net income, nor is the corporation of learning engaged (avowedly, at least) in an enterprise that looks to a net income.[16] At the same time, such increased enrolment as comes of this competitive salesmanship among the universities is made up almost wholly of wasters, accessions from the genteel and sporting classes, who seek the university as a means of respectability and dissipation, and who serve the advancement of the higher learning only as fire, flood and pestilence serve the needs of the husbandman.

Competitive publicity, therefore, and its maid-servant conventional observance, would appear in all this order of things to have no serious motive, or at least none that can freely be avowed; as witness the unwillingness of any university administration formally to avow that it seeks publicity or expends the corporate funds in competitive advertising. So that on its face this whole academic traffic in pub-

c. "Education is the one kind of human enterprise that cannot be brought under the action of the economic law of supply and demand. It cannot be conducted on 'business principles.' There is no 'demand' for education in the economic sense. . . . Society is the only interest that can be said to demand it, and society must supply its own demand. Those who found educational institutions or promote educational enterprise put themselves in the place of society and assume to speak and act for society, not for any economic interest."—Lester Frank Ward (1841–1913), *Pure Sociology: A Treatise on the Origins and Spiritual Development of Society* (1903), 575. [Ward was an American botanist, paleontologist, and sociologist, who was also first president of the American Sociological Association. –Ed.]

16. Between 1900 and 1910, the nation's eighteen- to twenty-four-year-old population attending college rose from 2.3 percent to 2.9 percent; by 1930, it hit 7.2percent. Not until the post–World War II era was there a comparable surge in enrollment. Veblen associated increased undergraduate enrollment in his time exclusively with the spreading business mentality in American universities. But increased undergraduate numbers during the first three decades of the twentieth century can also be viewed, as the historian Roger Geiger has suggested, as a vote of confidence on the part of the principal clientele of the American universities. Increased undergraduate enrollment made a powerful argument for increased financial support from state legislators, university alumni, and local and national benefactors. See Roger Geiger, *To Advance Knowledge: The Growth of American Research Universities, 1900–1940* (New Brunswick, NJ: Transaction, 2004), 13.

licity and genteel conventionalities appears to be little else than a boyish imitation of the ways and means employed, with shrewd purpose, in business enterprise that has no analog with the pursuit of knowledge. But the aggregate yearly expenditure of the universities on this competitive academic publicity runs well up into the millions, and it involves also an extensive diversion of the energies of the general body of academic men to these purposes of creditable notoriety; and such an expenditure of means and activities is not lightly to be dismissed as an unadvised play of businesslike fancy on the part of the university authorities.

Unquestionably, an unreflecting imitation of methods that have been found good in retail merchandising counts for something in the case, perhaps for much; for the academic executives under whose surveillance this singularly futile traffic is carried on are commonly men of commonplace intelligence and aspiration, bound by the commonplace habits of workday intercourse in a business community. The histrionic[17] afflatus[18] is also by no means wanting in current university management, and when coupled with commonplace ideals in the dramatic art its outcome will necessarily be a tawdry, spectacular pageantry and a straining after showy magnitude. There is also the lower motive of unreflecting clannishness on the part of the several university establishments. This counts for something, perhaps for more than one could gracefully admit. It stands out perhaps most baldly in the sentimental rivalry—somewhat factitious, it is true—shown at intercollegiate games and similar occasions of invidious comparison between the different schools. It is, of course, gratifying to the clannish conceit of any college man to be able to hold up convincing statistical exhibits showing the greater glory of "his own" university, whether in athletics, enrolment, alumni, material equipment, or schedules of instruction; whether he be an official, student, alumnus, or member of the academic staff; and all this array and circumstance will appeal to him the more unreservedly in proportion as he is gifted with a more vulgar sportsmanlike bent and is unmoved by any dispassionate interest in matters of science or scholarship; and in proportion, also, as his habitual outlook is that of the commonplace man of affairs. In the uncritical eyes of the commonplace men of affairs, whose experience in business has trained them into a quasi-tropismatic[19] approval of notoriety as a means of advertising, these puerile demonstrations will, of course, have a high value simply in their own right. Sentimental chauvinism[20] of this kind is a good and efficient motive to emulative enterprise, as far as it goes,

---

17. Deliberately affected; theatrical.
18. A strong creative impulse, considered to be divine in origin, as in "divine afflatus."
19. Almost automatic.
20. Belief that your own country, ethnic group, race, and so forth is superior to any other.

but even when backed with the directorate's proclivity to businesslike make-believe, it can, after all, scarcely be made to cover the whole voluminous traffic that must on any consistent view go in under the head of competitive publicity.

III

The abiding incentives to this traffic in publicity and genteel observance must be sought elsewhere than in the boyish emotions of rivalry and clannish elation that animates the academic staff, or even in the histrionic interest which the members of the staff or the directorate may have in the prestige of their own establishment. The staff, indeed, are not in any sensible degree accountable for this pursuit of prestige, since they have but little discretion in these matters; in substance, the government of a competitive university is necessarily of an autocratic character, whatever plausible forms of collective action and advisement it may be found expedient to observe. The seat of discretion is in the directorate; though many details of administration may be left to the deliberations of the staff, so long as these details do not impinge on the directorate's scheme of policy. The impulse and initiative to this enterprise in publicity, as well as the surveillance and guidance in the matter, radiates from this center, and it is here, presumably, that the incentives to such enterprise are immediately felt. The immediate discretion in the conduct of these matters rests in the hands of the directive academic head, with the aid and advice of his circle of personal counsellors, and with the backing of the governing board.

The incentives that decide the policy of publicity and guide its execution must accordingly be such as will appeal directly to the sensibilities of the academic head and of the members of the governing board; and this applies not only as regards the traffic in publicity by print and public spectacles, but also as regards the diversion of the corporation of learning to utilitarian ends, and as regards the traffic in conventional observances and conformity to popular opinion. What these incentives may be, that so appeal to the authorities in discretion, and that move them to divert the universities from the pursuit of knowledge, is not altogether easy to say; more particularly it is not easy to find an explanation that shall take account of the facts and yet reflect no discredit on the intelligence or the good faith of these discretionary authorities.

The motives that actuate the members of the governing boards are perhaps less obscure than those which determine the conduct of the academic executive. The governing boards are, in effect, made up of businessmen, who do not habitually look beyond the "practical" interest of commercial gain and the commonplaces of commercial routine and political bravado. It is (should be) otherwise with the academic management, who are, by tradition, presumed to be animated with scholarly ideals, and whose avowed ulterior motive is in all cases the single-minded furtherance of the cause of learning.

On its face it should not seem probable that motives of personal gain, in the form of pecuniary or other material interest, would have a serious part in the matter. In all probability there is in no case a sensible pecuniary gain to the university as such from its expenditures on publicity, and there is still less question of gain in any other than the pecuniary respect. There is also commonly no very substantial pecuniary gain to be derived from this business either by the academic head or by the members of the board—an exceptional instance to the contrary will not vitiate this general proposition. It all brings no appreciable pecuniary return to them, particularly so far as it is concerned with the pursuit of prestige; and apart from exceptional, and therefore negligible, cases it admits of no appreciable conversion of funds to private use. At the same time it seems almost an affront to entertain the notion that these impassively purposeful men of affairs are greatly moved by personal motives of vanity, vaingloriously seeking renown for efficiently carrying on a traffic in publicity that has no other end than renown for efficiently carrying it on. And yet it will be found extremely difficult to take account of the facts and at the same time avoid such an odiously personal interpretation of them.

Such, indeed, would have to be the inference drawn by anyone who might ingenuously take the available facts at their face value—not counting as facts the dutiful protestations of the authorities to the contrary. But it should be kept in mind that a transparent ingenuousness is not characteristic of business phenomena, within the university or without. A degree of deviation, or "diplomacy," may be forced on the academic management by the circumstances of their office, particularly by the one-eyed business sense of their governing boards. Indeed, admissions to such an effect are not altogether wanting.

Rated as they are, in the popular apprehension, as gentlemen and scholars, and themselves presumably accepting this rating as substantially correct, no feature of the scheme of management imposed on the academic executive by business principles should (presumably) be so repugnant to their sensibilities and their scholarly judgment as this covert but unremitting pursuit of an innocuous notoriety, coupled as it necessarily is with a systematic misdirection of the academic forces to unscholarly ends; but prudential reasons will decide that this must be their chief endeavor if they are to hold their own as a competitive university. Should the academic head allow his sense of scholarly fitness and expediency to hamper this business of reputable notoriety, it is, perhaps with reason, feared that such remissness would presently lead to his retirement from office; at least something of that kind seems a fair inference from the run of the facts. His place would then be supplied by an incumbent duly qualified on this score of one-eyed business sagacity, and one who would know how to keep his scholarly impulses in hand. It is at least conceivable that the apprehension of some such contingency may underlie current university management at some points, and it may therefore in some instances have given the administration of academic affairs an air of light-headed futility, when it should rather be credited with a sagaciously disingenuous yielding to circumstance.

The run of the facts as outlined above, and the line of inference just indicated as following from them, reflect no great credit on the manly qualities of the incumbents of executive office; but the alternative, as also noted above, is scarcely preferable even in that respect, while it would be even less flattering to their intellectual powers. Yet there appears to be no avoiding the dilemma so presented. Of disinterested grounds for the common run of academic policy there seem to be only these two lines to choose between: either a short-sighted and headlong conformity to the vulgar prejudice that does not look beyond "practical" training and competitive expansion, coupled with a boyish craving for popular display; or a strategic compromise with the elders of the Philistines,[21] a futile doing of evil in the hope that some good may come of it.

This latter line of apology is admissible only in those cases where the university corporation is in an exceptionally precarious position in respect of its endowment, where it is in great need and has much to hope for in the way of pecuniary gain through stooping to conventional prejudices, that are of no scholastic value, but that are conceived to bind its potential benefactors in a web of fatally fragile bigotry; or, again, where the executive is in sensible danger of being superseded by an administration imbued with (conceivably) yet lower and feebler scholarly ideals.

Now, it happens that there are notable instances of universities where such a policy of obsequiously reputable notoriety and aimless utilitarian management is pursued under such circumstances of settled endowment and secure tenure as to preclude all hazard of supersession on the part of the executive and all chance of material gain from any accession of popular renown or stagnant respectability. There is a small class of American university corporations that are so placed, by

---

21. People guided by material values and are usually disdainful of artistic and intellectual values. Today usually not capitalized.

the peculiar circumstances of their endowment, as to be above the apprehension of need,[22] so long as they are content to live anywhere nearly within the domain of learning; at the same time that they have nothing to lose through alienating the affections of the vulgar, and nothing to gain by deferring to the sentimental infirmities of elderly well-to-do persons. This class is not a numerous one; not large enough to set the pace for the rest; but evidently also not numerous enough to go on their own recognizances, and adopt a line of policy suited to their own circumstances and not bound to the fashion set by the rest. Some of the well-known establishments of this class have already been alluded to in another connection.

Statistical display, spectacular stage properties, vainglorious make-believe and obsequious concessions to worldly wisdom, should seem to have no place in the counsels of these schools; which should therefore hopefully be counted on to pursue the quest of knowledge with that single mind which they profess. Yet such is eminently, not to say preeminently, not the case. Their policy in these matters commonly differs in no sensible degree from that pursued by the needier establishments that are engaged in a desperate race of obsequiousness, for funds to be procured by favor of well-to-do donors, or through the support of worldly-wise clergymen and politicians. Indeed, some of the most pathetic clamor for popular renown, as well as instances of the most profligate stooping to vulgar prejudice, are to be credited to establishments of this, potentially independent, class. The management, apparently, are too well imbued with the commonplace preconceptions of worldly wisdom afloat among the laity, to admit of their taking any action on their own deliberate initiative or effectually taking thought of that pursuit of learning that has been entrusted to their care. So, perhaps through some puzzle-headed sense of decorum, they have come to engage in this bootless conventional race for funds which they have no slightest thought of obtaining, and for an increased enrolment which they advisedly do not desire.

In the light of these instances, one is constrained to believe that the academic executive who has so been thrown up as putative director of the pursuit of learning must go in for this annexation of vocational schools, for amateurish "summer sessions," for the appointment of schoolmasters instead of scholars on the academic staff, for the safe-keeping and propagation of genteel conventionalities at the cost of scholarship, for devout and polite ceremonial—one is constrained to believe that such a university executive goes in for this policy of tawdry routine

22. In 1918, the "small class" of private American universities "above the apprehension of need" included Harvard, MIT, Yale, Columbia, Penn, Princeton, Cornell, Johns Hopkins, Chicago, and Stanford.

because he lacks ordinary intelligence or because he lacks ordinary courage.[23] His discretion is overborne either by his own store of unreflecting prejudice, or by fear of losing personal prestige among the ignorant, even though he has no substantial ground, personal or official, for so yielding to current prejudice. Such appears to be the state of the case in these instances, where the exigencies of university politics afford no occasion for strategic compromise with the worldly-wise; which pointedly suggests that the like threadbare motives of unreflecting imitation and boyish make-believe may also have unduly much to do with academic policy, even in that common run of cases that might otherwise have best been explained as an effect of shrewd strategy, designed to make terms with the mischievous stupidity of an underbred laity.

But any discussion of motives necessarily has an invidious air, and so cannot but be distasteful. Yet, since this executive policy can be explained or understood only as the outcome of those motives that appeal decisively to the discretionary officials, it is necessary to pursue the inquiry a degree farther at this point, even at the cost of such slight odium as may not be avoided, and at the risk of a certain appearance of dispraise. It is perhaps needless to say that this question of motivation is not gone into here except as it may serve to exhibit the run of the facts. The run of the facts is not intelligible except in the light of their meaning as possible motives to the pursuit of that policy of which they are the outcome.

On the above considerations, it follows that the executive heads of these competitive universities are a picked body of men, endowed with a particular bent, such as will dispose them to be guided by the run of motives indicated. This will imply that they are, either by training or by native gift, men of a somewhat peculiar frame of mind—peculiarly open to the appeal of parade and ephemeral celebrity, and peculiarly facile in the choice of means by which to achieve these gaudy distinctions; peculiarly solicitous of appearances, and peculiarly heedless of the substance of their performance. It is not that this characterization would imply exceptionally great gifts, or otherwise notable traits of character; they are little else than an accentuation of the more commonplace frailties of commonplace men.[24] As a side light on this spiritual complexion of the typical academic

23. During Veblen's years at Chicago, perhaps the most prominent example of an "academic executive" appointing a "schoolmaster" instead of a scholar to the faculty was William Rainey Harper's appointment of Richard G. Moulton (1849–1924) as full professor in the University Extension program. Moulton was one of several popular lecturers without advanced academic training who began successful careers in England and then came to teach in American universities as extension programs came into fashion in the 1890s.

24. Cf. chapter III, "The Academic Administration," note 18.

executive, it may be worth noting that much the same characterization will apply without abatement to the class of professional politicians, particularly to that large and long-lived class of minor politicians who make a living by keeping well in the public eye and avoiding blame.[d]

There is, indeed more than a superficial or accidental resemblance between the typical academic executive and the professional politician of the familiar and more vacant sort, both as regards the qualifications requisite for entering on this career and as regards the conditions of tenure. Among the genial make-believe that goes to dignify the executive office is a dutiful protest, indeed, a somewhat clamorous protest, of conspicuous self-effacement on the part of the incumbent, to the effect that the responsibilities of office have come upon him unsought, if not unawares; which is related to the facts in much the same manner and degree as the like holds true for the maneuvers of those wise politicians that "heed the call of duty" and so find themselves "in the hands of their friends." In point of fact, here as in political office-seeking, the most active factor that goes to decide the selection of the eventual incumbents of office is a tenacious and aggressive self-selection. With due, but by no means large, allowance for exceptions, the incumbents are chosen from among a self-selected body of candidates, each of whom has, in the common run of cases, been resolutely in pursuit of such an office for some appreciable time, and has spent much time and endeavor on fitting himself for its duties. Commonly it is only after the aspirant has achieved a settled reputation for eligibility and a predilection for the office that he will finally secure an appointment. The number of aspirants, and of eligibles, considerably exceeds the number of such executive offices, very much as is true for the parallel case of aspirants for political office.

---

d. Indeed, the resemblance is visible. As among professional politicians, so also as regards incumbents and aspirants for academic office, it is not at all unusual, nor does it cause surprise, to find such persons visibly affected with those characteristic pathological marks that come of what is conventionally called "high living"—late hours, unseasonable vigils, surfeit of victuals and drink, the fatigue of sedentary ennui. A flabby habit of body, hypertrophy of the abdomen, varicose veins, particularly of the facial tissues, a blear eye and a coloration suggestive of bile and apoplexy—when this unwholesome bulk is duly wrapped in a conventionally decorous costume it is accepted rather as a mark of weight and responsibility, and so serves to distinguish the pillars of urbane society. Nor should it be imagined that these grave men of affairs and discretion are in any peculiar degree prone to excesses of the table or to nerve-shattering bouts of dissipation. The exigencies of publicity, however, are, by current use and wont, such as to enjoin not indulgence in such excursions of sensual perversity, so much as a gentlemanly conformity to a large routine of conspicuous convivialities. "Indulgence" in ostensibly gluttonous bouts of this kind—banquets, dinners, etc.—is not so much a matter of taste as of astute publicity, designed to keep the celebrants in repute among a laity whose simplest and most assured award of esteem proceeds on evidence of wasteful ability to pay. But the pathological consequences, physical and otherwise, are of much the same nature in either case. [In Veblen's day, what might be described more politely as a stout mid-drift was viewed as a sign of economic prosperity and professional success. It also was commonplace for affluent Americans to gather at huge banquets and consume heavy meals. –Ed.]

As to the qualifications, in point of character and attainments, that so go to make eligibility for the executive office, it is necessary to recall what has been said in an earlier chapter[e] on the characteristics of those boards of control with whom rests the choice in these matters of appointment. These boards are made up of well-to-do businessmen, with a penchant for popular notability and the qualifications necessary to be put in evidence by aspirants for executive office are such as will convince such a board of their serviceability. Among the indispensable general qualifications, therefore, will be a "businesslike" facility in the management of affairs, an engaging address and fluent command of language before a popular audience, and what is called "optimism,"—a serene and voluble loyalty to the current conventionalities and a conspicuously profound conviction that all things are working out for good, except for such untoward details as do not visibly conduce to the vested advantage of the well-to-do businessmen under the established law and order. To secure an appointment to executive office it is not only necessary to be possessed of these qualifications, and contrive to put them in evidence; the aspirant must ordinarily also, to use a colloquialism, be willing and able to "work his passage"[25] by adroit negotiation and detail engagements on points of policy, appointments and administration.

The greater proportion of such aspirants for executive office work their apprenticeship and manage their campaign of office-seeking while engaged in some university employment. To this end the most likely line of university employment is such as will comprise a large share of administrative duties, as, e. g., the deanships that are latterly receiving much attention in this behalf; while of the work of instruction the preference should be given to such undergraduate class-work as will bring the aspirant in wide contact with the less scholarly element of the student body, and with those "student activities" that come favorably under public observation; and more particularly should one go in for the quasi-scholarly pursuits of "university extension"; which will bring the candidate into favorable notice among the quasi-literate leisure class; at the same time this employment conduces greatly to assurance and a flow of popular speech.[26]

e. See chapter II, "The Governing Boards," 81–83, 88–90.

25. Someone willing to "work his passage" pays for his journey with work instead of money.

26. Supporters of university extension programs viewed them as a way to establish the immediate public usefulness of universities, as well as to gain support from civic leaders and state legislatures. William Rainey Harper envisioned Chicago's extension lectures and correspondence courses as vehicles to infuse higher levels of quality in the nation's chaotic school system. Educating urban and rural teachers, he believed, would better prepare more of their students to go on to college and university-level study. (During his first year at Chicago, Veblen apparently did not endear himself to Harper when he abandoned in midstream a commitment to prepare a correspondence course on political economy. He informed Harper that he considered the terms of his payment inadequate.)

It is by no means here intended to convey the assumption that appointments to executive office are currently made exclusively from among aspiring candidates answering the description outlined above, or that the administrative deanships that currently abound in the universities are uniformly looked on by their incumbents as in some sort a hopeful novitiate to the presidential dignity. The exceptions under both of these general propositions would be too numerous to be set aside as negligible, although scarcely numerous enough or consequential enough entirely to vitiate these propositions as a competent formulation of the typical line of approach to the coveted office. The larger and more substantial exception would, of course, be taken to the generalization as touching the use of the deanships in preparation for the presidency.

The course of training and publicity afforded by the deanships and extension lectures appears to be the most promising, although it is not the only line of approach. So, e. g., as has been remarked in an earlier passage, the exigencies of academic administration will ordinarily lead to the formation of an unofficially organized corps of counsellors and agents or lieutenants, who serve as aids to the executive head. While these aids, factors, and gentlemen-in-waiting are vested with no official status proclaiming their relation to the executive office or their share in its administration, it goes without saying that their vicarious discretion and their special prerogatives of access and advisement with the executive head do not commonly remain hidden from their colleagues on the academic staff, or from interested persons outside the university corporation; nor, indeed, does it appear that they commonly desire to remain unknown.

In the same connection, as has also been remarked above, and as is sufficiently notorious, among the large and imperative duties of executive office is public discourse. This is required, both as a measure of publicity at large and as a means of divulging the ostensible aims, advantages and peculiar merits of the given university and its chief. The volume of such public discourse, as well as the incident attendance at many public and ceremonial functions, is very considerable; so much so that in the case of any university of reasonable size and spirit the traffic in these premises is likely to exceed the powers of any one man, even where, as is not infrequently the case, the "executive" head is presently led to make this business of stately parade and promulgation his chief employment. In effect, much of this traffic will necessarily be delegated to such representatives of the chief as may be trusted duly to observe its spirit and intention; and the indicated bearers of these vicarious dignities and responsibilities will necessarily be the personal aids and counsellors of the chief; which throws them, again, into public notice in a most propitious fashion.

So also, by force of the same exigencies of parade and discourse, the chief executive is frequently called away from home on a more or less extended itinerary; and the burden of dignity attached to the chief office is such as to require that its ostensible duties be delegated to some competent lieutenant during these extensive absences of the chief; and here, again, this temporary discretion and dignity will most wisely and fittingly be delegated to some member of the corps of personal aids who stands in peculiarly close relations of sympathy and usefulness to the chief. It has happened more than once that such an habitual "acting head" has come in for the succession to the executive office.

It comes, therefore, to something like a general rule, that the discipline which makes the typical captain of erudition, as he is seen in the administration of executive office, will have set in before his induction into office, not infrequently at an appreciable interval before that event, and involving a consequent, more or less protracted, term of novitiate, probation and preliminary seasoning; and the aspirants so subjected to this discipline of initiation are at the same time picked men, drawn into the running chiefly by force of a facile conformity and a self-selective predisposition for this official dignity.

The resulting captain of erudition then falls under a certain exacting discipline exercised by the situation in which the exigencies of office place him. These exigencies are of diverse origin, and are systematically at variance among themselves. So that the dominant note of his official life necessarily becomes that of ambiguity. By tradition—indeed, by that tradition to which the presidential office owes its existence, and except by force of which there would apparently be no call to institute such an office at all—by tradition the president of the university is the senior member of the faculty, its confidential spokesman in official and corporate concerns, and the "moderator" of its town meeting like deliberative assemblies. As chairman of its meetings he is, by tradition, presumed to exercise no peculiar control, beyond such guidance as the superior experience of the senior member may be presumed to afford his colleagues. As spokesman for the faculty he is, by tradition, presumed to be a scholar of such erudition, breadth and maturity as may fairly command something of filial respect and affection from his associates in the corporation of learning; and it is by virtue of these qualities of scholarly wisdom, which give him his place as senior member of a corporation of scholars, that he is, by tradition, competent to serve as their spokesman and to occupy the chair in their deliberative assembly.

Such is the tradition of the American College President—and, in so far, of the university president—as it comes down from that earlier phase of academic history from which the office derives its ostensible character, and to which it owes its hold on life under the circumstances of the later growth of the schools. And it will be noted that this office is distinctly American; it has no counterpart elsewhere, and there appears to be no felt need of such an office in other countries, where no similar tradition of a college president has created a presumptive need of a similar official in the universities—the reason being evidently that these universities in other lands have not, in the typical case, grown out of an underlying college.[27]

In the sentimental apprehension of the laity out of doors, and in a degree even in the unreflecting esteem of men within the academic precincts, the presidential office still carries something of this traditionally preconceived scholarly character; and it is this still surviving traditional preconception, which confuses induction into the office with scholarly fitness for its dignities, that still makes the office of the academic executive available for those purposes of expansive publicity and businesslike management that it has been made to serve. Except for this uncritical esteem of the office and its incumbency, so surviving out of an inglorious past, no great prestige could attach to that traffic in spectacular solemnities, edifying discourse and misdirected business control, that makes up the substantial duties of the office as now conducted. It is therefore of the utmost moment to keep up, or rather to magnify, that appearance of scholarly competence and of intimate solidarity with the corporation of learning that gives the presidential office this prestige value. But since it is only for purposes external, not to say extraneous, to the corporation of learning that this prestige value is seriously worthwhile, it is also only toward the outside that the make-believe of presidential erudition and scholarly ideals need seriously be kept up. For the common run of the incumbents today to pose before their faculties as in any eminent degree conversant with the run of contemporary science or scholarship, or as rising to the average even of their own faculties in this respect, would be as bootless as it is uncalled for. But the faculties, as is well enough understood, need of course

27. As a historian, Veblen is right on target in these two paragraphs. The American system of collegiate education that emerged in the middle of the eighteenth century relied chiefly on small staffs of young tutors, and several decades passed before regular professors with some length of tenure outnumbered mostly transient tutors. In this setting, the only secure and sustained professional office in American collegiate education was that of the college president. Moreover, unlike rectors who headed European universities and schools at the time, American college presidents were not elected by the teaching staff nor in any fundamental way accountable to them. It is true that college trustees held power to appoint and replace college presidents. They could not rule in his place, however, because it was largely the reputation and promoting energy of the president that determined a college's reputation in a community. The upshot, as the historian Richard Hofstadter observed, was that the American college president was the institution's main symbol and spokesman, as well as its dynamic center. See Richard Hofstadter and Walter P. Metzger, *The Development of Academic Freedom in the United States* (New York: Columbia University Press, 1955), 124–25.

entertain no respect for their executive head as a citizen of the republic of learning, so long as they at all adequately appreciate his discretionary power of use and
abuse, as touches them and their fortunes and all the ways, means and opportunities of academic work. By tradition, and in the genial legendary lore that colors
the proceedings of the faculty-meeting, he is still the senior member of an assemblage of scholarly gentlemen; but in point of executive fact he is their employer,
who does business with and by them on a commercial footing. To the faculty, the
presidential office is a business proposition, and its incumbent is chiefly an object of circumspection, to whom they owe a "hired-man's loyalty."[28]

It is toward the outside, in the face of the laity out of doors, that the high
fence—"the eight-fold fence"[29]—of scholarly pretension is to be kept up. Hence
the indicated means of its upkeep are such as will presumably hold the (transient) respect and affection of this laity, quasi-scholarly homiletical discourse, frequent, voluminous, edifying and optimistic; ritualistic solemnities, diverting and
vacant; spectacular affectations of (counterfeit) scholastic usage in the way of droll
vestments, bizarre and archaic; parade of (make-believe) gentility; encouragement
and (surreptitious) subvention of athletic contests; promulgation of (presumably
ingenuous) statistics touching the volume and character of the work done.

It is only by keeping up these manifestations toward the outside, and making
them good in the esteem of the unlearned, that the presidential office can be
made to serve the ends of the board of control and the ambitions of the incumbent; and this large apparatus and traffic of make-believe, therefore, is the first
and most unremitting object of executive solicitude. It is the "place whereon to
stand" while moving the academic universe. The uses to be made of the standing-place so achieved have already been set out in some detail in earlier chapters.
They center about three main considerations: visible magnitude, bureaucratic
organization, and vocational training.

As already noted in earlier passages, the boards of control are bodies of businessmen in whose apprehension the methods successfully employed in competitive
business are suitable for all purposes of administration; from which follows that
the academic head who is to serve as their general manager is vested, in effect,
with such discretionary powers as currently devolve on the discretionary officials

---

28. Cf. chapter III, "The Academic Administration," note 28.
29. Title and subject of first poem in *Kojiki*, the oldest survey book of Japanese myths and stories by
an anonymous eighth-century Japanese poet. The "eight-fold fence" consisted of multitudinous clouds
behind which newly married deities could retire from public scrutiny.

of business corporations; from which follows, among other things, that the members of the faculty come to take rank as employees of the concern, hired by and responsible to the academic head.

The first executive duty of the incumbent of office, therefore, is to keep his faculty under control, so as to be able unhampered to carry out the policy of magnitude and secularization with a view to which the governing board has invested him with his powers. This work of putting the faculty in its place has by this time been carried out with sufficient effect, so that its "advice and consent" may in all cases be taken as a matter of course; and should a remnant of initiative and scholarly aspiration show itself in any given concrete case in such a way as to traverse the lines of policy pursued by the executive, he can readily correct the difficulty by exercise of a virtually plenary power of appointment, preferment and removal, backed as this power is by a nearly indefeasible black-list. So well is the academic black-list understood, indeed, and so sensitive and trustworthy is the fearsome loyalty of the common run among academic men, that very few among them will venture openly to say a good word for any one of their colleagues who may have fallen under the displeasure of some incumbent of executive office. This work of intimidation and subornation may fairly be said to have acquired the force of an institution, and to need no current surveillance or effort.[f]

The subservience of the faculty, or of a working majority, may safely be counted on. But the forms of advisement and responsibility are still necessary to be observed; the president is still, by tradition, the senior member of the faculty, and its confidential spokesman. From which follows a certain, at least pro forma, disingenuousness in the executive's coercive control of academic policy, whereby the ostensible discretion and responsibility comes to rest on the faculty, while the control remains with the executive. But, after all, this particular run of ambiguity and evasions has reached such settled forms and is so well understood that it no longer implies an appreciable strain on the executive's veracity or on his diplomatic skill. It belongs under the category of legal fiction, rather than that of effectual prevarication.

So also as regards the business-like, or bureaucratic, organization and control

f. As bearing on this "hired-man's loyalty" of the academic staff and the means of maintaining it, see George Cram Cook (1873–1924), "The Third American Sex," *Forum* (October, 1913), 450–455. [Cook was an American novelist, playwright, and poet who taught at Iowa and Stanford. His paper's curious title is explained in its opening sentences: "In America there are three sexes—men, women, and professors. It is the saying of European scholars looking from those self-governing democracies, their universities, upon ours. They see ours ruled without the consent of the governed through presidential autocrats without the consent of the governed—not a part of the world of learning, but superimposed on it." –Ed.]

of the administrative machinery, and its utilization for vocational ends and statistical showing. All that has been worked out in its general features, and calls, in
any concrete case, for nothing much beyond an adaptation of general practices
to the detail requirements of the special case. It devolves, properly, on the clerical
force, and especially on those chiefs of clerical bureau called "deans," together
with the many committees-for-the-sifting-of-sawdust into which the faculty of a
well-administered university is organized. These committees being, in effect if
not in intention, designed chiefly to keep the faculty talking while the bureaucratic
machine goes on its way under the guidance of the executive and his personal
counsellors and lieutenants. These matters, then, are also well understood, standardized, and accepted, and no longer require a vigilant personal surveillance
from the side of the executive.[30]

As is well and seemly for any head of a great concern, these matters of routine
and current circumlocution are presently delegated to the oversight of trusted subalterns, in a manner analogous to the delegation of the somewhat parallel duties
of the caretakers of the material equipment. Both of these hierarchical corps of
subordinates are in a somewhat similar case, in that their duties are of a mechanically standardized nature, and in that it is incumbent on both alike to deal in
a dispassionate, not to say impersonal, way each with the particular segment of
apparatus and process entrusted to his care; as is right and good for any official
entrusted with given details of bureaucratic routine.

The exacting duties that remain personally incumbent on the academic executive, and claiming his ordinary and continued attention, therefore, are those of
his own official prestige on the one hand, and the selection, preferment, rejection
and proscription of members of the academic staff. These two lines of executive
duty are closely correlated; not only in that the staff is necessarily to be selected
with a view to their furthering the prestige of their chief and his university, but
also in that the executive's experience in the course of this enterprise in publicity
goes far to shape his ideals of scholarly endeavor and to establish his standards
of expediency and efficiency in the affairs of learning.

---

30. In these two paragraphs, Veblen suggests that the underlying reality of American university
faculty taken as a group is embodied and revealed in an unequal system of "divided responsibility." The
American university's administrative side draws on the principles and practices of the business world;
its academic side depends on the expertise of individual faculty. While there is regular interaction between the two sides, the spheres are distinct. The practical upshot, as Christopher Newfield describes
it, is a "reciprocal hands-off ethic" that makes for a system of divided governance that effectively excludes faculty as a group from any direct university-wide budgetary and managerial power. See Newfield, *Ivy and Industry: Business and the Making of the American University* (Durham, NC: Duke University
Press, 2003), 80–81.

By usage, guided, no doubt, by a shrewd sense of expediency in the choice of means, it has, in the typical case, come to be the settled policy of these incumbents of executive office to seek the competitively requisite measure of public prestige chiefly by way of public oratory. Now and again his academic rank, backed by the slow-dying tradition that his office should be filled by a man of scholarly capacity, will bring the incumbent before some scientific body or other; where he commonly avoids offence. But, as has been remarked above, it is the laity that is to be impressed and kept propitiously in mind of the executive and his establishment, and it is therefore the laity that is to be conciliated with presidential addresses; it is also to the laity that the typical academic executive is competent to speak without stultification. Hence the many edifying addresses before popular audiences, at commencements, inaugurations, dedications, club meetings, church festivals, and the like. So that an executive who aspires to do his whole duty in these premises will become in some sort an itinerant dispensary of salutary verbiage; and university presidents have so come to be conventionally indispensable for the effusion of graceful speech at all gatherings of the well-to-do for convivial deliberation on the state of mankind at large.[g]

Throughout this elocutionary enterprise there runs the rigorous prescription that the speaker must avoid offence, that his utterances must be of a salutary order, since the purpose of it all is such conciliation of goodwill as will procure at least the passive good offices of those who are reached by the presidential run of language. But, by and large, it is only platitudes and racy anecdotes that may be counted on to estrange none of the audiences before which it is worthwhile for the captains of erudition to make their plea for sanity and renown. Hence the peculiarly, not to say exuberantly, inane character of this branch of oratory, coupled with an indefatigable optimism and good nature. This outcome is due neither to a lack of application nor of reflection on the part of the speakers; it is, indeed, a

g. Unfortunately, the language wants a competent designation for public-minded personages of this class; which comprises something appreciably more than the homiletical university executives alluded to above, and their understudies, while it is also not strictly inclusive of all these executives. There is indeed a fairly obvious contingent comes in from among those minor politicians and clergymen who crave the benefit of an inoffensive notoriety, and who are at the same time solicitous to keep their fellow-men in mind of the unforgotten commonplaces. One will necessarily have misgivings about putting forward a new technical term for adoption into a vocabulary that is already top-heavy with technical innovations. "Philandropist" has been suggested. It is not a large innovation, and it has the merit of being obviously self-explanatory. At the same time its phonetic resemblance to an older term, already well accepted in the language, should recommend it to the members of the craft whom it is designed to signalize, and with whom phonetic considerations are habitually allowed weight. The purists will doubtless find "philandropist" a barbarism; but that is an infirmity that has attached to many technical designations at their inception, without permanently hindering their acceptance and serviceability; it is also not wholly unfitting that the term chosen should be of such a character.

finished product of the homiletical art and makes up something of a class of its own among the artistic achievements of the race. At the same time it is a means to an end.[h]

However, the clay sticks to the sculptor's thumb, as the meal-dust powders the miller's hair and the cobbler carries sensible traces of the pitch that goes into his day's work, and as the able-bodied seaman "walks with a rolling gait."[31] So also the university executive, who by pressure of competitive enterprise comes to be all things to all audiences, will come also to take on the color of his own philan-dropic pronouncements; to believe, more or less conveniently, in his own blame-less utterances. They necessarily commit him to a pro forma observance of their tenor; they may, of course, be desired as perfunctory conciliation, simply, but in carrying conviction to the audience the speaker's eloquence unavoidably bends his own convictions in some degree. And not only does the temper of the audi-ence sympathetically affect that of the speaker, as does also his familiar contact with the same range of persons, such as goes with and takes a chief place in this itinerant edification; but there is also the opportunity which all this wide-ranging itinerary of public addresses affords for feeling out the state of popular sentiment, as to what ends the university is expected to serve and how it is expected best to serve them. Particularly do the solemn amenities of social intercourse associated with this promulgation of lay sermons lend themselves felicitously to such a pur-pose; and this contact with the public and its spokesmen doubtless exercises a powerful control over the policies pursued by these academic executives, in that it affords them the readiest, and at the same time the most habitual, indication as to what line of policy and what details of conduct will meet with popular ap-proval, and what will not.

Since, then, it is necessarily the endeavor of the competitive executives to meet the desires of their public as best they can, consistently with the demands of mag-

h. "The time has come, the walrus said,
   To talk of many things."

Within the last few years one of the more illustrious and fluent of the captains of erudition hit upon the expedient of having a trusted *locum tenens* [Latin: place-holder. –Ed.] appointed to take over the functions of the home office for a term of years, while the captain himself "takes the road"—on an appreciably augmented salary—to speak his mind eloquently on many topics. The device can, however, scarcely yet be said to have passed the experimental phase. This illustrious exponent of philandropism commands an extraordinary range of homily and is a raconteur of quite exceptional merit; and a device that commends itself in this special case, therefore, may or may not prove a feasible plan in general and ordinary usage. But in any case it indicates a felt need of some measure of relief, such as will en-able the run of presidential speech to gain a little something in amplitude and frequency. [Quotation from Lewis Carroll's "The Walrus and the Carpenter"; cf. chapter VII, "Vocational Training," note d.]

31. Phrase sometimes used in federal maritime law to describe features once considered charac-teristic of an ordinary seaman.

nitude and éclat imposed by their position as chiefs of these competitive concerns, it becomes a question of some moment what the character of this select public opinion may be, to which their peregrinations expose them; and how far and with what limitations the public opinion that so habitually impinges on their sensibilities and shapes their canons of procedure may be taken as reflecting the sentiments of the public at large, or of any given class of the population.

The public that so contributes to the habitual bent of the academic executives is necessarily a select fraction of the laity, of course—self-selected by virtue of membership in the various clubs, churches and other like organizations under whose auspices the edification and amenities in question are commonly brought into bearing, or by virtue of voluntary attendance at these occasions of quasi-culture and gentility. It is somewhat exclusive fragment of the public, pecuniarily of a middling grade, as is indeed also its case in other than the pecuniary respect. Apart from the (very consequential) convivial gatherings where businessmen will now and again come together and lend a genial ear to these executive spokesmen of philandropism, it will be found that at the audiences, and at their attendant solemnities of hospitality, the assembly is made up of very much the same elements as make up the effective constituency of the moderately well-to-do churches.[i] Neither the small minority of the wholly idle rich, nor the great majority who work with their hands, are present in appreciable force; particularly not the latter, who are busy elsewhere; nor do the learned class come in evidence in this connection—except, of course, the "scholars by appointment,"[32] within whose official competency lie precisely such occasions of public evidence.

Doubtless, the largest, tone-giving and effective, constituent in this self-selected public on whose temper the university president typically leans, and from whose bent his canons of circumspection are drawn, is the class of moderately well-to-do and serious-minded women who have outlived the distractions of maternity, and so have come to turn their parental solicitude to the common good, conceived as a sterilization of the proprieties. The controlling ideals of efficiency

i. So, e. g., a certain notably self-possessed and energetic captain of erudition has been in the habit of repeating ("on the spur of the moment") a homily on one of the staple Christian virtues. [Possible allusion to William Rainey Harper, whose public rhetoric about the larger mission of the University of Chicago was informed by the tenets of what would be more accurately described as late-nineteenth-century Protestant liberalism. The most essential religious attribute of a university, Harper believed, was its commitment to the pursuit of reason, knowledge, and truth. It was a belief widely shared by the architects of the American university system. –Ed.]

32. Cf. note 23, *supra*. In the first decades of the twentieth century, examples of "scholars by appointment" also included numerous nonacademic social reformers who were hired to staff new university-housed schools of social work. The practice of "scholars by appointment," continues to this day, expanding to include prominent journalists and media figures, as well as former politicians and statesmen.

and expediency in the affairs of the higher learning accordingly, in so far as they are not a precipitate of competitive business principles simply, will be chiefly of this derivation. Not that the captains of erudition need intimately harbor precisely those notions of scholarship which this constituency would enjoin upon them, and for which they dutifully speak in their conciliatory sermons before these audiences; but just as happens in all competitive retail business that has to deal with a large and critical constituency, so here—the captains find themselves constrained in their management of the affairs of learning to walk blamelessly in the sight of this quasi-public spirited wing of the laity that has by force of circumstances come to constitute the public, as seen in the perspective of the itinerant philandropist.

The executive and all his works and words must avoid blame from any source from which criticism might conceivably affect the traffic with which he is occupied, such is the first of those politic principles that govern the conduct of competitive business. The university must accordingly be managed with a first view to a creditable rating in those extraneous respects, touching which that select laity that make up the executive's effective public are competent to hold convictions. The resulting canons of management will be chiefly of the nature of taboos, since blame is best avoided by a code of avoidance. and since the forum in which these taboos are audited is a forum in which the matronly negations of piety, propriety and genteel usage take precedence of work, whether scholarly or otherwise, a misdirected cowardice not infrequently comes to rule the counsels of the captains of erudition—misdirected not only in the more obvious sense that its guidance is disserviceable to the higher learning, but also (what is more to the immediate point) in the sense that it discredits the executive and his tactics in the esteem of that workday public that does not habitually give tongue over the cups at five-o'clock.[j]

It is perhaps unnecessary, as it would assuredly be ungraceful, to pursue this quasi-personal inquiry into the circumstances that so determine that habitual at-

j. These resulting canons of blameless anility will react on the character of the academic personnel in a two-fold way: negatively and by indirection they work out in an (uncertain but effectual) selective elimination of such persons as are worthwhile in point of scholarship and initiative; while positively and by direct incitement it results that the tribe of Lo Basswood has been elected to fill the staff with vacancy. ["Lo Basswood" is unidentified. –Ed.]

At the same time the case is not unknown, nor is it altogether a chance occurrence, where such an executive with plenary powers, driven to uncommonly fatuous lengths by this calculus of expedient notoriety, and intent on putting a needed patch on the seat of his honor, has endeavored to save some remnant of good-will among his academic acquaintance by protesting, in strict and confidential privacy, that his course of action taken in conformity with these canons was taken for the sake of popular effect, and not because he did not know better; apparently having by familiar use come to the persuasion that a knave is more to be esteemed than a fool, and overlooking the great ease with which he has been able to combine the two characters.

titude of the executive. The difficulties of such an ambiguous position should be sufficiently evident, and the character of the demands which this position makes on the incumbent should be similarly evident, so far as regards conduciveness to clean and honest living within the premises of this executive office. It may, however, not be out of place to call to mind one or two significant, and perhaps extenuating, traits among those conventions that go to make up the situation. Unlike what occurs in the conduct of ordinary business and in the professions, there has hitherto been worked out no code of professional ethics for the guidance of men employed in this vocation—with the sole exception of that mandatory inter-presidential courtesy that binds all members of the craft to a strict enforcement of the academic black-list[33]—all of which leaves an exceptionally broad field for casuistry. So that, unlike what happens in the business community at large, no standardization has here determined the limits of legitimate prevarication; nor can such a standardization and limit be worked out so long as the executive is required, in effect, to function as the discretionary employer of his academic staff and hold them to account as agents for whom he is responsible, at the same time that he must, in appearance, be their confidential spokesman and their colleague in the corporation of learning. And it is impossible to forego either of these requirements, since the discretionary power of use and abuse is indispensable to the businesslike conduct of the enterprise, while the appearance of scholarly co-partnery with the staff is indispensable to that prestige on which rests the continued exercise of this power. And so also it has similarly proved unavoidable (perhaps as an issue of human infirmity) that the executive be guided in effect by a meretricious subservience to extra-scholastic conventions, all the while that he must profess an unbiased pursuit of "the increase and diffusion of knowledge among men."

IV

With all due endeavor to avoid the appearance of a study in total depravity,[34] the foregoing analysis has come, after all, to converge on the growth and derivation of those peculiar ambiguities and obliquities that give character to the typical academic executive. Not that all academic executives, without exception, are (in the historical present) to be found fully abreast of that mature phase of the type that would so be reflected by the exigencies of their office as outlined above. Nor need

33. Cf. chapter III, "Academic Administration," note h.
34. Corrupt act or practice; evil or immoral act. Veblen's original choice for the subtitle of *The Higher Learning in America* was "a study in depravity."

it be believed or argued that no man may enter on these duties of office but such as are specially fitted, by native gift and previous training, for just such an enterprise in meretricious notoriety as these official duties enjoin. The exceptions to such a rule are not altogether rare, and the incumbent may well have entered on the duties of office with preconceptions and aims somewhat at variance with what its discipline inculcates. But, it should be called to mind, the training that makes a typical executive comes with the most felicitous and indefeasible effect not in the predisposing discipline of candidature but in the workday conduct of office. And so consistent and unremitting is this drift of the duties of office, overt and covert, that, humanly speaking, anyone who submits to its discipline through an appreciable period of years must unavoidably come to conform to type. Men of unmanageably refractory temperament, such as cannot by habituation be indued[35] with the requisite deviation and self-sufficiency, will of necessity presently be thrown out, as being incompetent for this vocation. Instances of such rejection after trial will come to mind, but such instances are, after all, not so frequent or so striking[36] as to throw doubt on the general rule. The discipline of executive office will commonly shape the incumbent to its uses. It should seem beyond reason to expect that a decade of exposure to the exigencies of this high office will leave the incumbent still amenable to the dictates of commonplace tolerance and common honesty.

As intimated above, men with ingrained scholarly ideals and a consistent aim to serve the ends of learning will still occasionally be drawn into the executive office by force of circumstances—particularly by force of the slow-dying preconception that the preferences of the academic staff should count for something in the choice of their senior member; and this will happen in spite of the ubiquitous candidature of aspirants who have prepared themselves for this enterprise by sedulous training in all the arts of popularity and by a well-organized backing of influential "friends." The like happened more frequently a quarter of a century ago, at the time when the current situation was taking shape under the incipient incursion of business principles into university policy. But it does not appear that those incumbents who so enter on these duties, will fare notably otherwise in the

35. Provided with a quality or trait.
36. During Veblen's lifetime, there were two particularly well-publicized instances of college or university presidents being "rejected" after crossing swords with boards of trustees. In 1897, E. Benjamin Andrews (1844–1917) was forced to resign from the presidency of Brown University after a controversy with some members of the Brown Corporation regarding his views on the coinage of silver, which had been a divisive issue in the 1896 presidential campaign. In 1923, Alexander Meikeljohn (1872–1964) was forced to resign from the presidency of Amherst College by its board of trustees, partly because of his mishandling of his office's finances and partly because of his high-handed treatment of the faculty.

end than do the others whose previous training has already bent them to the typical policy of deviation, from the outset.

An illustrative instance or two may well be to the point. And the same illustrations will perhaps also serve to enforce the view that anything like an effectual university—a seminary of the higher learning, as distinct from an assemblage of vocational schools—is not a practicable proposition in America under current conditions. Such seems to be the conclusion vouched for by the two most notable attempts of the kind during the past quarter-century. The two instances in question should appear to afford clear experimental evidence to that effect, though it is always possible to allege that personal or local conditions may so far have affected these experimental instances as still to leave the case in doubt.

In these two instances, in the Middle West and in the Far West, the matter has been tried out under conditions as favorable to the cause of learning as the American community may hope to offer, barring only the possible inhibition due to an untoward local color of sentiment. Each of these two great establishments has been favored with an endowment of such magnitude as would be adequate to the foundation of an effectual university,[37] sufficient to the single-minded pursuit of the higher learning, with all the "modern appliances" requisite to scientific and scholarly work, if only their resources had been husbanded with a single mind to that end; and in either case the terms of the endowment have been sufficiently tolerant to admit such pursuit of knowledge without *arrière pensée*.[38] The directive hands, too, under whose discretionary control each of these establishments entered on its adventures and attained its distinctive character, were men who, at one point or another in their administration of academic policy, entertained a sincerely conceived scholarly ambition to create a substantial university, an institution of learning.[k] And, in a general way, the two attempts have equally failed of their avowed initial purpose.

37. The "two great establishments" Veblen alludes to here are Chicago and Stanford. In 1919, Chicago's endowment value was $39.6 million, and Stanford's was $33.2 million. Only the endowments of Harvard ($44.5 million) and Columbia ($39.6 million) were higher.

38. French: mental reservation.

k. In all fairness it should be noted, as a caution against hasty conclusions, that in both of these cases this initial scholarly intention has been questioned—or denied—by men well informed as to the later state of things in either of the two universities in question. And it may as well be admitted without much reservation that the later state of things has carried no broad hint of an initial phase in the life-history of these schools, in which ideals of scholarship were given first consideration. Yet it is to be taken as unequivocal fact that such was the case, in both instances; this is known as an assured matter of memory by men competent to speak from familiar acquaintance with the relevant facts at the time. In both cases, it is only in the outcome, only after the pressure of circumstances has had time to act, that a rounded meretricious policy has taken effect. What has misled hasty and late-come observers in this matter is the relatively very brief—inconspicuously brief—time interval during which it was found practicable to let the academic policy be guided primarily by scholarly ideals. [The two "cases" alluded

In the persons of their discretionary heads, the two enterprises were from the outset animated with widely divergent ideals and aspirations in matters of scholarship, and with singularly dissimilar and distinctive traits of character, resembling one another in little else than a sincere devotion to the cause of scholarship and an unhampered discretion in their autocratic management of affairs;[39] but it is an illuminating comment on the force of circumstances governing these matters, that these two establishments have gone down to substantially the same kind and degree of defeat—a defeat not extreme but typical, both in kind and degree. In the one case, the more notorious, the initial aim (well known to persons intimately in touch with the relevant facts at the time) was the pursuit of scholarship, somewhat blatant perhaps, but none the less sincere and thoughtful; in the companion-piece it was in a like degree the pursuit of scientific knowledge and serviceability, though, it is true, unschooled and puzzle-headed to a degree. In both enterprises alike the discretionary heads so placed in control had been selected by individual businessmen of the untutored sort, and were vested with plenary powers. Under pressure of circumstances, in both cases alike, the policy of forceful initiative and innovation, with which both alike entered on the enterprise, presently yielded to the ubiquitous craving for statistical magnitude and the consequent felt need of conciliatory publicity; until presently the ulterior object of both was lost in the shadow of these immediate and urgent maneuvers of expediency, and it became the rule of policy to stick at nothing but appearances.

So that both establishments have come substantially to surrender the university ideal, through loss of effectual initiative and courage, and so have found themselves running substantially the same course of insidious compromise with "vocational" aims, undergraduate methods, and the counsels of the Philistines. The life-history of each, while differing widely in detail of ways and methods, is after all made up, for the greater part, of futile extensions, expansions, annexations, ramifications, affiliations and pronunciamentos, in matters that are no more germane to the cause of learning than is the state of the weather. In the one case, the chase after a sufficient notoriety took the direction of a ravenous megalomania,

---

to here are University of Chicago (about which Veblen is right) and Stanford (where things were not quite as he recalls). At Chicago, William Rainey Harper's early public rhetoric did highlight the prominence of graduate education and research. At the first meeting of the faculty, Harper expressed a hope that the first two years of undergraduate study in time would be transferred to a separate campus, leaving the main campus for the final two years of undergraduate study and graduate education. Stanford was launched with the different assumption that during its first year most registering students would be freshmen. Of 595 who enrolled in 1891, only 37 registered as graduate students. –Ed.]

39. William Rainey Harper relished academic costume and pageantry, and used Chicago's then quarterly convocations to make well-publicized formal statements on the condition of the university.

the busiest concern of which presently came to be how most conspicuously to prolong a shout into polysyllables; and the further fact that this clamorous raid on the sensibilities of the gallery was presently, on a change of executive personnel, succeeded by a genial surrender to time and tide, an aimless gum-shod pusillanimity, has apparently changed the drift of things in no very appreciable degree.[1]

In the companion-piece, the enterprise has been brought to the like manner and degree of stultification under the simple guidance of an hysterically meticulous deference to all else than the main facts. In both cases alike the executive solicitude has come to converge on a self-centered and irresponsible government of intolerance, differing chiefly in the degree of its efficiency. Of course, through all this drift of stultification there has always remained—*decus et solamen*[40]—something of an amiably inefficient and optimistic solicitude for the advancement of learning at large, in some unspecified manner and bearing, some time, but not to interfere with the business in hand.

It is not that either of these two great schools is to be rated as useless for whatever each is good for, but only that that pursuit of learning on which both set out in the beginning has fallen into abeyance, by force of circumstances as they impinge on the sensibilities of a discretionary executive. As vocational schools and as establishments for the diffusion of salutary advice on the state of mankind at large, both are doubtless all that might be desired; particularly in respect of their statistical showing. It is only that the affairs of the higher learning have come definitively to take a subsidiary, or putative, place. In these establishments; and to all appearance irretrievably so, because both are now committed to so large and exacting a volume of obligations and liabilities, legal and customary, extraneous and alien to their legitimate interest, that there is no longer a reasonable chance of their coming to anything of serious import in the way of the higher learning,

1. As a commentary on the force of circumstances and the academic value of the executive office, it is worth noting that, in the case cited, an administration guided by a forceful, ingenious and intrepid personality, initially imbued with scholarly ideals of a sort, has run a course of scarcely interrupted academic decay; while the succeeding reign of astute vacuity and quietism as touches all matters of scholarship and science has, on the whole, and to date, left the university in an increasingly hopeful posture as a seminary of the higher learning. All of which would appear to suggest a parallel with the classic instance of King Stork and King Log. Indeed, at the period of the succession alluded to, the case of these fabled majesties was specifically called to mind by one and another of the academic staff. It would appear that the academic staff will take care of its ostensible work with better effect the less effectually its members are interfered with and suborned by an enterprising captain of erudition. [King Stork and King Log: characters in "The Frogs Who Wished for A King," a morality tale in *Aesop's Fables* (late to mid-sixth century BCE), which tells of frogs who tired of governing themselves and petitioned Jupiter to give them a king. In response, Jupiter first threw down a huge log, which young frogs used as a diving platform and older frogs employed as a meeting place where in time they came to complain that Jupiter had sent them a tame and ineffectual "King Log." To show the frogs what fools they had been, Jupiter then sent a crane—"King Stork"—who immediately began to consume the witless frogs. –Ed.]

40. Latin: an ornament and safeguard.

even, conceivably, under the most enlightened management in the calculable future.[41] In their bootless chase after a blameless publicity, both have sunk their endowment in conspicuous real estate, vocational, technical and accessory schools, and the like academic side-issues, to such an extent as to leave them without means to pursue their legitimate end in any adequate manner, even if they should harbor an effectual inclination to pursue it.[m]

These remarks on the typical traits of the academic executive have unavoidably taken the color of personalities. That such is the case should by no means be taken as intentionally reflecting anything like dispraise on those persons who have this (unavoidable) work of stultification in hand. Rather, it is dispassionately to be gathered from the run of the facts as set out above that those persons on whom these exigencies impinge will, by force of habituation, necessarily come to take the bent which these current conditions enforce, and without which this work could not well be done; all on the supposition—and it is by no means an extravagant assumption—that these persons so exposed to these agencies of spiritual disintegration are by native gift endowed with the commonplace traits of human nature, no more and no less. It is the duties of the office, not a run of infirmities peculiar to the incumbents of office, that make the outcome. Very much like that of the medicine-man, the office is one which will not abide a tolerant and ingenuous incumbent.[n]

41. Veblen was a poor prophet here. Chicago and Stanford have long since joined the ranks of the world's finest research universities.

m. There is a word to add, as to the measure of success achieved by these enterprises along their chosen lines of endeavor. Both of the establishments spoken of are schools of some value in many directions, and both have also achieved a large reputation among the laity. Indeed, the captains under whose management the two schools have perforce carried on their work, are commonly held in considerable esteem as having achieved great things. There is no desire here to understate the case; but it should be worth noting, as bearing on the use and academic value of the presidential office, that the disposal of very large means—means of unexampled magnitude—has gone to this achievement. A consideration of these results, whether in point of scholarship or of notoriety, as compared with the means which the captains have disposed of, will leave one in doubt. It should seem doubtful if the results could have been less excellent or less striking, given the free disposal of an endowment of 20 or 30 million, and upward, even under the undistinguished and uneventful management of commonplace honesty and academic traditions without the guidance of a "strong man." It is, indeed, not easy to believe that less could have been achieved without the captain's help. There is also evidence to hand that the loss of the "strong man" has entailed no sensible loss either in the efficiency or in the good repute of the academic establishment; rather the reverse.

n. Within the precincts, it is not unusual to meet with a harsher and more personal note of appraisal of what are rated as the frailties of the executive. There are many expressions to be met with, touching this matter, of a colloquial turn. These will commonly have something of an underbred air, as may happen in unguarded colloquial speech; but if it be kept in mind that their personal incidence is duly to be read out of them, their tenor may yet be instructive, and their scant elegance may be overlooked for once, in view of that certain candor that is scarcely to be had without a colloquial turn. They should serve better than many elaborate phrases to throw into relief the kind and measure of esteem accorded these mature incumbents of executive office by the men who assist behind the scenes. So, in bold but intelligible metaphor, one hears, "He is a large person full of small potatoes," "The only white

V

In all the above argument and exposition, touching the executive office and its administrative duties, the point of the discussion is, of course, not the personal characteristics of the typical executive, nor even the spiritual fortunes of the persons exposed to the wear and tear of executive office; although these matters might well engage the attention of any one given to moralizing. The point is, of course, that precarious situation in which the university, considered as a corporation of the higher learning, is placed under these current conditions, and the manner in which these current conditions give rise to this situation. Seen from the point of view of the higher learning, and disregarding considerations extraneous to that interest, it is evident that this run of events, and the conditions which determine them, are wholly untoward, not to say disastrous.

Now, this inquiry is nowise concerned to reform, deflect or remedy this current drift of things academic away from the ancient holding ground of the higher learning; partly because such an enterprise in reform and rehabilitation lies beyond its competence; and partly, again, because in all this current move to displace the higher learning there may conceivably be other ends involved, which may be worthwhile in some other bearing that is alien to the higher learning but of graver consequence for the fortunes of the race—urgent needs which can only be served by so diverting effort and attention from this pursuit. Yet, partly out of a reasonable deference to the current prejudice that any mere negative criticism and citation of grievances is nothing better than an unworthy experiment in irritation; and more particularly as a means to a more adequate appreciation of the

---

thing about him is his liver," "Half-a-peck of pusillanimity," "A four-flusher." Something after this kind is this aphoristic wisdom current in the academic community, in so far as it runs safely above the level of scurrility. In point of taste, it would be out of the question to follow the same strain of discourteous expressions into that larger volume of more outspoken appraisal that lies below that level; and even what has so been sparingly cited in illustration can, of course, not claim a sympathetic hearing as being in any way a graceful presentment of the sense intended to be conveyed in these figures of speech. Yet the apology may be accepted, that it conveys this sense intelligibly even if not elegantly.

Indeed, a person widely conversant with current opinion and its expression among the personnel of the staff, as touches the character and academic value of a capable and businesslike executive, might unguardedly come to the persuasion that the typical academic head, under these latter-day conditions, will be a feeble-minded rogue. Such is, doubtless, far from being the actual valuation underlying these many artless expressions that one meets with. And doubtless, the most that could be said would be that, in point of orientation, the typical executive, qua executive, tends to fall in with the lines so indicated; that the exigencies of the executive office are of a kind that would converge upon such an issue "in the long run" and "in the absence of disturbing causes"; not that the effectual run of circumstances will at all commonly permit a consummation of that kind and degree.

"Indeed . . . we may say . . . as Dr Boteler said of strawberries. 'Doubtless God could have made a better berry, but doubtless God never did.'" [Quotation from *The Complete Angler* (1613), Izaak Walton (1593–1683), credited to "Dr. Boteler," generally believed to be the English physician Dr. William Butler (1563–1618). –Ed.]

rigorous difficulties inherent in this current state and drift of things; it may not be out of place to offer some consideration of remedial measures that have been attempted or projected, or that may be conceived to promise a way out.

As is well known, diverse and various remedial measures have been advocated by critics of current university affairs, from time to time; and it is equally evident on reflection that these proposed remedial measures are with fair uniformity directed to the treatment of symptoms—to relieve agitation and induce insensibility. However, there is at least one line of aggressively remedial action that is being tried, though not avowedly as a measure to bring the universities into line with their legitimate duties, but rather with a view to relieving them of this work which they are no longer fit to take care of. It is a move designed to shift the seat of the higher learning out of the precincts of the schools. And the desperate case of the universities, considered as seminaries of science and scholarship, is perhaps more forcibly brought in evidence by what is in this way taking place in the affairs of learning outside the schools than by their visible failure to take care of their own work. This evidence goes to say that the difficulties of the academic situation are insurmountable; any rehabilitation of the universities is not contemplated in this latter-day movement. And it is so coming to be recognized, in effect though tacitly, that for all their professions of a single-minded addiction to the pursuit of learning, the academic establishments, old and new, are no longer competent to take the direction of affairs in this domain.

So it is that, with a sanguine hope born of academic defeat, there have latterly been founded certain large establishments, of the nature of retreats or shelters for the prosecution of scientific and scholarly inquiry in some sort of academic quarantine, detached from all academic affiliation and renouncing all share in the work of instruction.[42] In point of form the movement is not altogether new. Foundations of a similar aim have been had before. But the magnitude and comprehensive aims of the new establishments are such as to take them out of the category of auxiliaries and throw them into the lead. They are assuming to take over the advance in science and scholarship, which has by tradition belonged under the tutelage of the academic community. This move looks like a desperate surrender of the university ideal. The reason for it appears to be the proven inability of the schools, under competitive management, to take care of the pursuit of knowledge.

Seen from the point of view of the higher learning, this new departure, as well

---

42. Allusion to the Carnegie Institution of Washington and the Rockefeller Institute of Medical Research, both generously endowed by the men for whom they were named.

as the apparent need of it, is to be rated as untoward; and it reflects gravely enough on the untoward condition into which the rule of business principles is leading the American schools. Such establishments of research are capable, in any competent manner, of serving only one of the two joint purposes necessary to be served by any effective seminary of the higher learning; nor can they at all adequately serve this one purpose to the best advantage when so disjoined from its indispensable correlate. By and large, these new establishments are good for research only, not for instruction; or at the best they can serve this latter purpose only as a more or less surreptitious or supererogatory side interest. Should they, under pressure of instant need, turn their forces to instruction as well as to inquiry, they would incontinently find themselves drifting into the same equivocal position as the universities, and the dry rot of business principles and competitive gentility would presently consume their tissues after the same fashion.

It is, to all appearance, impracticable and inadvisable to let these institutions of research take over any appreciable share of that work of scientific and scholarly instruction that is slipping out of the palsied hands of the universities, so as to include some consistent application to teaching within the scope of their everyday work. And this cuts out of their complement of ways and means one of the chief aids to an effectual pursuit of scientific inquiry. Only in the most exceptional, not to say erratic, cases will good, consistent, sane and alert scientific work be carried forward through a course of years by any scientist without students, without loss or blunting of that intellectual initiative that makes the creative scientist. The work that can be done well in the absence of that stimulus and safeguarding that comes of the give and take between teacher and student is commonly such only as can without deterioration be reduced to a mechanically systematized task work—that is to say, such as can, without loss or gain, be carried on under the auspices of a businesslike academic government.

This, imperatively unavoidable, absence of provision for systematic instruction in these newfound establishments of research means also that they and the work which they have in hand are not self-perpetuating, whether individually and in detail or taken in the large; since their work breeds no generation of successors to the current body of scientists on which they draw. As the matter stands now, they depend for their personnel on the past output of scholars and scientists from the schools, and so they pick up and turn to account what there is ready to hand in that way—not infrequently men for whom the universities find little use, as being refractory material not altogether suitable for the academic purposes of notoriety. When this academic source fails, as it presently must, with the increasingly efficient application of business principles in the universities, there should seem to be small recourse for establishments of this class except to run into the sands of intellectual quietism where the universities have gone before.

In this connection it will be interesting to note, by way of parenthesis, that even now a large proportion of the names that appear among the staff of these institutions of research are not American, and that even the American-born among them are frequently not American-bred in respect of their scientific training.[43] For this work, recourse is necessarily had to the output of men trained elsewhere than in the vocational and athletic establishments of the American universities, or to that tapering file of academic men who are still imbued with traditions so alien to the current scheme of conventions as to leave them not amenable to the dictates of business principles. Meantime, that which is eating the heart out of the American seminaries of the higher learning should in due course also work out the like sterilization in the universities of Europe, as fast and as far as these other countries also come fully into line with the same pecuniary ideals that are making the outcome in America. And evidence is not wholly wanting that the like proclivity to pragmatic and popular traffic is already making the way of the academic scientist or scholar difficult and distasteful in the greater schools of the Old World. America is by no means in a unique position in this matter, except only in respect of the eminent degree in which this community is pervaded by business principles, and its consequent faith in businesslike methods, and its intolerance of any other than pecuniary standards of value. It is only that this country is in the lead; the other peoples of Christendom are following the same lead as fast as their encumbrance of archaic usages and traditions will admit; and the generality of their higher schools are already beginning to show the effects of the same businesslike aspirations, decoratively colored with feudalistic archaisms of patriotic buncombe.[44]

As will be seen from the above explication of details and circumstances, such practicable measures as have hitherto been offered as a corrective to this sterilization of the universities by business principles, amount to a surrender of these institutions to the enemies of learning, and a proposal to replace them with an imperfect substitute. That it should so be necessary to relinquish the universities, as a means to the pursuit of knowledge, and to replace them with a second-best, is due, as has also appeared from the above analysis, to the course of policy (nec-

43. Allusion to the Rockefeller Institute for Medical Research. There is no evidence to support Veblen's claim that a "large proportion" of the Institute's staff at the time were "not American," although many had done graduate training at German universities.
44. Variant of bunkum: empty or insincere talk.

essarily) pursued by the executive officers placed in control of academic affairs; and the character of the policy so pursued follows unavoidably from the dependence of the executive on a businesslike governing board, backed by a businesslike popular clamor, on the one hand, and from his being (necessarily) vested, in effect, with arbitrary power of use and abuse within the academic community, on the other hand. It follows, therefore, also that no remedy or corrective can be contrived that will have anything more than a transient palliative effect, so long as these conditions that create the difficulty are allowed to remain in force.

All of which points unambiguously to the only line of remedial measures that can be worth serious consideration; and at the same time it carries the broad implication that in the present state of popular sentiment, touching these matters of control and administration, any effort that looks to reinstate the universities as effectual seminaries of learning will necessarily be nugatory; inasmuch as the popular sentiment runs plainly to the effect that magnitude, arbitrary control, and businesslike administration is the only sane rule to be followed in any human enterprise. So that, while the measures called for are simple, obvious, and effectual, they are also sure to be impracticable, and for none but extraneous reasons.

While it still remains true that the long-term common-sense judgment of civilized mankind[45] places knowledge above business traffic, as an end to be sought, yet workday habituation under the stress of competitive business has induced a frame of mind that will tolerate no other method of procedure, and no rule of life that does not approve itself as a faithful travesty of competitive enterprise. And since the quest of learning cannot be carried on by the methods or with the apparatus and incidents of competitive business, it follows that the only remedial measures that hold any promise of rehabilitation for the higher learning in the universities cannot be attempted in the present state of public sentiment.

All that is required is the abolition of the academic executive and of the governing board. Anything short of this heroic remedy is bound to fail, because the evils sought to be remedied are inherent in these organs, and intrinsic to their functioning.

Even granting the possibility of making such a move, in the face of popular prejudice, it will doubtless seem suicidal, on first thought, to take so radical a departure; in that it would be held to cripple the whole academic organization and subvert the scheme of things academic, for good and all—which, by the way, is precisely what would have to be aimed at, since it is the present scheme and

45. Cf. chapter II, "The Governing Boards," note 1.

organization that unavoidably work the mischief, and since, also (as touches the interest of the higher learning), they work nothing but mischief.

It should be plain, on reflection, to anyone familiar with academic matters that neither of these official bodies serves any useful purpose in the university, in so far as bears in any way on the pursuit of knowledge. They may conceivably both be useful for some other purpose, foreign or alien to the quest of learning; but within the lines of the university's legitimate interest both are wholly detrimental, and very wastefully so. They are needless, except to take care of needs and emergencies to which their own presence gratuitously gives rise. In so far as these needs and difficulties that require executive surveillance are not simply and flagrantly factitious—as, e. g., the onerous duties of publicity—they are altogether such needs as arise out of an excessive size and a gratuitously complex administrative organization; both of which characteristics of the American university are created by the governing boards and their executive officers, for no better purpose than a vainglorious self-complacency, and with no better justification than an uncritical prepossession[46] to the effect that large size, complex organization, and authoritative control necessarily make for efficiency; whereas, in point of fact, in the affairs of learning these things unavoidably make for defeat.

Objection to any such measure of abolition is not to be grounded in their impracticability or their inefficiency—supposing only that they could be carried out in the face of the prejudices of the ignorant and of the selfishly interested parties; the obstacles to any such move lie simply in the popular prejudice which puts implicit faith in large, complicated, and formidable organizations, and in that appetite for popular prestige that animates the class of persons from which the boards and executives are drawn.

This unreasoning faith in large and difficult combinations has been induced in the modern community by its experience with the large-scale organization of the mechanical industries, and still more particularly by the convincing pecuniary efficiency of large capital, authoritative control, and devious methods, in modern business enterprise; and of this popular prejudice the boards of control and their executive officers have at least their full share—indeed they owe their place and power in great part to their being animated with something more than an equitable share of this popular prepossession. It is undeniable, indeed it is a matter of course, that so long as the university continues to be made up, as is now customary, of an aggregation of diverse and sundry schools, colleges, divisions, etc., each and several of which are engaged in a more or less overt rivalry, due to

46. Attitude, belief, or impression formed beforehand; prejudice.

their being so aggregated into a meaningless coalition—so long will something formidable in the way of a centralized and arbitrary government be indispensable to the conduct of the university's affairs; but it is likewise patent that none of the several constituent schools, colleges, etc., are any the better off, in respect of their work, for being so aggregated in such an arbitrary collective organization. The duties of the executive—aside from the calls of publicity and self-aggrandizement—are in the main administrative duties that have to do with the interstitial adjustments of the composite establishment. These resolve themselves into a coordinated standardization of the several constituent schools and divisions, on a mechanically specified routine and scale, which commonly does violence to the efficient working of all these diverse and incommensurable elements; with no gain at any point, excepting a gain in the facility of control for control's sake, at the best. Much of the official apparatus and routine office work is taken up with this futile control. Beyond this, and requisite to the due working of this control and standardization, there is the control of the personnel and the checking-up of their task work; together with the disciplining of such as do not sufficiently conform to the resulting schedule of uniformity and mediocrity.

These duties are, all and several, created by the imposition of a central control, and in the absence of such control the need of them would not arise. They are essentially extraneous to the work on which each and several of the constituent schools are engaged, and their only substantial effect on that work is to force it into certain extraneous formalities of routine and accountancy, such as to divert and retard the work in hand. So also the control exercised more at large by the governing board; except in so far as it is the mere mischief-making interference of ignorant outsiders, it is likewise directed to the keeping of a balance between units that need no balancing as against one another; except for the need which so is gratuitously induced by drawing these units into an incongruous coalition under the control of such a board; whose duties of office in this way arise wholly out of the creation of their office.

The great and conspicuous effect of abolishing the academic executive and the governing board would be, of course, that the university organization as now known would incontinently fall to pieces. The several constituent schools would fall apart, since nothing holds them together except the strong hand of the present central government. This would, of course, seem a monstrous and painful outrage to all those persons who are infatuated with a veneration of big thing; to whom a "great"—that is to say voluminous—university is an object of pride and loyal affection. This class of persons is a very large one, and they are commonly not given to rejection on the merits of their preconceived ideals of "greatness."

So that the dissolution of this "trust"-like university coalition would bitterly hurt their feelings. So intolerable would the shock to this popular sentiment presumably be, indeed, that no project of the kind can have any reasonable chance of a hearing.

Apart from such loss of "prestige value" in the eyes of those whose pride centers on magnitude, the move in question would involve no substantial loss. The chief direct and tangible effect would be a considerable saving in "overhead charges," in that the greater part of the present volume of administrative work would fall away. The greater part—say, three-fourths—of the present officers of administration, with their clerical staff, would be lost; under the present system these are chiefly occupied with the correlation and control of matters that need correlation and control only with a view to centralized management.

The aggregate of forces engaged and the aggregate volume of work done in the schools would suffer no sensible diminution. Indeed, the contemplated change should bring a very appreciably heightened efficiency of all the working units that are now tied up in the university coalition. Each of these units would be free to follow its own devices, within the lines imposed by the work in hand, since none of them would then be required to walk in lock-step with several others with which it had no more vital articulation than the lock-step in question.

Articulation and co-ordination is good and requisite where and so far as it is intrinsic to the work in hand; but it all comes to nothing better than systematized lag, leak and friction, so soon as it is articulation and coordination in other terms and for other ends than the performance of the work in hand. It is also true, the coalition of these several school units into a pseudo-aggregate under a centralized control gives a deceptive appearance of a massive engine working to some common end; but, again, mass movement comes to nothing better than inhibition and misdirection when it involves a coalition of working units whose work is necessarily to be done in severalty.[47]

Left to themselves the several schools would have to take care each of its own affairs and guide its endeavors by the exigencies of its own powers and purposes, with such regard to intercollegiate comity and courtesy as would be required by the substantial relations then subsisting between them, by virtue of their common employment in academic work.

In what has just been said, it is not forgotten that the burden of their own affairs would be thrown back on the initiative and collective discretion of the several

---

47. Quality or condition of being separate and distinct.

faculties, so soon as the several schools had once escaped from the trust-like co-alition in which they are now held. As has abundantly appeared in latter-day prac-tice, these faculties have in such matters proved themselves notable chiefly for futile disputation; which does not give much promise of competent self-direction on their part, in case they were given a free hand. It is to be recalled, however, that this latter-day experience of confirmed incompetence has been gathered under the overshadowing presence of a surreptitiously and irresponsibly autocratic executive, vested with power of use and abuse, and served by a corps of adroit parliamentarians and lobbyists, ever at hand to divert the faculty's action from any measure that might promise to have a substantial effect. By force of circum-stances, chief of which is the executive office, the faculties have become deliber-ative bodies charged with power to talk. Their serious attention has been taken up with schemes for weighing imponderables and correlating incommensurables, with such a degree of verisimilitude[48] as would keep the statistics and accoun-tancy of the collective administration in countenance, and still leave some play in the joints of the system for the personal relation of teacher and disciple. It is a nice problem in self-deception, chiefly notable for an endless proliferation.

At the same time it is well known—too well known to command particular attention—that in current practice, and of necessity, the actual effective organiza-tion of each of these constituent school units devolves on the working staff, in so far as regards the effectual work to be done. even to the selection of its working members and the apportionment of the work. It is all done "by authority" of course, and must all be arranged discreetly, with an ulterior view to its sanction by the executive and its due articulation with the scheme of publicity at large; but in all these matters the executive habitually comes into bearing only as a (power-ful) extraneous and alien interference—almost wholly inhibitory, in effect, even though with a show of initiative and creative guidance. And this inhibitory sur-veillance is exercised chiefly on grounds of conciliatory notoriety towards the outside, rather than on grounds that touch the efficiency of the staff for the work in hand. Such efficiency is commonly not barred, it is believed, so long as it does not hinder the executive's quest of the greater glory. There is, in effect, an inhib-itory veto power touching the work and its ways and means.

But even when taken at its best, and when relieved of the inhibition and de-flection worked by the executive, such an academic body can doubtless be counted on to manage its collective affairs somewhat clumsily and incompetently. There can be no hope of trenchant policy and efficient control at their hands; and, it

48. The appearance of being true or real.

should be added, there need be no great fear of such an outcome. The result should, in so far, be nearly clear gain, as against the current highly efficient management by an executive. Relatively little administration or control would be needed in the resulting small-scale units; except in so far as they might carry over into the new régime an appreciable burden of extra-scholastic traffic in the way of athletics, fraternities, student activities, and the like; and except so far as regards those schools that might still continue to be "gentlemen's colleges," devoted to the cultivation of the irregularities of adolescence and to their transfusion with a conventional elegance; these latter, being of the nature of penal settlements, would necessarily require government by a firm hand. That work of intimately personal contact and guidance, in a community of intellectual enterprise, that makes up the substance of efficient teaching, would, it might fairly be hoped, not be seriously hindered by the ill-coordinated efforts of such an academic assembly, even if its members had carried over a good share of the mechanistic frame of mind induced by their experience under the régime of standardization and accountancy.

Indeed, there might even be ground to hope that, on the dissolution of the trust, the underlying academic units would return to that ancient footing of small-scale parcelment and personal communion between teacher and student that once made the American college, with all its handicap of poverty, chauvinism and denominational bias, one of the most effective agencies of scholarship in Christendom.[49]

The hope—or delusion—would be that the staff in each of the resulting disconnected units might be left to conduct its own affairs, and that they would prove incapable of much concerted action or detailed control. It should be plain that no other and extraneous power, such as the executive or the governing boards, is as competent—or, indeed, competent in any degree—to take care of these matters, as are the staff who have the work to do. All this is evident to anyone who is at all conversant with the run of academic affairs as currently conducted on the grand scale; inasmuch as it is altogether a matter of course and of common notoriety within the precincts, that this is precisely what these constituent schools and units now have to do, each and several; with the sole qualification that they

49. Veblen's admiring view of the traditional nineteenth-century American college in part may have reflected his local experience as a Yale graduate student in the early 1880s. Between 1830 and 1890, two generations of Yale humanists and social scientists—whom the historian Louise Stevenson has termed the "New Haven Scholars"—assimilated advanced German university learning and methods and adapted them to the practices of leading American undergraduate college of the time. See Stevenson, *Scholarly Means to Evangelical Ends: The New Haven Scholars and the Transformation of Higher Learning in America, 1830–1890* (Baltimore: Johns Hopkins University Press, 1986).

Figure 6. Thorstein Veblen, 1920. Carleton College Archives

now have to take care of these matters under the inhibitory surveillance of the executive and his extraneous interests, and under the exactions of a super-imposed scheme of mechanical standardization and accountancy that accounts for nothing but its superimposition. At the same time the working force of the staff is hampered with a load of dead timber imported into its body to administer a routine of control and accountancy exacted by the executive's need of a credit-able publicity.[o]

This highly conjectural tracing of consequences to follow from this hypothet-ical dissolution of the trust, may as well be pursued into a point or two of detail, as touches those units of the university coalition that have an immediate interest

o. It will be objected, and with much reason, that these underlying "school units" that go to make up the composite American university habitually see no great evil in so being absorbed into the trust. They lend themselves readily, if not eagerly, to schemes of coalition; they are in fact prone to draw in under the aegis of the university corporation by "annexation," "affiliation." "absorption," etc. [On quoted words, cf. chapter I, "Introductory," note 5.] Anyone who cares to take stock of that matter and is in a position to know what is going on can easily assure himself that the reasons which decide in such a case are not advisedly accepted reasons intrinsic to the needs of efficiency for the work in hand, but rather reasons of competitive expediency, of competitive advantage and of prestige; except in so far as it may all be—as perhaps it commonly is—mere unreflecting conformity to the current fashion. In this connection it is to be remarked, however, that even if the current usage has no intrinsic advantage, as against another way of doing, failure to conform with the current way of doing will always entail a disadvantage.

in point of scholarship—the Collegiate ("Arts") division and the Graduate School. The former being left to its own devices and, it might be hoped, being purified of executive megalomania, it should seem probable that something of a reversion would take effect, in the direction of that simpler scheme of scholarship that prevailed in the days before the coming of electives. It was in the introduction of electives, and presently of alternatives and highly flexible curricula,[50] that the move first set in which carried the American college off its footing as a school of probation and introduction to the scholarly life, and has left it a job lot of ostensibly conclusive short-cuts into the trades and professions. It need not follow that the ancient curriculum would be re-established, but it should seem reasonable that a move would take effect in the direction of something like a modern equivalent. The Graduate School, on the other hand, having lost the drag of the collegiate division and the vocational schools, should come into action as a shelter where the surviving remnant of scholars and scientists might pursue their several lines of adventure, in teaching and in inquiry, without disturbance to or from the worldly-wise who clamor for the greater glory.

Now, all this speculation as to what might happen has, of course, little else than a speculative value. It is not intended, seriously and as a practical measure, to propose the abolition of the president's office, or of the governing board; nor is it intended to intimate that the captain of erudition can be dispensed with in fact. He is too dear to the commercialized popular imagination, and he fits too convincingly into the businessmen's preconceived scheme of things, to permit any such sanguine hope of surcease from skilled malpractice and malversation. All that is here intended to he said is nothing more than the *obiter dictum*[51] that, as seen from the point of view of the higher learning, the academic executive and all his works are anathema, and should be discontinued by the simple expedient of wiping him off the slate; and that the governing board, in so far as it presumes to exercise any other than vacantly perfunctory duties, has the same value and should with advantage be lost in the same shuffle.

50. Cf. chapter VII, "Vocational Training," note a.
51. Latin: an incidental or collateral opinion cited by a judge that is not binding.

Page numbers in italics indicate figures.